THE WAY OF
THE HUNTER

Also by Thomas McIntyre

DAYS AFIELD

The Way of the Hunter

Thomas McIntyre

THE WAY OF
THE HUNTER

The Art and the Spirit of Modern Hunting

 E. P. DUTTON   NEW YORK

Published in the United States by E. P. Dutton,
a division of NAL Penguin Inc.,
2 Park Avenue, New York, N.Y. 10016.

Published simultaneously in Canada by
Fitzhenry and Whiteside, Limited, Toronto.

Library of Congress Cataloging-in-Publication Data

McIntyre, Thomas.
    The way of the hunter: the art and the spirit of modern hunting
Thomas McIntyre.—1st ed.
        p.   cm.
    Bibliography: p.
    Includes index.
    ISBN 0-525-24718-1.
    1. Hunting.   I. Title.
SK33.M4   1988
799.2—dc19   88-10293
                                                            CIP

1 2 3 4 5 6 7 8 9 10

First Edition

Grateful acknowledgment is made for permission to quote from the following
works:

Thomas McGuane, "Midstream," *Harper's* (April 1987), reprinted by
permission of Harper's.

Evelyn Waugh, "A Journey to Brazil in 1932," in *When the Going Was Good*
(Boston: Little, Brown, 1984), reprinted by permission of Little, Brown and
Company.

Chapter 18 originally appeared in somewhat different form as two separate
articles in *Sports Afield:* "My Only Leopard" (December 1981) and "On the
Nitro Express" (July 1986). Copyright © 1981, 1986 by The Hearst Corporation. All rights reserved. Reprinted by kind permission of *Sports Afield*.

For three "old" hunters, forever young, Roy Cooper, Walter H. White, and the Reverend Anderson Bakewell, S.J.

And to the memory of John Francis McIntyre

Nevertheless, I am sensible, there is no becoming *Sportsmen* by Book. You may here find the Rules and proper Direction for that End; but Practice alone can make you *Masters.* . . . You must sweat and be cold, must sweat again, and be cold again, before you can arrive at any Degree of Perfection in this Art.

MR. GEORGE MARKLAND
"Pteryplegia: Or, the Art of Shooting-Flying"

CONTENTS

Introduction   1

1   Rabbits and Squirrels: First Steps   7

2   Migrants I: Doves   18

3   Migrants II: Waterfowl   27

4   Means I: Shotguns   38

5   Means II: Rifles   53

6   Exotica   62

7   Deer   71

8   Bone, Skin, Meat   83

9   Meditations   97

10   Horseflesh   105

11   Bears   114

12   Elk   129

13   The Bestiary   138

14   Uplanders   153

15   "Turkie Cocke"   162

16   Ramifications   170

17   "Municipal Paleolithic Man"   178

18   The Nitro Express   187

    Conclusion   205

    Bibliography   207

    Index   211

THE WAY OF
THE HUNTER

INTRODUCTION

Following three fall days of hunting upland birds; of getting up at
5:00 A.M. and coming in at 9:00 P.M.; of clambering for six and ten
and even seventeen miles a day over steep slopes of lava rock so sharp
that the setter's paws had to be booted; of unseasonably warm weather
that left my shirt banded with white rings of dried salt; of sleep so
hard I half expected to awaken each morning to find that the boys
from the forensics lab had been called in during the night to draw a
chalk outline around my motionless body; after all that—*and*, it must
be said, of chukar partridge rising in singles and doubles and coveys
of a dozen and two dozen and more; of a battered but reliable 12-
gauge brought to my shoulder and the safety let off and the trigger
pulled and the action pumped; of, for the most part, birds then sailing
away unscathed; but every so often against all conceivable odds, and
with perhaps no inalienable right to on my part, of seeing one or, at
the absolute outside, *two* fold up and plummet into the dry sagebrush
where the dog, breaking only then from his head-raised point, would
run and lift gently a hot feathered body in has jaws to deliver it to

my hand—after *all* that I am sitting on a Sunday morning at a picnic table in a municipal park, watching young children toss bread to the mallards and American widgeons (wondering, only in passing, how those wild birds would look cupped and webbed over the front bead of my shotgun) and beginning the writing of a book about not what I do, but what I am: a hunter. How did I ever come to such a place? How does anyone, in what can so easily be viewed as these increasingly abnormal days, still come to it, still follow the way of the hunter?

There was a time, not so very long ago, when that was a question that did not seem to demand overly much to be answered. It barely, in fact, demanded to be asked. A child was born among hunters, and with little or no premeditation he—and more frequently than might be imagined, she—would find himself initiated into that clan that is as old as the human animal, to learn from his elders the hunter's way. Simple as that.

Today, though, nothing looks simple, and the old hunters seem somehow further from us than ever before. The wild country, at first glance, looks to have shrunk markedly, and our connections to it, and to that life we also categorize as "wild" that dwells upon it, seem to have shrunk by a similar proportion. A certain class of intractable moralists, who tend to perceive existence in terms far more streamlined than the woefully complex and ambiguous actuality of it would really seem to dictate, admonish us that the chase is at best ignorant carnival, at worst a heinous crime, and in any case a dark urge long ago to have been put behind us. Yet there persists in so *many* of us an insatiable hunger to set off, in spite of it all—the lack of experience, the lack of familiarity with the land, the abundance of reproach—in pursuit of animals, to locate them on their native grounds and on their own terms, to "take" them (capturing their flesh as they capture our souls—as fair a trade-off as there ever was), and to partake once more of a feast as old as every hill and every hunter, whether naked and carrying a spear or down-jacketed and packing an '06, who ever crept over a ridge crest to look for wildlife—and to live the "wild life." It is one of the finest mysteries our species retains from our "primitive" past, and maybe one of the most inexplicable, yet one that is well worth attempting to write about.

This book, then, is for those who need, far more than want, to take up this course, and who through circumstance may never have been able to spend time among the old hunters. It is also a book for the more experienced hunter who wishes to recall his own discovery of the way as I attempt to describe the route a hunter follows in his education, a hunter's experience progressing, often, in logical steps— at least by the hunt's special logic—few, if any, of us starting out our hunting lives on the trail of rogue elephants, for example. This is meant to be, as well, a book of information, of knowledge gained through personal experience. By definition this will make it a book of eccentric views, but those are the views all hunters eventually come to. Every hunter has ultimately to learn the way himself. No one individual can show him where, exactly, he should put each foot as he moves through the trees. The truest hunter must go beyond rote lessons to a degree of knowledge that has become thoroughly in-grained, become an instinctual quality of his being, something beyond mere consciousness. He must, finally, be able to cross over from *un-derstanding* to *knowing*. *That* is what ultimately cannot be taught; the best that can be achieved is to offer one's impressions of the territory one has seen, describing as best one can for another hunter the land-marks he should keep an eye out for as he enters the country of the game. (And these are sights that it might even be of value for non-hunters to see, to better understand why humans still give chase to animals.)

These landmarks have, to be sure, every bit as much to do with the spirit of the chase, the "heart of the hunter," as with the arts that are employed in it; and in this book I shall commence with that spirit and try never to lose sight of it even when I am talking about ways and means.

It was that spirit that drew me to hunting when as a young boy I discovered a maddening infatuation with animals. They were at first rabbits and the like, the so-called small game, which after the inevitable tempering of the innate bloodthirstiness the young of all predator species possess—that fearsome, genetic egomania that in their own minds sets them above the entire rest of nature and is a birthright granted to help ensure their early survival—came to loom far larger than the adjective *small* would imply.

Out of small game came flights of doves and ducks, and I came to see, through them, that my attraction was not, above all else, to the killing, but to the sighting of the animal, the "reading" of his flight, the knowing of where he would be and how I could find him and perhaps reach him in the sky with a few tiny pellets of chilled lead shot. It was from these birds that I first came to see that I loved animals and being at large in the open in pursuit of them, being an active participant in the timeless round of the hunter and the hunted, choosing not to try to place myself beyond the wild, *not* to hope to be able to observe it at some sterile, heightened remove, but rather to wade right into it and get some of its mud on my boots, and sometimes some of its blood on my hands.

Although the pursuit has always seemed more essential than the kill, there continues an inescapable linkage to the means of capture, to weaponry—which on the level of the hunting weapon remains the technological fine art with the longest unbroken human tradition, just ahead of the manufacture of the musical instruments that evolved out of weaponry, the bow being the prototype of the harp—a fascination with it and a desire to learn more about it. There were at the outset .22s and shotguns, certainly, then rifles for big game.

With his rifle a hunter looks for his first large mammal to hunt. Which animal this will be is not so easy a decision for many of us today as it once was when the hunter's way began when he stepped out the backdoor. We would like that first animal to be a deer or perhaps a pronghorn, but often we find that an animal like the wild boar, not even native to this land, but remarkably wild all the same, can teach us much about the way of the hunter.

Yet we will all come to the deer, sooner rather than later. There are four kinds of deer for us to hunt in North America, and far more than four ways to hunt them. There are also the deer's antlers to contemplate, their hides to look after, and their meat to take care of, and, finally, the inescapable question of death that we must confront in the hunt for the deer, and in our hunts for all game.

Luckily for us, one man has looked at that question, and all the other questions the hunt raises, intensely and brilliantly in the single most important work on hunting in this century. That man's name is José Ortega y Gasset, and the book-length essay he wrote, titled *Meditations on Hunting,* is one that no hunter can entirely ignore.

From the pages of Ortega y Gasset, we move along the hunter's way even further into the wild and can find ourselves in the decidedly strange position of sitting astride a horse, having united with another species, as we do with the dog, to pursue a third, and trying to figure out how to make the best of that predicament.

The country the horse may carry us into is frequently that of the bear—both black and brown—and the greatest cervid the Americas have to offer, the elk; and we find that with these our hunting has entered a highly intense realm of passion. There are any number of other animals upon this continent that our hunter's passion may involve us with at this stage, big-game animals like the moose and pronghorn and mountain lion and mountain goat, and others, all possessing the ability to draw us off to wild places.

Often when a hunter finds himself at this place along the way, he may, even though he undoubtedly hunted them as a child, begin as well to take an intensified interest in upland birds—from pheasant to quail to the various forest and plains grouse to the Hungarian partridge and the incomparable chukar—that is nothing *less* than passionate. From having a passionate interest to being consumed by passion is what often happens to the hunter when he sets out next to find the wild turkey, a nominally upland bird who, as anyone who has ever hunted him can attest, is actually one of our most challenging native *big-game* animals, without benefit of even being a *mammal.*

A big-game animal who is thoroughly mammalian is the wild mountain sheep, and here is a precinct of hunting where intensity can give way to absolute fanaticism. There is much in the pursuit of the wild mountain sheep that involves what is best *and* worst in modern hunting.

Yet the most primitive and pure kinds of hunting, with hounds and falcons and simple Pleistocene cunning, still go on today; and there remains outside of North America a distant wild place the hunter will want to see, the place where the long course of his way had its origins, and of which every hunter has dreamed, that place being Africa. When he stalked his first rabbit, every young hunter believed in his heart that it was actually the spoor of a leopard he was on. On occasion, this can lead that young hunter, once grown, to go look for a leopard's spoor in fact.

From rabbit to leopard may not be the way all hunters take, but it is a direction they all can recognize. At a second glance it can even be seen that wild country still *does* exist and that it is still possible for us to bond to it and to its wild life. There are old hunters, still marvelously up and about, who are left to know and a hunter's arts to learn. The hunter's remains, as well, as honorable a way today as any human occupation—more honorable than most, I would say. Finally, though, it is just something so *utterly* human.

We arose over ten thousand centuries ago from hunters who loped, with weapons in hand and animal flesh on their minds, across yellow plains, and it may be every bit as long before the need to hunt is in any way quenched within us. When, and if, it ever is, it will probably mean that for better or worse we are no longer human but have become something quite different. For now, though, human we tenaciously remain. And the hunter's way we follow. I hope that this book may offer a rough outline, a map drawn in the dust, of the territory that might lie ahead for someone choosing to travel on the way of the hunter, or reveal that territory to those who merely wish to comprehend better what it could possibly mean to be a hunter in these days.

1

RABBITS AND SQUIRRELS: FIRST STEPS

A way begins, quite often enough, without our fully realizing. At the start of the hunter's way there was, for many of us, a gun. Practically none of us could see, then, what *that* was going to lead to.

Before the cool days that he will come to know, a young boy will receive his first gun.* There will be an understanding, here, that while this gun may not yet be his "property" in any pinched, legalistic sense, it will, all the same—provided he always conducts himself with it with due care and caution, and with the clear knowledge that into his hands has been delivered a tool whose purpose is very much a matter of living and dying—be his as outrightly as anything he will ever come to hold a bill of sale to in this life.

My first gun, as it was for so many others who have found themselves on the way of the hunter, was a small-caliber rifle, in my specific case a Remington .22 Bolt Action Repeater Model 34. It was

---

* Though there is a substantive difference between a gun and a rifle, as will be explained, *gun* remains a far more evocative term than the drably generic *firearm,* and so is being used here in that sense.

of a rather plain takedown design with a twenty-four-inch round tapered barrel; a tubular magazine with the capacity to hold fifteen lubricated .22 long-rifle rimfire cartridges—which owed their existence to one Louis Nicolas Flobert, a French gun maker who in the mid-1800s developed a round based on the percussion caps for black powder muskets and the French size 3-0 shotgun pellet that measured twenty-two one-hundredths of an inch in diameter—automatic shell ejector; chromium-plated bolt, bolt handle, and trigger; white-metal-bead front sight and adjustable rear sight; and a shotgun-style steel butt plate on a "genuine American Walnut military type stock," as the ad copy from 1934, when the gun was purchased new for my then-fourteen-year-old father for "$14.60 (Including Tax)," reads.

The magazine advertisement depicts this Judge Hardy parent speaking on a black telephone to his local weapons merchant. Both men wear ties. The white-haired father says, "Say, Bill, that Model 34 I got for the boy's Christmas just came in. Have you another like it? I want one for myself, too. It's the sweetest little rifle I ever saw." The copy goes on to describe a rifle "put together like a clock," whose "bolt action is smooth as grease and as certain as Christmas." Who could not have wished to possess so estimable an implement, or to take up a way in which it served an ancient and honorable function, the function of acquiring meat?

I was four, I guess, when my dad first held this rifle up to my shoulder and passed on his knowledge of it to me. We were together in a bright hot desert place off a lonesome dirt road. He was the owner of a '56 Nomad station wagon, one Winchester Model 70 .30-'06 rifle, a .22 semiautomatic pistol (a Colt Woodsman), a semiauto 12-gauge shotgun, and the Model 34. Before he ever permitted me to squeeze the trigger, he told me, in the first serious words he ever addressed to me, always to treat a gun, *any* gun, as if it were loaded, even when I was certain it was not (*especially* when I was certain, because that is when a rifleman can become careless); never to point it at anything I did not intend to shoot; to be alert at all times to where the muzzle was pointing; always to be sure that there was a solid background behind my target to halt the bullet's flight safely; and to be conscious that a gun was made to kill, as surely as any spear or arrow ever was.

Dad showed me then how with my eye to nest the front bead into the notch of the rear sight and to settle my target atop it; and when I fired that first shot, the sound was like the ripping of some

A jackrabbit makes a dash for it. (*Photo: Durwood Hollis*)

thick fabric, and I was irreparably embarked on something that would occupy the rest of my life. That desert day was as much a boy's Christmas as any day could be.

It would be some years before I would be old enough to hunt with this gun. But when I was, it was with my father, to begin with— I undoubtedly going sleepless the night before my first hunt, in that state of anticipatory excitement Southerners of another time knew as being "journey proud"; and then, when I was older still, I hunted with other friends who, to greater or lesser degrees, found themselves on the hunter's way, too; or alone if I could find no one else to hunt with me; but always for the game appropriate to that Model 34. If M. Flobert's .22 rimfire cartridge had been created with one particular class of game in mind, it would have been those smaller gnawing mammals, the rabbits and hares and tree squirrels.

Rabbits and hares, the lagomorphs, or "hare-shaped" animals, range in size in North America from the Arctic hare—as big as a snowy-furred house cat—to the pygmy rabbit—a sort of teacup of a hopper. For the majority of hunters, though, the two most important groups of lagomorphs are the jackrabbits and the cottontails.

The jackrabbit is a predominantly trans-Mississippian animal comprising three species, the whitetail, antelope, and blacktail jack-rabbit (*Lepus townsendi, L. alleni,* and *L. californicus*).* The last is the one I know best from my carrying the Model 34 through the deserts of my native California.

Hunter-gatherer Indians of the Great Basin gave chase to jack-rabbits to good effect in the past with throwing sticks and by driving them en masse into large nets woven out of sagebrush; and, as we shall see, the jackrabbit is game well suited to being pursued by the so-called long dogs. He is, as well, first-rate quarry for a boy with a .22. I think there could be few more challenging animals to teach one the skills of successful stalking, or from which to begin to gain some glimmer of what geniuine hunting may be about, than the jackrabbit.

A jackrabbit is a visually oriented animal whose basic survival technique is to remain hidden, motionless, usually seated in the shade of something, such as sagebrush or a clump of creosote bush, until he concludes that the jig is very much up—then to make a dash for it with a frantic joie de vivre. For this reason, many rabbit hunters choose to carry shotguns with No. 6 shot† loaded in the shells so they can tumble a jackrabbit on the fly, as it were, should they kick one up as they mosey about the territory.

While this may be the more expedient course, there seems too great a reliance upon happenstance in it by my lights, which have an expressed preference for hunting hares with weapons with a narrower field. The thorough inspection of the terrain, the knowledge of the jackrabbit's behavior, the ability to "think" like a rabbit—to see the surroundings as a wild animal would—that are demanded in order to know ahead of time where a jackrabbit might possibly be, so that a hunter can be prepared to kill with a single projectile, are what make

---

* The varieties of many animals named in this book are so numerous that to latinize them all would leave these pages looking like Caesar's *Gallic Wars.* So we will confine the use of binomials to allusions where one particular species needs to be distinguished from others, and to the first reference to an animal that is discussed in some detail. A knowledge of natural science is not without value to a hunter, but the wild is a classroom of another kind. It is more important to know the animal itself than to know its binomial, and the best way to know any animal is to hunt it.

† Briefly, shotgun shot is classified by size numbers, the smaller the number, the larger the shot, with some of the smallest, for clay targets and little birds, being No. 9, with a diameter of 0.08 inches, up to the 0, or "aught," sizes, 0.33 inches in 00 or "double-aught," used mainly for hunting deer, thus the name *buckshot,* and thus the inaccuracy of referring to all shotgun shot *as* buckshot. It is all shot, but only *some* is appropriate for deer—and then only at extremely close ranges.

this *hunting* and make it a valuable method by which a boy can learn the ways of the hunter.

The population of rabbits runs in a natural cycle of highs and lows, with the rabbits up one year, or for several years, and nowhere to be seen the next. This can be the result of weather (such as wet years versus dry, with the consequent increase or decrease in available feed), predation, or the normal "boom-and-bust" trend all wild species are subject to: once a population of animals reaches the carrying capacity of an area it is, if left to its own devices, likely to crash shortly thereafter, like someone leaning too far back in a chair and suddenly toppling over. Jackrabbits will do some agricultural "damage"—never mind, just yet, the far more widespread damage most agriculture has done to the natural lands jacks, and all other wild species, inhabited long before those lands were subjected to the dragline, the plow, and the wonders of modern chemistry—because of their taste for fresh greens. Therefore, it is one of the greater benefits that planted fields have to offer that along their edges a hunter is likely to find lagomorphs.

Jackrabbit hunting is frequently carried out in the late summer, as a prelude to the prime hunting seasons of the fall. Being for the most part nocturnal, jackrabbits are most active, from the hunter's standpoint, in the early morning and late afternoon and evening— assuming that a hunter (make that, instead, a "shooter," that being what one—who has come to treasure striking things with bullets above actually engaging in that mysterious union with animals that is hunting—has in truth made himself into in such an instance) does not say to himself, To hell with it all, and set out after rabbits in the black of night, laying down fields of fire from the open back of a floodlight-equipped pickup truck. The true hunting of jackrabbits—or any animal—has nothing to do with quartz-halogen-lighted armored assaults, but is a matter of walking long distances with an eye always open for the sight of the animal, and whatever else the Out There has to show. If he is lucky, a hunter may spot a jackrabbit at sufficient range for the animal to feel secure in remaining still. Often, the jackrabbit's long ears, exposed above the growth he has confidently taken cover behind, will give him away. What is called for then is that the hunter work into position to make a killing shot. If the shot is missed, or the rabbit, as they are wont to do, bolts before the hunter can fire, this is when the art of hitting running game starts to be learned.

The mistake most made by small-game hunters in the matter of running animals is to believe that a bullet, somehow, travels at a velocity approximating the instantaneous, when actually it is, in the case of the .22, barely into the supersonic range; and so the shots tend to land harmlessly behind the animal, kicking up talcumy dust at the rabbit's flying heels. It takes real time for any bullet to travel to a target, so leading a moving animal—that is, aiming far enough ahead of the fleeing rabbit, and remembering to keep swinging the muzzle, even after the shot has been fired, to maintain that necessary lead, so that the bullet will intercept his course—is critical (particularly when it comes to killing birds on the wing with a shotgun: what the shotgun was made for—see Chapter 4). It is like passing a football: a quarterback does not throw the spiraling ball to where the receiver *is*, but to where he will be by the time the football has flown its course through the air. If a young hunter can learn to kill jackrabbits on the run, he should have little difficulty when the moment comes for him to kill a bounding deer. Now, if one wished to make the conditions of the hunt more challenging, he might attempt to hunt his jackrabbits with a handgun or a bow.

All the jackrabbits are quite edible, but all are also susceptible to assorted contagions, tularemia, or "rabbit fever," merely the most lurid. If a hunter is genuinely concerned, then he should only handle dead jackrabbits while wearing gloves, especially when cleaning and skinning them. Not even this, however, will absolutely ensure that a jackrabbit's flesh will not exact some toll from the human who kills and eats it; but one of the primary features of all hunting, we shall come to understand, is the wide diversity of risk involved in it. Yet while no one should go in search of guarantees in the Out There, discretion is, nonetheless, always in order.

The cottontail rabbit (*Sylvilagus floridanus,* et al.) is found, in a number of minor variations, throughout the continental United States; and he is arguably superior table fare to the lanky jackrabbit—though both, as with most game meat, must be kept moist in the cooking to bring out the best in them. I have enjoyed some memorable rabbit stews formulated out of cottontails—and even achieved some success in barbecuing them—and can recall numerous July Firsts, when the rabbit season usually opens in California, spent tramping happily around the high desert of Joshua trees and mirror-white granite, hunting them.

The cottontail, like the jackrabbit, will try to flee when he feels threatened; and though his escape lacks some of the high-performance dazzle of the jack's, his smaller size makes shooting him about on a par with trying to shoot a sprinting, zigzagging jackrabbit. The cottontail does seem, though, more inclined to count on concealment

For many, if not most, boys in North America, their hunting experience begins with the cottontail rabbit. (*Photo: Daniel Hernandez*)

over speed as a defense strategy, appearing to "hold tighter" to cover than a jackrabbit when he is crouched down in his form or under a bush—with his puff of a tail tucked out of sight beneath him, an evolutionary bit of legerdemain learned in the starkest of ways from being preyed on for ages by the sharp-eyed likes of coyotes and bobcats who are forever on the qui vive for that telltale flare of white—so a hunter can walk directly over him without noticing in the slightest. In many areas, east of the Mississippi in particular, a cottontail hunter will link up with beagles to help scare up the rabbits and send them running in a wide circle back to where the hunter waits.

If there were not rabbits, it would be impossible to envision any other small-game animal so fundamentally American as the tree squirrel. He is a creature of the wild heart of this country, of that time when an unbroken deciduous woodland Arcadia (or so it is recalled in legend) spread from the Atlantic seaboard to the banks of what the Ojibwa called "Big River"—and across the breadth of which, it has been said, that squirrel could travel without once finding it in the least necessary to set a four-toed front foot on the ground. It was the extremely accurate black powder "Kentucky" squirrel rifle (crafted in Pennsylvania by German gunsmiths)—normally of .36 or .45 caliber—and the training gained from the hunting of the squirrel that made the American Revolutionary army such a redoubtable guerrilla force. Take Brunswick stew, add Boone and Crockett, segue into Nick Adams up in Michigan and Boon Hogganbeck under the Gum Tree, and you can begin to see just how the squirrel might fit into the entire scheme of things.

The name *squirrel* is derived from the Greek word *skiouros*, meaning "he who sits in the shadow of his tail." Among the shadows of hardwood trees many a young boy has gone looking for the fox and the gray squirrel (*Sciurus niger* and *S. carolinensis*)—the latter sometimes called a cat squirrel. These rodents are found primarily in the eastern half of the country and are among the most important of small-game species. They taught any number of boys how to hunt, how to slip through a forest, eyes and ears attuned to the spectrum and the pitch of the environment. They set many a young hunter's heart to beating.

There are occasions in the hunt when a hunter's best tactic is to do what seems like nothing at all, but is actually the intensely skilled task of sitting and looking and awaiting the arrival of the game; and in the hunting of fox and cat squirrels, a hunter able to seat himself and remain motionless against the base of an oak tree may, after initial moments of a silent woods, hear the sound of moving squirrels and begin to catch sight of them. At other times, squirrel hunting involves the painstakingly slow *and* arduous chore of moving and looking very thoroughly. This is called *still-hunting*, and it is what many take to be the essence of hunting. Sometimes, the only thing a squirrel will reveal of himself is the flick of a bushy tail as he presses flat against a tree limb; but it is bits of information as minute as this that the hunter, seated or moving, will have to learn to detect if he hopes to kill a squirrel. Frightened, a squirrel may rush headlong back into his leafy ball of a nest, known as a *dray*, or into the hollow of a tree. Sometimes, a hunter's pounding on the trunk, pulling on vines hanging from the tree, and, yes, hissing like a cat may spook a squirrel out; but hitting him cleanly with a .22 after that, as he flies through the treetops, remains as speculative a venture as any that hunting has to offer.

Perhaps the most symbiotic relationship in hunting is that in which two predatory species are joined, that relationship between dog and man when they hunt together. The late Spanish philosopher José Ortega y Gasset, author of the inescapable *Meditations on Hunting,* holds that the ancient addition of the dog to the human activity of hunting (though it may very well have been the addition of the human to the dog's hunting, for all any of us can know from our bipedal perspective) was the ultimate admission of the limitations of consciousness when it came to the matter of pursuing game. Hunting with dogs represents "man's accepting reason's insufficiency," according to Ortega y Gasset, accepting, I might add, at least in the case of the mature hunter, perfectly gladly. Hunting is much too basic and important a human activity to be considered "reasoned" behavior—which is where the smarmy apologist, who sanctimoniously contends that human hunters, acting solely out of what he would claim to be a selfless sense of duty, are no more than impassive regulatory mechanisms used to control "excess" animal populations ("It's a dark and lonely business, but somebody's got to do it"), *and* the bewildered critic, who, seeing hunting as cruel senseless *fun,* points out the complete irrelevancy that it fails to conform to some Platonic ideal, when it has nothing whatsoever to do with Plato or his dullard ideas, both very much miss the trolley—but is, rather, the recapturing of a mode of being predating conscious thought. At no time is this made clearer to a hunter than when he hears the sound of baying dogs, and once more his animal soul claws up out of his center and allows him to operate beyond the tyranny of his consciousness, a pure predator once again. In hunting with dogs, as Ortega y Gasset says, "the orgiastic element shoots forth, the dionysiac, which flows and boils in the depth of all hunting." With dogs "hunting acquires a certain kind of symphonic majesty," and the fact that true hunters can hear this symphony so acutely is what causes them to make so many other folks just a tad jumpy.

Humans hunt birds in the company of both flushing dogs and pointers, but the grandest crescendo of the symphony comes in the hunting of big game—bears and large wild cats, for the most part—with hounds. In microcosm, though, its strains are also to be unmistakably heard in the hunting of cat squirrels with fice dogs.

The word *fice,* or *fyce* or *feist* (as in "feisty"), is well known in the South and comes from the earlier term *fisting dog,* referring to a small mongrel, customarily of some conglomeration of terrier breeds. (The implication of the name would appear to be a dog no larger than one's fist, although, unfortunately, the word's origins go back to even older English words referring, it seems, to the passing of wind: to wit, a wee fart of a dog.) He is a dog very much of the southern hardwood tracts, with their remnant memories of that unbroken forest canopy that once tented the eastern half of North America, where he is still used extensively for the hunting of cat squirrels.

It is a strange and thrilling sight to see fice dogs trotting along on their "bench legs," looking *up* for game, somehow in direct opposition to our accepted notions of canine noses doggedly to the ground. More often, though, a hunter turns his dogs loose and listens for their voices to tell him when a squirrel has been found. Then it is time for the hunter to run like something wild himself, splashing across shallow creeks and plunging through underbrush until he arrives at the tree where the dogs stand on their hind legs, their front paws up on the trunk, heads thrown back, barking for all they are worth. Killing a squirrel poised forty or fifty feet up in the branches of a tree is no easy chore, either. In late summer and early fall, the foliage of the trees gives the squirrels a greater sense of security than they have after all the leaves have shed; and they are less likely, at the first sight of a human, to try to escape—either into nests or hollows or in frenzied leaps from limb to limb. They are, though, also much harder to detect in this season, especially in the fading light of late afternoon when they become most active; but this only helps to remind a hunter that among the first of his tools that he must hone is his vision.

I think that out of all the hunting of small game, hunting tree squirrels in his local woods with a small-caliber rifle—one handed him by his father who has come to trust him to handle it and himself responsibly in the Out There—would be the perfect way for a boy (who, out of a desire that has arisen from within himself for reasons that may never be entirely fathomable to him, wants to learn the hunter's way) to begin his study. For one thing, it is hunting that requires no elaborate preparation or travel or expense or prolonged physical effort; and it is hunting a boy can do on his own, or accompanied only by his dog. He can make his own mistakes and locate his own truths himself, free of the good-natured impatience he might sense if he were to hunt with older, more experienced hunters who have already learned the shortcuts. From such hunting a young hunter can gain an intimate knowledge of a small stretch of the wild and of a manageable quarry. He can gain confidence in himself and in his own skills and abilities, so that he can return home in the evening light with that prize that always astounds hunters no matter how many times they have won it, the gift of wild meat from game fields, what the father of "game management" (a wretched title; think of him instead as a harkener-back to the old notion of the "natural philosopher"), Aldo Leopold, calls "our meat from God."

There may come a time when such a young hunter will view the hunting of small game as being of minor importance when compared with the hunting of large mammals, but there is every likelihood of its remaining a lifelong source of happiness to him, a happiness whose significance is calculable in terms that are in geometric proportion to the few ounces of animal flesh that stand to be gathered. Those woods, or deserts or plains, he slipped through as a boy, armed and alert, drawn taut as a bow, will be the places where he was born as a hunter. You never lose your feeling for that, for where, you will come to realize in time, it all began for you.

2

MIGRANTS I: DOVES

The mathematical elegance of hunting small game by oneself is undeniable. Yet a young hunter must soon come to learn that the chase
also has its communal aspect. The human, no less than the dog, is by
nature an animal of the pack, and never more so than when he is in
pursuit of wild game in the company of other humans. One of the
earliest and most fundamental units of human society, in fact, is the
hunting party. The rabbit drives of those hunter-gatherer Indians, for
instance, were in no way single-handed enterprises, but extremely
coordinated tribal affairs. For a young hunter, his introduction into
the association of the hunting party may come on that fiercely hot
September morning when his first dove hunt begins.

Through my memory there runs an unbroken line of over twenty
seasons of dove hunts with the same party, from hunts in years even
before I had obtained my hunting license at eleven and could legally
carry a gun into the field, restricted before that time to the role of
bird boy fetching others' downed birds, through those of the years
of high school and college and work, to the final ones before the banal
commonplaces of age and distance and death disrupted this contin-

uum. The hunting fields were outside the San Joaquin Valley town of Tulare, in acres of harvested corn and milo and in pastures of wild turkey millet. The party was nearly always composed of my father, my brother, my father's friend Roy, his daughter, Pam, the Tulare rancher Elmer (farmers in the West adamant about being known as "ranchers"), and me. Others would be a part, too, added and subtracted each season, but those six were the core, almost never failing to be in a dove field, together, on September 1.

The doves we were looking for were mourning doves, in terms of birds killed, the most hunted game-bird species in North America. For some hunters, doves may be the only animal they pursue all season, while for others opening day marks the official New Year's of their annual chase.

The mourning dove (*Zenaidura macroura marginella* and *carolinensis,* to get Linnaean about matters) is a migratory bird found widely between Canada and Central America. He delights in warm climes, his southward movements inspired by the cooler temperatures of fall; but a few of his number are always to be found in the most absurdly frigid northern conditions, winging incongruously over snowbanks and the stubble of wheat fields come December. To see him at his best, though, demands our being in a hot September place of grain or seed crops where at dawn he will flock in in flights of a dozen or so birds, one flight following hard on another so that a hunter will have barely time enough between each to retrieve his dead birds and reload for the next onslaught.

A young hunter will begin his hunting of mourning doves when he is awakened at an hour so insensibly before light that it will be a foreign land to him, both far too late to be awake still and much too early to have gotten up yet. Breakfast will not even be a consideration for hours to come; and as the cars and pickups are loaded with hunters and guns, in the chill air, along with the distinct sensation of the day's formidable heat drawing in from the east, will be the smell of alfalfa and moonlight. Not a rooster will be crowing; but in not too many seasons to come, the young boy will have become familiar with this as the hour when every hunting day is meant to begin.

After a long drive to the hunting grounds, a young hunter will be set off at his assigned position in the darkness, perhaps in some brush along a field's or pasture's edge, or beside a tree or a fence post or almost anything he can crouch or sit behind—a shooting stool a comfortable appurtenance for any dove field—to break up his silhouette and so not deflect the doves from passing within range of him.

Dove hunting. (*Photo: Robert Robb*)

The other hunters will be spaced out at thirty- to fifty-yard intervals along the firing line, well apart but at no more than comfortable hailing distance. The young hunter should, as he does when doing any shooting, be wearing proper hearing and eye protection—earplugs and impact-resistant shooting glasses—and should know not to fire at any low-flying birds or swing his shotgun in the direction of another hunter. There ought to be a sufficiency of birds, anyway, so he should not allow his innate eagerness to see them fall from the sky override any considerations of safety. (Even if the birds are few, there is still no reason for his not exercising caution.) As he waits for dawn, slapping at mosquitoes alighting on him, there will be no need for his loading his shotgun before the legal shooting hour, and even then he should wait until he can clearly distinguish that any birds flying over him are indeed mourning doves.

Mourning doves do not make the plaintive cooing from which their name derives while in flight, but travel with a sound from their wings like the hurried creaking of oarlocks. They may fly straight, but seldom true, dipping and banking as they advance, their wing beats continuous, their streamlined airframes ill-suited to the luxury of gliding. At the sight of a human they will veer off, so a hunter must remain low and at least partially hidden until they are within range, before rising up, letting off the safety, and trying for a bird. Camouflage clothing is also helpful in this regard, though not a make-or-break point with doves.

Number 8 or 7½ shot—0.09 to 0.095 inches in diameter—out of a fairly open barrel—a barrel choked* no more than cylinder (no choke) or improved (only slightly choked)—works well on mourning doves because it does not take a good many pellets to bring one down, and a wider pattern of shot can do much to compensate for the sudden and unforeseen deviations in the bird's line of flight.

As his first morning of hunting doves progresses, a young hunter will twist madly, trying to catch the far sight of the approaching birds so he can be ready to rise up and take them when they reach him. More birds than he can imagine, though, will slip right by him as he

---

* *Choking* is the constricting of the muzzle of a shotgun to some minor degree to alter the spread of the shot pattern, "on the same principle that makes a stream of water from a hose narrow down when you compress it," as the writer Stephen Bodio explains, and, therefore, increase or decrease the effective range of the shotgun: more choke, smaller pattern (see p. 40) and longer range; less choke, larger pattern and shorter range.

turns, too late, and sees only their departing shapes. Then he will notice the voices of the other hunters calling to him—"Behind you! Coming over!"—and he will begin to appreciate how this hunting of doves is a joint venture of all the assembled hunters, one hunter's eyes becoming the eyes for every hunter; and he will begin calling to the other hunters himself, "Coming over! Behind you!" Later, when they are all gathered together under the big sycamore behind Elmer's weathered barn, cleaning the day's birds—plucking and singeing and drawing being the best way, because this leaves the skin intact, that skin needed to keep the flesh of the birds moist when they are cooked at that time when all the hunters have once more come together to eat them—he will see even better how no one here hunts alone. A hunter could, but it would not be the same.

While still in the field, though, the young hunter will have filled his limit, or simply decided, even if it is not filled, that he has taken enough birds for this morning, and will unload his shotgun and have time to sit and wait for the others to finish their hunting. He will find himself still watching the sky, though, and shouting to the other hunters as doves pass near them; and there may begin to mount in him a fascination with these birds, a wonderment at what they are and where they came from on those beating wings.

Small and looking deceptively delicate for birds capable of lengthy migrations, mourning doves are of the Columbidae family of birds, which includes in North America the white-winged dove and the band-tailed pigeon, besides some 286 other species worldwide. They eat seeds and grain and build in almost any locale, city or country, a rickety nest of twigs in which they lay two white eggs. A hunter can scout for doves a day or two before the opening of the season, to see where they are coming in to feed or water in huntable quantities, and then set up his party there on opening morning. A grainfield is best for a morning shoot, while for the afternoon he might try a watering hole. (Dove hunting actually benefits from having a fair number of hunters around a field, because this keeps the birds "stirred up" and not nestled down and feeding in one unhunted area of that field.)

Knowing things like that will answer for a young hunter some of the *whats* and *wheres* of the dove, but not the *whys* that he may also begin to ask when he feels himself in the grip of that animal. He may wonder what it could be like to conduct one's life on the wing, surging through air the way a fish must fin through water. He may feel the beating of imagined flight muscles in his own arms and chest; he may imagine his own skin coated by the refined scales of feathers, how cool and dry they must be when stroked by the wind. Hunkered on the ground, he may even feel himself lightened and lifted above his surroundings by the sweep of doves overhead, drawn up to mingle with them. He may realize that what is around him is no longer just stagnant geography but, when seen from the bird's vantage, terrain pulsing with meaning, each contour communicating some message: here is food, here is drink, here is a place of safe rest. He may begin to wonder whether this is how all animals view the world, how humans did once, too, and whether, somehow, he can learn to view it again this way himself. Because of doves, now even the sky has taken on meaning for him.

When he first hunted small game, much of what drove the young hunter on was, frankly, childish blood lust, and anything he learned of the wild was almost incidental to satisfying that urge. Comprehending a rabbit or squirrel did not seem to require much reflection, because both traveled the earth more or less in the same fashion as he did. Both were bound to it, and he could more easily recognize himself in them. Now he is confronted by an animal who defies gravity in a way he never can, and yet in its otherness he still feels a connection to it. Is this what hunting is? Seeing the difference but sensing the sameness?

If he can recognize himself in a bird, or, rather, recognize the bird in himself, then there is every likelihood of his becoming *inalterably* lost to the wild. He will begin to suspect that there are other animals lurking within himself as well, goose and deer and bear and mountain sheep and leopard. He may be too young, yet, to give himself over totally to this suspicion, but the inexorable slide will have begun for him, all while sitting firmly on his butt in the dirt of a dove field.

If the American Southwest is where a young hunter grew up, his first encounter with doves would probably have been with the white-winged variety (*Zenaida asiatica*). Heavier and appearing sturdier, their wings marked by a large bar of white feathers, their tails wider and blunter than the mourning dove's pointed one, the whitewing, *paloma blanca* in Spanish, is, in south Texas and Mexico, very much the dove of choice. The birds are seed- and grain-eaters like the mourning dove, attracted to sunflowers and milo and sorghum, capable of eating each day two ounces apiece of such feed. For Texan and Mexican ranchers, the sight of a million or so whitewings settling like blue smoke over a money crop is, obviously, a thoroughly baleful one. Hunters, therefore, are seldom unwelcome. Does a million birds in one place sound excessive? Sometimes that is what a hunter is fortunate enough to see, although with modern-day agriculture's penchant for exhausting the land—drawing down water tables and "clearing" the mesquite and palo verde thickets and bosques the whitewings need for roosting and nesting—it is a progressively rarer display.

In the mornings the birds will come out of the thickets they spent the night in and pass over the huisache brakes, heading for the fields, coming in such an outlandish flurry that a befuddled hunter is prone to commit the venial sin of all wing shooting: drawing a bead on the entire flock and invariably hitting nothing more than empty sky. It would be well to take a young hunter out to the skeet-shooting range before the season to help him master the skills of swing and lead needed to kill birds in flight (skills that are discussed in greater detail in Chapter 4). He must also be taught that when in the field he should select just one bird out of each flight and kill it, cleanly, a lost cripple being wing shooting's, and all hunting's, original sin.

In the fields, whitewings perch on the stalks of the plants to dine. As "tree-feeders," they knock grain into the furrows; and in those areas where the two species overlap, their ground-feeding relative, the mourning dove, can come along and tidy up after them. The same shot size and chokes that are used for mourning doves are advisable for whitewings, though in the later season (and this applies to mourning doves as well), when the birds have been shot at and climb to higher elevations for safety, tighter choking, such as modified—the next step up from improved—gives a shooter the added range he may require to reach the birds. And like the mourning dove, the whitewing is also very temperamental about weather, a late-summer thunderstorm or cold snap being all that it may take to drive every bird out of the region.

Along the Pacific littoral a young hunter may be lucky enough to know the band-tailed pigeon (*Columba fasciata*), the monarch of North Amerian Columbidae. These purplish-gray, teal-size birds, bearing a band of black across their tails, are as far from city pigeons (actually rock doves) as buffalo wolves are from poodles. They are most often found at altitude along the Coast Range—though they can be seen as far east as the Divide—where they feed on acorns and berries and piñon nuts, and are moved south by the turning of the season, so that September may be the hunter's time for them in British Columbia, whereas in Southern California they may not be hunted until mid-December. High mountain passes are profitable sites to lie in wait for them; but the band-tail is dauntingly hard to bring down, so No. 6 shot—preferably a magnum load—out of a shotgun of no

Band-tailed pigeons. (*Photo: Durwood Hollis*)

Band-tailed pigeon markings. (*Photo: Durwood Hollis*)

"Doves coming over!" (*Photo: Robert Robb*)

less than 20-gauge (see p. 40) with a barrel choked modified or full is a good band-tail combination.

Patience is demanded of a hunter when he first sees band-tails high in the clear late-fall sky, because he must wait for the birds to descend in a gyre into shooting range if he is to kill them well, their deserving nothing less from him. Rather than considering it a virtue, though, a hunter should look on patience as only another of the innumerable skills that his chosen occupation calls upon him to possess.

3

MIGRANTS II: WATERFOWL

It can, and has, been argued that doves as a sporting proposition probably represent more *shooting* than hunting; but the undeniable charm of pursuing all the migratory birds, however one chooses to classify that pursuit, as a means of introducing youths to the cooperative, clanlike hunting party is the opportunity it affords of being able to sit the shifty little bastards down in one spot and know what they are up to—at least to the extent that kids ever allow anyone to know anything about what they are *really* up to. A very young hunter is not likely to appreciate fully the subtle pleasures of having to lug a heavy shotgun around while trying to maintain the rigorous, daylong pace of often wearying walking needed to *hunt* upland birds with any degree of success, for instance. But in a dove field one can plant him like a geranium and watch him bloom. The very same thing can be accomplished in a duck blind.

One can, of course, hunt waterfowl exactly like upland game. On one of my first duck hunts, my father's friend Roy and I were in Siskiyou County, California, a few miles from the Oregon line and a few days shy of Christmas. We had spotted a cattle pond, frozen over except for some open water in the middle where what looked from the distance to be a small flock of mallards paddled and dabbled.

"Now remember," Roy admonished as we skulked toward the pond behind the cover of the dike, "*no flock shooting.*"

We drew up opposite the pond, then clambered over the dike. Our estimate of the flock's size had been insufficient by a magnitude of, oh, say 10 or so, and no more than a hundred quacking ducks rose up in a huge shower of silvered pond water. I fired two flummoxed shots from my Charles Daly 12-gauge over-and-under, and Roy got off three from his old Model 12 meat gun. Between us we killed fully one duck. *Uno. Eins.*

My jump shooting (as this hunting technique is called) improved painfully slowly, but in later years I *was* able to sneak across a brushy pasture on a snowy morning and, armed with my Remington 870 pump, kill two blue-winged teal and a mallard as they flushed wild together out of a creek bottom; and then on an Idaho pheasant hunt the year after, pushing across broken ground on a hot October afternoon, I put up a couple of dozen mallards out of a slough I had not even known was there and managed to pick the greenhead drake— vibrant as a traffic light, with blood-orange feet and the smell of Canadian prairies still clinging to him—right out of the center of the rising flock, killing him dead. Geese can be stalked similarly, or a hunter can float waterways or scull out in a so-called sneakboat in pursuit of them. (When jump shooting ducks and geese over water— in fact, in all overwater hunting of waterfowl—a hunter should be sure to have good boots, a good set of chest waders, so he can wade out to retrieve his birds, or a good dog to do the job for him.)

While jump shooting ducks and geese is admittedly not *much* more enjoyable than being in a circus parade or dancing through the streets of Rio during Carnival would be, *waterfowling* in its classic form means setting out spreads of decoys, or "dekes" or "blocks"; building a blind of some persuasion; and trying to lure the birds down into gun range. (It is in this way, as well as in jump shooting, that waterfowling may represent a truer notion of hunting than does the shooting of doves.)

The use of decoys for waterfowling is an ancient practice that predates the use of firearms. American Indian waterfowlers might use decoys cunningly fashioned from bundled reeds to draw waterfowl in close enough for them to be netted or speared or shot with arrows. Indians of the north today mold decoys from the mud of the tidal flats where they are hunting and adorn them with a few feathers, or

Setting out duck decoys. (*Photo: Durwood Hollis*)

prop up the carcasses of birds killed by *pass shooting*—birds who happened to fly within range of the blind—in lifelike poses to attract in other birds. In the days of the market hunters—who supplied waterfowl to meat markets and restaurants during the nineteenth and the early part of this century—live ducks might be used as decoys, a practice outlawed since 1935.

When decoys succeed in drawing ducks and geese down to where hunters wait, dressed in camouflage as well as concealed in a blind, careful not to turn their shiny faces skyward to flash like heliographs and flare away the birds, the prime reason has less to do with the humans' extraordinary skills than it does with those ducks and geese having meant to light there all along. Decoys, no matter how cleverly formed or arranged, will not entice waterfowl to go where they have absolutely no intention of going to begin with. So, the first law of decoying in birds is to place the decoys where the *birds,* in their infinite wisdom, have already gotten it into their heads to land, *not* where the hunter would find it most *convenient* for them to land. It is surprising the number of experienced waterfowlers to whom this simple premise never seems to occur.

A Mississippian friend of mine, when I go down to hunt ducks with him, always spends the late afternoon before our hunt traveling the farm roads of the Delta, finding out exactly which water-filled pothole the ducks are "pitching into." As we drive together in his Jeep in the January light, he points off to a skein of black specks in the gray distance.

"Gadwalls," he pronounces.

A little later there is another ragged V of dots above the black line of hardwoods, as identifiable to me as Morse code.

"Mallards," is how my friend classifies these.

He notes my amazement at his knack—he is always proved right—and explains, "You know, it used to impress me, too, when I saw someone else who was able to do that. But, shoot, there is not any trick to it. All it takes to tell ducks that way is to hunt 'em 'bout every day of the season for fifteen years or so. Even *you,*" he smiles sidelong, hunched over the steering wheel and staring out the mud-splattered windshield, "could do it then."

After a hunter has determined where his decoys ought to go, then he has a number of options with regard to how to distribute them. There are numerous attractive arrangements of "hook" and J and double o patterns hunters swear by, but blind faith in one complicated design or another can be carried to extremes. Basically, if a hunter can have the sun at his back and a crosswind in front of him, he is in about as ideal a situation as he can hope for. The sun at his back will help hide him from the ducks by shining into their eyes—which is why he would not care to have the wind blowing in from behind: subject to the laws of aerodynamics no less than any (other) aircraft, waterfowl land into the wind, and if a hunter is directly in front of the birds, he is more likely to be detected, the resulting evasive maneuvers being about like what you would expect a MiG pilot to execute if he suddenly discovered himself flying into a hidden *mujahidin* rocket emplacement. (With the wind blowing into his face, a hunter is going to have the ducks coming in from behind him, and he will have difficulty seeing them in time, and the birds will tend to land too far out.) A crosswind, as well, makes it easier for a hunter to judge his leads as the ducks pass in front of him.

At its most bare bones, then, decoying-in waterfowl is a matter of a hunter's finding where the birds are putting in, situating his blind to take fullest advantage of wind and light, putting out a lot of dekes—he cannot have *too* big a spread—remembering to leave an opening on the water where he wants the live birds to land—and not setting his blocks so far away that the outer edge of the spread is beyond gun range—and being prepared to move his blind and dekes, even in the middle of the morning, if the birds are "maple-leafing" in somewhere else: he should not be worried about frightening birds off by his movements in this circumstance; they certainly are not going to be drawn to him where he is, so he might as well risk moving over to them.

Decoys can be as plain or extravagant as a hunter likes, from painted bleach bottles to hand-carved wooden gallery art—some goose hunters go as far as employing full-body mounts of honkers, taxidermyed to within one inch of reincarnation, for their spreads—and it is often effective to mix species together, mingling "divers" with "puddlers," as it is to sprinkle in a few "security" birds, such as heron or gallinule decoys. At day's end, though, the decoys should all be taken up until the next shoot, even if it will only be the next morning, ducks touching down amid glassy-eyed mannequins of their own kind tending to be rather chary about returning to such a science-fiction movie set ("a signpost up ahead: *The Duck Zone*") in the near future.

Blinds can vary from a few bullrushes gathered around a hunter, to some brush pulled over him, to a pit merely augered into the ground or with a fifty-gallon drum set into it, to a wooden-frame or permanent concrete structure only slightly more luxurious than your average big-league dugout. I do not think that permanence, though, is really desirable, as long as hunters have to key their position to the waterfowl's whims. Simple and movable, and fitting in with the surrounding vegetation, is best. In snowy goose fields, no more than a white bed-sheet can provide excellent cover. Also, layout or mummy boats—that float low in the water and in which the hunter lies flat, until the waterfowl set in, then sits up to fire—work well when combined with camouflage netting or some plant material drawn over the hunter.

The theory of decoy placement for geese, whether over open water or in fields, is not appreciably different from that for ducks: put the decoys out where the birds want to land, have a good blind, and let them come. (In the way of a "trick," it is good to remember that goose decoys should not all be set with the heads erect because this is a natural sign of wariness and a signal that the birds are about to fly. A fair number of the decoys should be placed with their heads down in the unconcerned posture of feeding, notifying the incoming geese that all is well. In fields, the decoys should also be placed facing into the wind, because this is the way geese would stand in real life, preferring not to have the wind blowing up under their plumage. And mix up sizes, as geese mix in real life.)

Calling may be used to help attract geese in, as it can be with ducks. Once in Kentucky I shared a goose pit with a father and his two sons whose cracking adolescent voices were put to good use imitating the honking of Canada geese; and geese, who themselves sounded like cheering fans at a football game, actually did come into range as the boys bleated. To become genuinely skilled at calling waterfowl, though, one needs to listen to expert callers in actual hunting situations to learn the proper tones and rhythms and when and where the numerous calls ducks and geese produce are appropriate, and to practice dedicatedly, so that his calling will not, instead of drawing birds in, send them away shrieking in terror, the calling of the inexperienced being worse than no calling at all.

In hunting both ducks and geese, heavier shotgun loads are called for. For the small ducks, the teal and smaller diving ducks, No. 7½s are acceptable, but I prefer 6s; while for big ducks—mallards, pintails, widgeons, canvasbacks, and so on—No. 6 shot is about a minimum, with No. 4s, being even better. For geese, shot sizes between 4 and 2 in magnum loadings are most effective, both for added range and for killing power, while BBs, though deadly when birds are in range, can tempt hunters to *sky-bust,* to try to hit birds who are far too high up, the shot, at best, rattling off their breast feathers, at worst crippling them and causing them to be lost. Modified and full chokes are called for, but a fundamental rule is always to wait until the birds have unquestionably come into range before attempting to kill them—they, too, deserving nothing less.

One last migratory bird that does not get hunted much but is

Calling in Canada geese.
(*Photo: Robert Robb*)

The author with 10-gauge shotgun and sandhill crane in Oklahoma. (*Photo: Mike Evans*)

of enormous interest—at least to me—is the sandhill crane. Along
with the whooping crane, who can be differentiated immediately from
the sandhill by his white-white plumage, as the sandhill can from the
great blue heron in flight by the fact that the heron flies with his neck
tucked in and the crane with his stretched out—the sandhill is one of
only two crane species in North America, numbering into the hundreds
of thousands, while the "whooper" carries on with fewer than two
hundred representatives. A four-foot-tall, gray-feathered bird—the tips
of the feathers bronze colored, the crowns of the adults covered by a
patch of bald red scalp—the sandhill may be hunted in a number of
states along the Central Flyway—one of the several primary north-
south migration routes for waterfowl across the continent.

Just as with the other waterfowl, hunting sandhills involves moving about the country and looking for where they are congregating.
When a good concentration is located—and one December in southwest Oklahoma this meant my hunting companions, Tom and Mike,

Dawn: waiting for ducks. (*Photo: Durwood Hollis*)

and my finding three thousand of the towering birds hopping and feeding and flapping up and landing back down together in a single harvested peanut field, the sound of their trilled calling, like that of a nursery crowded with cooing babies "Not of this Earth!," so loud and so continuous that it would haunt us for days afterward. At four the next morning, having received permission to hunt there from the landowner, we were back in the peanut field, digging three-foot-deep pits in the sandy soil, piling tumbleweeds around them, then setting out our decoys—painted plywood silhouettes and full-body plastic imitations—a hundred yards in front of us, facing into the wind.

The cranes would never dream of landing in our decoys, but would come down low enough over us to inspect the spread—before invariably tacking away like twelve-meter yachts when they realized the deception. We could see them approaching for miles, and for what seemed forever, as slow as oceangoing vessels, wing tips almost touching. Huddled down in our pits, fearing to look up on the chance our faces would alert them to our presences, we would wait until the sound of them was directly overhead, then we would stand and, pointing straight up, would fire. I was shooting a Spanish Laurona 10-gauge side-by-side with three-and-a-half-inch magnum shells holding two-and-a-quarter ounces of copper-plated No. 4 shot; and when a twelve-pound bird would die above me he would come down like a fully rigged schooner scuttled in the Pacific, his feathers fluttering in the air the way canvas sails must as they sink through seawater.

Cranes, like ducks and geese, can be plucked, and also, as with ducks and geese, when it comes to removing all the down under the feathers, a hunter is in for considerable labor. The end result, however, once the bird has had all the feathers and down removed from it, and the tiny hairlike feathers below that singed off, and it has been drawn— and if feasible, all waterfowl should be bled immediately after killing, and in warm weather all birds should be eviscerated as soon as possible—with the skin left intact so the dark-fleshed bird can be rubbed with marjoram and stuffed with apples and onions and roasted until the joints are loose and served with wild rice and a bit of gooseberry sauce on the side is worth all the work as a hunter tastes all the miles of flight and far places the bird passed through to reach him.

Plucking waterfowl, these days, is among the least of the worries a waterfowler has to face, however. Although mammoth efforts, through international treaties, local wildlife programs, and the projects of such private organizations as Ducks Unlimited, are made to preserve, and in some cases expand them, wetlands—the irreplaceable cradle of all waterfowl—continue to be drained to be turned into farmlands. More prosaically, it simply becomes harder every season for a waterfowl hunter to find a place to hunt as game-rich areas are "developed" out

Hunting ducks in flooded timber. (*Author photo*)

of existence or bought up by private clubs, that often charge nearly extortionary membership fees, and the swelling numbers of disenfranchised hunters crowd onto the limited remaining accessible private and public hunting areas.

In some best of all possible worlds hunters would not have to deal with the twentieth century—hunting being a means of escaping, if only momentarily, from the modern world and all its attendant abominations and widespread chuckleheadedness. But these days, that we have no choice but to live in, insist on intruding on us, even when we go a-huntin'. More waterfowl hunters are in more cramped quarters, and the result is a buildup of lead shot that threatens to poison ducks and geese. Who would have ever thought?

Strange to say, modern technology seems to extend a solution to at least this toxic-shot syndrome: nontoxic steel shot. There is controversy over even this, though. Steel will not deform the way softer lead will, and, therefore, in some older, lighter- and high-carbon-steel-barreled shotguns there is the possibility that the string of hard shot will "bulge" the barrel where the choke constricts it. The damaging of a fine-quality, old shotgun is a genuine loss—no matter how venal some might wish to characterize such a sentiment when compared to lead-poisoned waterfowl—as much a loss as taking a claw hammer to an antique harp or a Queen Anne chair might be. Nor is retiring the old side-by-side shotgun—a gun whose every stylistic feature and mechanism, as we shall see, is the direct result of generations of wing shooting, whose only real *function* is to be pointed at flying birds—to the gun cabinet in favor of a more modern shotgun made to handle steel shot all that appealing an option. It is like owning a Bugatti and being told that from now on all you will be allowed to do is look at it. For driving, you will have to take the Mazda.

There is also a sincere concern that steel shot, lacking the density of lead, does not kill as well—according to some opponents of steel shot, the difference would seem to be about like trying to knock over an empty beer can with a handful of popcorn in place of pea gravel. This *can* be a problem, as can the perceived difference in the leads required of steel versus lead shot—steel flies faster and reaches the bird quicker—but it is quite curable if only No. 4, and larger, shot—the hunter's using steel shot a size or two larger than the size lead shot he would normally use for the game he is after; for example, No. 4 steel in place of No. 6 lead—is used out of no smaller than three-inch 20-gauge magnum shells, with 16-, 12-, and 10-gauges being much superior and more reliable choices, and if, again, waterfowlers will simply restrain themselves until the birds are *there,* about to set down and clearly within range. (The rule some waterfowlers follow when using steel is to wait *at least* until they can clearly see the decoying birds' feet, while some wait until they can see their *eyes*.)

So even as a young hunter waits hidden in a duck blind—shivering like a pup, though not from the cold at all, as around him the older hunters, some blowing deep from their centers through duck calls, and others, as the quacking grows louder and the whoosh of ducks circling lower into the decoys draws closer, whisper hoarsely to him, "Not yet, son. Wait. Wait."—as this young hunter waits, the modern world creeps up, and with it the first hint of the cool days that now make hunting more difficult, but perhaps even more necessary.

"Now, son. Now," someone says, and the cover of the blind is thrown back and the boy stands and there are ducks in front of him, their wings cupped and their feet webbed, the true art of waterfowling to be found in having brought the birds into this position. He raises his shotgun—remembering only sketchily all that he has been taught about shooting at birds in flight, but enough of it for now—and fires, seeing a duck, pedaling the air, tumble out of it to the water, as a black dog splashes out of the blind and begins to swim, and someone calls, "Good shot, son!"

4

MEANS I: SHOTGUNS

Although we may speak of a kind of technology that is "modern," at its heart there is nothing in the least modern about technology, particularly the technology of hunting weapons.

The first technologist, the mother of whose invention must have been the grimmest brand of necessity imaginable, was undoubtedly some famished protohuman ancestor of ours knuckling along, in this scenario, in pursuit of something both edible and fleet. Out of sheer frustration at the sight of lunch about to make a clean getaway, he scoops up a stone and stands erect to hurl it, knocking a small animal, perhaps feathered, dead. Within a cartoon balloon, a glowing primordial light bulb appears.

From this point the natural progression of technological innovation leads to that stone's being chipped into a laurel-leaf point and strapped with sinew and glued with animal blood to a stick to create the spear, the spear becoming a fletched arrow to be fired from a bow, the crossbow arising out of the bow, and then, with the arrival of gunpowder, both eventually giving way to the gun, some of the first ones being used, in fact, for firing arrows. Ultimately, the human mind—the very pattern of whose circuitry evolved out of a million-year history of hunting—arrives at balls of lead to be propelled from those guns and thereby extend the human predator's range of lethality further beyond the limits of his grasp than it has ever been before.

Yet a mind capable of such seemingly stark, utilitarian logic is, oddly enough, also capable of playfulness. The bow, therefore, could be not only a weapon, to be fired, but a harp, to be plucked. Gunpowder—widely invented-discovered, probably by Arab apothecaries and alchemists, between the eleventh and thirteenth centuries, its formula of saltpeter, charcoal, and sulfur first written down by the Franciscan Oxonian Roger Bacon in his *Epistola de Secretis Operibus Artis et Naturae* sometime before the mid-thirteenth—could be used not only to launch projectiles but to explode firecrackers. Then there is the shotgun, in particular the English side-by-side "game gun,"* whose development, we shall see, is almost entirely the product of hunters concerned not so much with the task of securing victuals as with a serious quest for sport.

The line of the descent of firearms that brings us to the game gun begins, then, with small cannons, called *crakys,* a word meaning "ravens," following a tradition of naming guns in honor of birds that was carried on for four hundred years. There follow in due course hand-culverins, matchlocks, harquebuses, calivers, muskets (after the medieval falconer's name for the male European sparrow hawk), wheel locks (designed by a Florentine known as Leonardo da Vinci), snaphances, miquelet locks, flintlocks, percussion guns (invented by the Reverend Dr. Andrew Forsyth, minister of Belhelvie parish, Aberdeenshire), and breechloaders.

For several thousand years prior to the arrival of the gun on the scene, hunters had taken birds in a workmanlike manner by the use of snares or traps, or sometimes throwing sticks or, later, the crossbow when, on occasion, a bird on the wing might astonishingly be brought down. The gun's arrival, though, did not suddenly make wing shooting all the rage. The bird hunters, or fowlers, of the early sixteenth century were hardly devil-may-care sporting types out for a few laughs, but were, instead, impoverished bogtrotters lugging about smoothbore matchlocks or hand cannons, surplus left over from recent religious strife or some punitive action, and intent upon putting *anything*

---

* While I chose *gun* in place of the term *firearm* in Chapter 1, it should be noted here that gun usually refers to a smoothbore weapon, whereas a rifle is one with a *rifled*—a spirally grooved—barrel.

into the pot. Their shot, such as it was, being made from sheets of lead chopped up into small pieces, could conceivably sustain a killing pattern* for all of a handful of yards, if that. Bird hunting at this time consisted of crawling up to the edge of ponds or rivers or roosts and letting fly at birds and hoping for the best, as hunter-gatherers had pretty much been doing since that first stone was cast.

(Yet in spite of the seeming haphazard quality of such fowling, these hunters were considered so adept at game-taking that the nobles feared that their own hunting, primarily for big game with dogs and horses and spears and bows, might be impinged on, and so passed numerous laws making it illegal for most of the peasantry to own guns or hunt, thus giving birth to the grand tradition of "poaching his lordship's pheasants" and outwitting the gamekeeper.)

Changes in bird hunting came inch by inch.

First, at the end of the 1500s arrived the knowledge of how to manufacture round, and therefore ballistically more accurate, shot by pouring molten lead, mixed with a small quantity of arsenic, through a plate pierced with holes and into a bowl of water: it would be some two centuries more before the *shot tower*—wherein a liquid lead-and-antimony alloy is poured through sieves, of different size openings for different size shot, and let fall some two hundred feet into large tanks of water, the surface tension on the lead droplets in flight through the air keeping them round—would be conceived of (coming to its inventor, my father always told me, in a dream).

The fowling, or birding, piece of the early 1600s was a formidable weapon of up to six feet in length, twenty pounds in weight, and of .80 to .85 caliber, or about 8 or 9 "bore" or, as we call it today in America, "gauge."† With weapons of such elephantine ponderousness

---

* *Pattern* is the way the shot disperses when it leaves the muzzle of a shotgun. In present-day terms, pattern is the percentage of the shot load that, fired at a thirty-inch circle at a distance of forty yards, stays within that circle, each choke having an ideal pattern: for example, 70 percent or more for a full choke. If a shotgun does not pattern well, the shot scattering every which way out of it, then the odds of enough shot's reaching a bird to ensure a kill are gravely reduced.

† Quickly, *gauge,* as well as *bore,* is derived from a system of "bore numbers" in use by 1540 to standardize the size of musket balls and is defined by the number of balls of pure lead of that diameter that would equal one pound. A "10-gauge" shotgun, therefore, has a barrel of a diameter that corresponds to ten lead balls of that size weighing a pound. For the 12-gauge, there would be twelve; 16-gauge, sixteen; and so on, until the .410—62.78-gauge—is reached, it for painfully obvious reasons being classified by "caliber" (see p. 53).

as these—and black powder elephant guns and heavy double express rifles for use in Africa were, in truth, direct descendants of such fowling pieces—wing shooting, or "shooting flying," was still fairly much a moot possibility. Stalking horses and portable tree disguises were all the rage. Fowling, as a sporting diversion for gentlemen of leisure, still was not.

Then came the development in France of the flintlock, a great advance in reliability over preceding ignition systems, and a general refinement of the fowling piece along more graceful and wieldy lines. And *then* came Oliver Cromwell, a man who was said to enjoy, to the extent his Calvinist precepts would allow, music, hunting, and small beer, who repudiated the medicinal benefits of quinine because the trade in it was the monopoly of the crafty Jesuits, and who at one point in his rise to power involved himself in a dispute between fowlers and the Crown over the drainage of fenlands. Subsequent activities of his, though, were what inspired a recently orphaned Charles II's seeking refuge in France, where the general shape of a big time was for the powdered aristos, on their vast game-laden estates, to slay driven birds right, left, and center *on the wing,* and for the most part leave their feathered carcasses in the fields to rot. (At this same time, the rabble of England, released from game laws as a result of the Civil Wars, was engaged in a wholesale slaughter of its own of *all* English game—a dismal pattern to be repeated in France after the Revolution, in India after the end of the Raj, and wherever the instincts of humans to hunt have been forcibly suppressed and then set loose without constraint.)

Restored to the English throne in 1660, Charles II brought back with him, in contrast to the Puritans, an attitude that "God will never damn a man for allowing himself a little pleasure," it being his particular pleasure to have Cromwell's malaria-ridden corpse exhumed and the head stuck on a pole atop Westminster Hall for twenty years or so, and to hunt birds in the new style of shooting flying. This latter fad soon spread through the court and nobility and to the gentry; and by 1686, one Richard Blome, in *The Gentleman's Recreation,* could describe (incorrectly, as it happened—he accounted leading a "vulgar Error") the new technique of wing shooting, a practice hardly even thought of in the England of a generation earlier.

Fortunately, the type of shooting flying the English carried out at this time lacked the wretched excessiveness of the French fashion. In character it was very similar to our own style of walking-up game— jump shooting. Fowling pieces were now sporting barrels between thirty-nine and forty-five inches long—such length being thought necessary to burn efficiently the entire charge of gunpowder; were eight to nine pounds in weight; and possessed decent balance.

In 1727, a Mr. George Markland, "late fellow of St. John's College in Oxford," could publish a 373-line poem titled "Pteryplegia: Or, the Art of Shooting-Flying," which along with advice that the "Weak and Crazy" should not be taken out into the field, but "fed with Jellies till their Strength is come," and how a "Gulp too much" of the "cordial Dram" is worse than "none at all, like one help'd *over* his Horse [italics mine]," is able to describe the basic technique of wing shooting in terms that are as applicable to today's bird hunting as they were to that of 260 years ago:

> FIVE GENERAL sorts of *Flying Marks* there are:
> The *Lineals* two, *Traverse,* and *Circular;*
> The Fifth *Oblique,* which I may vainly teach
> But Practice only perfectly can reach.
>
> WHEN A BIRD comes *directly to your Face,*
> Contain your Fire a while and let her pass,
> Unless some Trees behind you change the Case.
> If so, a little Space above her Head
> Advance the Muzzle, and you strike her dead.
> Ever let Shot pursue where there is room;
> Marks hard before thus easy will become.
>
> BUT WHEN the Bird *flies from you in a Line,*
> With little Care I may pronounce her thine:
> Observe the Rule before, and neatly raise
> Your Piece til there's no *Open under-space*
> Betwixt the Object and the *Silver Sight;*
> Then send away, and timely stop the Flight.
>
> TH' UNLUCKY *Cross Mark,* or the *Traverse Shoot,*
> By some thought easy (yet admits Dispute,
> As the most common Practice is to Fire
> Before the Bird) will nicest Time require:
> For, too *much* Space allow'd, the Shot will fly
> All innocent and pass too nimbly by;
> Too *little* Space, the Partridge, swift as Wind,
> Will dart athwart and bilk her Death behind.

This makes the Point so difficult to guess,
'Cause you must be exact in Time or miss.

From here we arrive at the start of the nineteenth century and the development by England's most famous gun maker, Joseph Manton—who taught the illustrious likes of James Purdey and Thomas Boss how to build fine shotguns—of the game gun, a light (around seven pounds), well-balanced, fast-handling, side-by-side shotgun with barrels—formed from old horseshoe nails (because they were thought to have been made stronger by the wear the horses' hooves had given them) that were heated and hammered together into strips and wound around mandrels to make "Damascus" barrels—of about thirty inches long, with an elevated rib, abbreviated fore end, a straight grip, and the overall stock configurations that English shotguns—at least those designed for upland-game hunting—have to this day. All of this the result of subsistence fowlers' being supplanted by stylish sportsmen and once again reinforcing the belief that the only acceptable reason for ever wanting to be English is if you can be assured of being an English gentleman.

Innovations beyond this, such as center-fire cartridges, the bolt and top-lever mechanism for opening and closing guns, internal hammers, and the shortening of the barrels to the present twenty-six- to twenty-eight-inch range, were not really advances but merely the finishing touches to the game gun—later *American* advancements on the shotgun, such as choking, the lever- and pump-action repeaters of the late 1800s, and that greatest of American gun designers John M. Browning's semiautomatic of 1911, all being products meant to correspond to the needs of the commercial waterfowlers and, therefore, industrial in origin rather than of strictly sporting value: about like a John Deere tractor versus a Jaguar XKE. The game gun's sole reason for existence in this world, the purpose that molded its classic, elegant lines, was so that flighting birds could be taken out of the air for a hunter's sporting happiness.

Sometime in the late Victorian era, and especially during the Edwardian, something about this estimable notion of sport got seriously out of whack, though. The sales of top-quality English game guns were as dependent on the presence of so-called discretionary income in the 1800s as sales of hot tubs and gold Rolexes are today. The politically revolutionary year of 1848, for example, was an arid one when it came to the purchase not only of game guns but of champagne as well, as princes, both royal and merchant, were reluctant to part with a spare franc or pound until they saw how current events would be resolved. But as the industrial revolution broadened and fortunes mounted, so too did the demand for game guns and the desire of wealthy landowners to acquire fame as the hosts of shooting parties where the biggest bags of game were taken. The somewhat dubious sport of shooting driven game, the *battue* the French originated, was perfected to unseemly heights by the English.

There arose at this time in England numerous earls and lords and sirs whose renown as wing shooters on driven game was, at least within their own class, the equal of that afforded a .380 batter in major-league baseball today. Rivalries among these shooters could be fierce. In order to set a record, a Lord Walsingham in 1888 would have his moors driven remorselessly so he might kill 1,075 grouse in a *single* day, or a Lord de Grey, the Marquis of Ripon, would have six pheasants dead in the air all at the same time, a "display that frequently drew subdued applause from his audience," as one writer describes the tableau. On one grouse shoot, a certain Lord Wemyss, in an effort to top Lord de Grey's bag for that day, persisted in shooting even after his black powder charges had succeeded in setting his "butt," or blind, ablaze. It subsequently took two weeks to extinguish the resulting range fire, but His Lordship did win top-gun honors that day. Purchases of ten thousand shotgun cartridges annually by such individuals were not uncommon, and the owners of country estates vied feverishly with each other for the privilege of having shots such as these grace their weekend affairs, one such, which the Prince of Wales attended on December 18, 1913, amassing a bag of 3,937 pheasants.

Although from the standpoint of bird populations it was probably a harmless custom—the landowners raising birds to shoot on their properties the way sheep were raised to be butchered—wing shooting at this extreme, whatever else it might have been, certainly was no longer hunting; it was hardly even pastime anymore. It could only be glazed, mindless rote—mount, swing, lead, fire; mount, swing, lead, fire, ad very much nauseam—no vital connection remaining between the predator and his prey, no acknowledgment anymore that a bird was in fact an animal and not just a self-propelled target. Nothing more than an exercise in extravagance and prodigality, this shooting was the sort of convulsively conspicuous consumption that might be expected from an age so smugly full of itself that it felt it could blithely squander a generation in the muddy trenches of the Great War.

If nothing else, that war did put a damper on the gluttonous

wing shooting that could allow a Lord de Grey alone to record a
lifetime bag of 556,813 head of game killed with the shotgun, before
he "dropped dead in the heather" during a grouse shoot in the fall of
1923, aged seventy-one. Such wealth and hubris as were required to
carry out this type of shooting with any really insolent jauntiness were
in rather short supply after 1918.

Huge bags of pheasants and partridges and doves can yet be
taken on shoots in many locales, but this is not what the game gun
was really meant for. Its real meaning and purpose, and joy, lie somewhere between the dour harvesting of the medieval fowler and the
fatuous exterminating carried out by the upper-class twit. It is to be
found, as it was in Mr. Markland's day, in carrying a gun down the
rows of an English wheat field or through an Irish woodcock woods
or in a covert in Vermont or through Georgia branch bottoms after
quail. It is about an individual bird and a hunter, the one-to-one
relationship they share.

If all we were interested in were how *many* birds we could kill,
how big a score we could rack up, we could certainly find a more
efficient means than wing shooting, which is why I say it is more an
outgrowth of sport than any other impetus. For all the pretenses of
its being a science, that can be taught scientifically, which some experts
want to bring to wing shooting, it remains far more an art, for which
one "must sweat and be cold, must sweat again, and be cold again"
before he can arrive at any "degree of perfection" in it.

There are, nonetheless, certain steps a wing shooter can take to make
his sweating, if not easier, at least more productive.

Shotguns are, to begin with, pointed at a target—unlike rifles,
which are aimed—and for the beginner this usually means that a more
open choke is better than too tight a one. A shotgun hunter keeps
both eyes open when he fires. This is necessary so he can retain his
depth perception to estimate the distance to the bird and to adjust his
lead accordingly, and also so he has his complete peripheral vision on
both sides of his head to detect the flight of birds. Before he even
picks up a shotgun, then, a hunter must determine which is his master
eye.

Just as most of us are either right- or left-handed, so we are right-
or left-*eyed*: one eye's perception being dominant over the other's, and
this eye being called the "master eye." A simple test can demonstrate
the effect of this on shotgun shooting.

Find a vertical line—where two walls meet or the edge of a

doorframe, for example—a few yards away from you. Now, with both eyes open, quickly point your finger at this line. Holding your finger on the line, close your left eye. Note how far, if at all, your finger appears to move off the line; then, without moving your finger, open your left eye and close your right. Again, note the distance of the movement off this line. If you are right-handed, it is likely that you are "right-eye dominant," and your finger should have been closer to the line when viewed through your right eye than it was when viewed through your left. If, however, your finger was closer with your left eye open, then that is your master eye; and if you are right-handed, then you may have a problem.

This problem is called *cross-eye dominance* and can cause you to point off your target when you bring up your shotgun. The tidiest remedy for this is to learn to mount your shotgun on the same side as your master eye. If you discover that you are cross dominant in your eyes after you have been shooting for a number of years, though, then changing over can be very difficult.

Another solution, therefore, is to squint, slightly, your cross-dominant eye before shooting. You do not want to close it completely, just enough to make your other eye assume dominance. There is also a mechanical method for achieving this.

You should wear shooting glasses in any case, so it is possible to patch over the cross-dominant eye and thereby force the other to take over its duties. In my own situation (and this is why I am devoting space here to the master eye, which some gun writers dismiss as a meaningless theory, but which has made a marked difference in my own shooting), I shoot right-handed and have a dominant left eye. So, *first making absolutely certain that my side-by-side shotgun is unloaded, and having a friend, who has agreed to help me, check it himself to confirm this,* I bring the gun up into shooting position; and while I look down the rib, my friend places a dime-size disk of frosted cellophane tape on the left lens of my shooting glasses, just covering the iris of my left eye. Now, when I mount my shotgun and point it at a winging bird, the center of the vision in my left eye is automatically blocked, but my peripheral vision *and,* although I cannot quite explain why, my depth perception remain intact.

Once the dominant eye has been determined, and the matter of shooting right- or left-handed has been settled, the next question is of gun fit. If you should ever find yourself in the Long Room at Purdey's being measured for your game gun by one of the Worshipful

Eye patch on shooting glasses to correct "cross-eye dominance." (*Photo: Daniel Hernandez*)

Company of Gunmakers of the City of London—recalling Manton and Bonnie Prince Charlie and the peasant fowling pieces that led to here—you will see how proper fit is much more akin to the tailor's art of proportion and cut than it is to mathematical calculation. Using a "try-gun," the gun maker will alter its dimensions ("I believe we could use a bit more castoff here, sir.") until he arrives at a proper configuration whose primary qualification is that it *feels* right to the shooter: so that the shotgun for the right-handed shooter (and I shall assume all shooters to be right-handed from here on out, to simplify matters) points where his left hand points; so that its butt comes smoothly to the shoulder without catching or being too short; so that the trigger finger will reach the forward trigger, on a double-triggered gun, comfortably; so that the *comb,* as the top edge of the stock is called, fits under the cheek so the head will not lift off the gun, the head needing to remain "down" on the gun to keep the right eye, which acts as the shotgun's rear sight, in the correct position so the rib will meet the line of sight and travel out it as of its own accord; so that a wood-and-steel weapon can become a natural extension of the hunter's hand and eye, and an extension of the human hunter's natural lethality. And how many of us will ever have our shotguns fitted and built for us by Purdey's?

Most of us will buy our shotguns over the counter in a gun shop somewhere far from London, or from any custom gun maker, for that

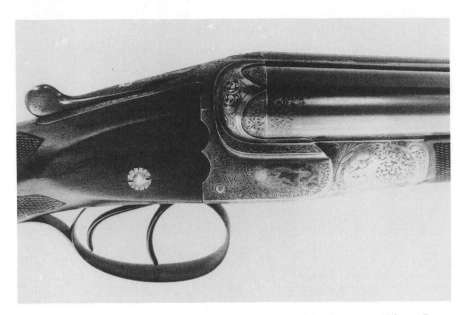

A high-grade 16-gauge English box-lock side-by-side shotgun. (*Photo: Larry Barnes*)

matter. Yet there is nothing to stop our looking for the same qualities of proper fit wherever we purchase our shotguns. (A very basic tenet to bear in mind when shopping for a shotgun is that we will tend to shoot better with a gun that is slightly on the long side, rather than one that is too short.) Most mass-produced shotguns are designed with some mythical Everyman in mind, and so we find ourselves "crawling" all over the stock to make ourselves fit it and get our eyes in line with the bird—when the idea is for us to be able to keep our eyes on the bird and bring the shotgun up into line with it.

We can search through factory guns until we find one that feels best, or have a gunsmith alter the stock to the dimensions we believe best suited to ourselves. And we can be sure to look for a gun with good balance, one in which the weight lies evenly between our two hands when the gun is raised. What we also need to do, though, is to *practice,* because even the most perfect of gun fits is only an adjunct to our becoming attuned to the physical movements, the *pas de shotgun,* of wing shooting.

A shotgun hunter needs to practice hour upon hour, day after day, to learn the art of pointing and swinging, until the motion becomes grooved into his subconscious, the way music is grooved into a record or the way one learns the movements of martial arts techniques. There is no substitute for this. A shotgun hunter can learn much from a shooting coach or school, if one is available to him. But at the very least he should practice on clay birds at the shotgun range, learning, particularly if he shoots "Continental" style with the stock held down before calling *"pull,"* how to mount the shotgun properly and to assume the proper stance: feet about shoulder-width apart; weight distributed evenly over them so that when the shooter swings he remains poised; the right shoulder put forward to meet the butt as the gun is raised; the shooter, no matter in which direction he turns to track a flying bird, never leaning *away* from the gun but keeping it held firmly, without being clutched in a tension-filled death grip, to his shoulder, so that the recoil can be absorbed by his entire body; the head remaining on the stock; the swing, a smooth follow-through.

Clays will also teach a shotgun hunter rudimentarily about lead, at least the lead required to shatter little black dishes flung from the windows of little wooden houses. There are tables, somewhere, that give the flight speeds of birds, the time shot takes to travel certain distances at certain velocities, and what appropriate leads should be; but these have always struck me as being every bit as useful for the shooting flying of live, wild, unpredictable birds as tables on meteorology are for forecasting what the wind will do ten minutes from now.

I am not sure any hunter knows beyond a shadow of all doubt how he has killed a bird every time he does it; and I am certain that I do not. Sometimes, it seems to me, I use a "sustained" lead, where I get what I perceive to be the correct length ahead of a bird and maintain that length as I fire, remembering to follow through; and I see a bird fall. Other times, I believe, I use a "swing-through" lead, swinging from behind the bird and accelerating through him, firing just as my muzzle passes his head. And I see him fall. At still other times, though, I cannot actually say *what* I have done; and the bird falls. And then, doing any or all of the above, or trying to lead just slightly ahead of an incoming bird, remembering that it is always better to lead for a bird's head rather than his whole body, or letting a bird going directly away rest, in my sight picture, on the muzzle of my shotgun (just as Markland says!), I fire, with every confidence in the world, and do *not* see a bird fall in the slightest.

All I do know beyond a shadow of all doubt about wing shooting—besides the enormous amount of time one must devote to practicing the art in order to be able to perform it even halfway well—is that if we do it enough there will be days when it seems a miracle that any birds fell at all, and others when we will have been—no other word for it—so at *one* with those sprightly feathered trajectories that it all seemed simply inevitable, that there was no way out of it for either of us, wing shooter or bird. As if the totality of our lives had led us to the moment of our conjunction.

I have fought shy of a discussion of the merits of the various shotgun gauges and loads till the end of this chapter because I find it so resolutely anticlimactic a part of the subject of shotguns and wing shooting: because I am of the opinion that there are almost no circumstances where a shotgun hunter could not get by quite satisfactorily with one well-fitted 12-gauge shotgun loaded with No. 6 lead shot that is able to leave the muzzle at a velocity between twelve hundred and thirteen hundred feet per second. Except, as I have previously noted, for the big waterfowl (and excluding wild turkeys— another kettle of bird altogether), which might call for No. 4 or No. 2 shot, or doves and quail and woodcock, who might be better served by No. 7½ or 8 shot, a "fowler's" preference for any shotgun-cartridge combination outside this is almost exclusively a question of aesthetics and personal prejudice. (For my own traveling gun—that is, one I am prepared to sacrifice on the altar of lost luggage—I use that Remington Model 870 12-gauge pump with a twenty-eight-inch modified barrel, having shot with it without complaint from Alaska to the Dakotas to Ireland to Mexico to Argentina.)

Of course, I must now hasten to add any number of exemptions to this rule, such as that some shotgunners perform better with the lessened recoil of a 20-gauge. And that for the waterfowler who wants a lighter gun to tote into the field, a 16-gauge—long a favorite of European shooters—is, especially with the advent of steel shot, an exquisite compromise between the 20- and the 12- (as well as being one of the most perfectly patterning of loads, one ounce of shot being "square" in the cartridge—recall the definition of gauge—that is, having the length and the diameter of the load of shot nearly equal and, therefore, subject to less of the deforming of the pellets that is encountered by a long column of shot). And that a "go-to-hell" (as a friend calls it) 10-gauge magnum will stop a goose in flight at fifty yards as surely as if a door had been slammed in its face. And that a 28-gauge makes a nonpareil fast-swinging easy-carrying upland-bird gun. And that for the expert shooter willing to risk no shots at birds beyond thirty yards, a .410 can significantly add to the sport of it all.

Chukar hunting. (*Photo: Durwood Hollis*)

I plead guilty: It's all true! Yet it remains, purely and simply, a matter *entirely* of taste.

Wing shooting at its truest—and why occupy oneself in any other way but the truest?—does not require more than one weapon with which to carry it out satisfactorily, one that when we are within proper range, and our point and our swing are right, we can kill a bird cleanly with; and a 12-gauge with a load of No. 6s is almost always such a weapon. If we choose to use something else, and argue a persuasive case for it, that is perfectly fine. All I am saying is that it is an argument outside the truth of wing shooting, whose heart remains unaffected by all questions of technology.

The heart of this game is not to be found in the particular technology we employ to bring about its intended outcome: the capturing of an animal. All our technology goes back, anyway, to that inborn lethality we, as evolved hunters, already have in our arms and legs and hands and eyes and brains. This is why, while we need to understand them clearly to be able, when we decide that it is time, to kill cleanly, we must not allow ourselves to become mired in all the numbers. Numbers are always a means, never the end. The end is far more complicated—and at the same time far more elegant—than any flock of numbers we can possibly imagine.

5

MEANS II:
RIFLES

What about rifles, then, for our native game? Again, should it happen to be our desire, there are numbers here to be played with as well, but in an even *more* Byzantine manner than with shotguns.

If it were a hunter's fondest wish to select a weapon to kill ducks with tomorrow morning, there would be the four gauges from 20 to 10 from which it would be reasonable for him to select. If on the other hand it were his desire to kill a deer, the number of reasonable calibers* that he could consider might be as high as four or five dozen. Which should it be? Does a .243 Winchester strike your fancy? What about a .250-3000 Savage? A .257 Roberts? 6.5 x 54 mm Mannlicher-Schoenauer? .270 Weatherby Magnum? 7 mm Mauser? 7 mm Remington Magnum? .30-40 Krag? .30-'06 Springfield? .308 Norma Magnum? .35 Whelan? There are at least four *times* as many calibers

---

* *Caliber,* just to keep things official, is, in general, the inner diameter of a firearm's bore, measured before the riflings have been cut—at which point a "firearm" becomes a "rifle"—and is expressed in hundredths or thousandths of an inch or in millimeters.

that could be named, not one of which would be an absolutely ludicrous choice for killing a deer; and if varied bullet weights are added to the calibers, the figure becomes nearly astronomical. All the numbers, all the twinkling numbers! As native technologists from our opposable thumbs to our prehensile toes, we do love them so.

And there is no denying that they can be diverting, and even quite romantic, when looked at in the context of an extravagantly varied hunting ground like Africa. But as with shotguns and wing shooting, it is necessary for us to understand rifles and the hunting of big game with them in a more fundamental way, without permitting ourselves to be blinded by science.

At their inception, smoothbore shoulder guns, when loaded with a single ball instead of shot, were simply iron tubes that spewed lead and smoke in no more than the general direction in which they were pointed, the discharged bullets tending to flutter through the air like knuckleballs. Such bullets might hit a deer at a hundred paces, but there was no telling where *on* the deer that hit might be.

There had long been an awareness—well before the football— that spin imparted stability to an object in flight. Hunting arrows, for instance, had for thousands of years been feathered, *fletched* or *fledged*, with the vanes set helically on the shafts so that they could spin and the arrows fly not only truer but farther.

Sometime in the 1400s straight grooves were first cut into gun bores to act as gutters, of a sort, to collect the fouling created by the burning of gunpowder—a progressive buildup of which made loading difficult and eventually impossible. With such grooves in it, a musketeer could fire more rounds in battle before having to stop to clean his barrel. Whether or not any connection between spin and bullet stability in flight had yet been made, at some point these grooves began to be cut in a spiral pattern, causing the balls to leave the muzzles spinning like tops; and, much to everyone's dismay, and to some's (namely the shooter's) delight, guns had suddenly taken on the novel attribute of accuracy. Once again, this was nothing more than another innovation the human's most important hunting weapon, his brain, was bound to come up with to extend his lethality. As were iron sights about this same time, and telescopic sights as early as the 1600s.

All of the above are involved in getting a bullet to an animal, but what needs to be considered next is what occurs when that bullet arrives. How do bullets kill?

*   *   *

An arrow or a spear kills by wounding. A wound to the heart of an animal will kill more quickly than one to the lungs or some other vital organ, but ultimately what allows a hunter to capture an animal is its loss of blood. A bullet, too, can kill by wounding in this fashion. But a bullet can also do things a spear or an arrow is not likely to.

First, a bullet can break bone, particularly such heavy bone as that found in the shoulders. With a broken shoulder a large mammal has tremendous difficulty in traveling fast or far, and a hunter is able then to overtake and capture it. If the spinal column can be hit, then this immobilization is instantaneous.

Then there is shock, to so-called hydrostatic shock that a high-velocity bullet creates in flesh when it strikes it, sending waves of impact radiating out through the predominantly liquid medium of an animal's body—the way a diver doing a "cannonball" can splash the water out of a pool. Such concussive shock can disrupt an animal's entire nervous system, shorting it all out and killing the animal where it stands. (Major Sir Gerald Burrard in his *Notes on Sporting Rifles* writes that this sort of massive shock is produced when a bullet strikes at a velocity in excess of twenty-four hundred feet per second.) The chief disadvantage—from a carnivore's point of view—to such high-speed shock is the extensive tissue damage it may cause, the speeding bullet creating a literal jellying of the meat surrounding the wound channel, making such meat far from palatable.

I am, for far from entirely sensible reasons, an inordinate fan of the old .45-70 Government round, whose hulking 405-grain bullet just sort of lumbers along at a velocity that would never see fifteen hundred feet per second, let alone *twenty-four* hundred, on its best day going downhill with a brisk tail wind. Yet of the several animals I have killed with this round—all, admittedly, at relatively close ranges out of a Browning 78 single-shot rifle with old-timey buckhorn sights— I do not believe I have ever lost so much as a chop to tissue damage, or "bloodshotting," as it is often called.

Once, on a wild-boar hunt in the coastal hills of central California with a friend of mine, I took a pig with one shot from my .45-70, and when that pig was skinned out its meat was in nearly perfect condition right down to the wound channel; while the three-hundred-pound boar my friend killed—with a 150-grain Nosler partition bullet traveling, out of a rifle chambered for the .270 Winchester Center Fire (W.C.F.) cartridge, over twice as fast as my .45-70 slug—died in midstride as if lightning-struck, but with a loss of the meat of the

Taking aim. (*Photo: Robert Robb*)

entire shoulder where the bullet entered, and most of the off shoulder where the bullet came out: massive damage by anyone's standards.

For all that, though, the .45-70 is patently too limited a rifle for me to use consistently and is certainly not the one for such open-country game as mule deer or pronghorn or, sometimes, elk are. There is no evading the need for a high-velocity round in the vast majority of our big-game hunting situations. The question is, What form should this round take?

There are, essentially, two approaches to this, one that is more or less European in origin and outlook, and the other that is un-questionably American. In the early eighteenth century the epitome of the European hunting rifle was probably some enormous wheel lock, its stock as ornately carved as the pulpit in a Gothic cathedral, firing a .75-caliber bullet meant to knock an animal flat, even if the shot were not quite perfectly placed. Such extremely heavy rifles, shot from rests or stands, *were* accurate to good distances—two to three hundred yards or more—but were usually very difficult to load and intended, frankly, to be carried by one's manservant until the quarry was in sight, and were part of a notion of hunting as purely a pleasure outing, the "game" it very much was not in the America of this time.

Because here hunting equaled survival, and wild animals equaled provender, and an "outing" could amount to months in the woods, a season as long as a farmer's—and often taken up by farmers after the harvest to increase their stocks of food—a rifle a scythe for reaping a crop of mammals. So, pragmatic American hunters needed those "Kentucky" rifles to be light—which meant, perforce, of comparatively small caliber; fast—both in velocity and loading *and* in aiming (there being hardly any time in the forest for the retainer—who was not there in the first place—to set up the rest for his hunter); and accurate. There was ample enough wildlife at large in the American wilderness of this day both for a hunter to have plenty of practice at killing game—to learn how to place his small-caliber bullet in a vital spot with confidence and precision (something, to put it coldly, the modern hunter, who may kill only a single big-game animal a year, does not have nearly the opportunity of learning)—*and* for him not to fret overly if a wounded animal got away: another was likely to be along in a moment or two to take its place. Modern rifles, cartridges, and propellants changed the two approaches, European and American, somewhat; but the basic idea of heavy versus light for big game lingers.

Anyone who read any American hunting or shooting writing from the 1930s through the 1970s could not help but be aware of the embodiments of each side of this heavy-light question: Elmer Keith and Jack O'Connor, the *Monitor* and the *Merrimack* of American gun writers.

O'Connor, thin-lipped and unsmiling forever behind his wire-rimmed spectacles, always looked in his photographs like the editor of a small-town gazette (he was for a time a professor of journalism, as well as a novelist) or a priest, with a hope for the purple, who could never seem to rise beyond the parish level. It was O'Connor's belief that while fast heavy* bullets could, without question, kill well, few hunters were able either to pack the weight, particularly in moun-tainous terrain, of the stout rifles that fired such bullets, or to withstand the kind of "mule kick" recoil such rifles generated, and still shoot accurately. His reasoning was that for almost all North American big game a hunter needed a rifle of such a caliber that its recoil was tolerable enough that flinching would not affect his shooting, and still of such

---

* Actually, *relatively* heavy, the game of North America not requiring the gen-uinely heavy—400- to 500-grain and above—bullets the dangerous megafauna of Africa, such as buffalo and rhino and elephant, demand.

high velocity that its flat trajectory would enable a hunter, if he needed to, to take long shots and deliver accurately a bullet, with good shocking power, to the vital heart-lung area of an animal.

The ideal of such a rifle for O'Connor, as should come as no surprise to almost anyone, was the .270 W.C.F. firing a 130-grain bullet, a combination he shot and popularized for half a century. It was the kind of rifle and bullet he felt comfortable climbing into the Rockies and killing elk at six hundred yards with, and was very much in the American tradition of the Kentucky rifle.

The full-blown figure of Elmer Keith is one that it would be nearly impossible to burlesque, the reality of the man being outlandish beyond all hope of exaggeration. Here was an old cowpoke and western hunting guide, never without the stub of a cigar in the corner of his mouth, his trademark jeroboam of a Stetson cocked over one eye, and a .44 Magnum revolver perpetually on his hip, who wrote an autobiography with the thoroughly unironic title *Hell, I Was There!*, purportedly shot polar bear with handguns, and classified the .375 H&H Magnum as a "very adequate" little deer rifle. For Keith recoil accounted for naught—although he would confess that after firing a round or two of 900-grain ammo out of a .600 Nitro Express Jeffrey sidelock double he did notice "a slight numb sensation" around the right side of his chest, but even in this instance the kick was no more than a "huge push" that did not, he was quick to add, bother him in the least, especially after he learned to clench his teeth before firing.

Keith rated the .270 a fair choice for use on "thin shelled game only." For "all-around" use, ol' Elmer preferred heavy rifles, often of .35 caliber and above, feeling that they gave a hunter greater self-assurance in his ability to kill game—an attribute never to be undervalued—especially at ranges exceeding four hundred yards when impact velocity had decreased, and expansion and penetration were lessened, stating that "a large-caliber bullet kills after expansion has stopped, because of the size of the bullet hole and weight of the bullet," a heavier bullet having more momentum than a lighter.

But O'Connor and Keith both advocated a hunter's practicing regularly with whatever rifle he chose, not just at the shooting bench, but from the sitting, prone, and offhand positions; that in the field he should always try to find a solid rest for his gun before shooting; and neither ever suggested that a hunter should shoot from vast ranges unless there appeared to be no human way for him to get closer. Long-range shooting calls for an intimate knowledge of your bullet's trajectory, the effect wind will have on it (adjusting for this effect known as "wind doping") as well as the effect of shooting uphill and downhill,* and your utmost skills as a marksman.

As an all-around rifle—and although there really is no such creature, a hunter who uses only a single rifle and knows how to use it with consummate skill will always be a better hunter than one who has half a dozen different ones at his disposal that he knows only indifferently—for myself for hunting the big game of North America, from deer to sheep to elk to moose to grizzly bear, I assuredly want a flat-shooting one with good long-range accuracy and killing power. As to the question of caliber, I personally tolerate recoil fairly well and so I am more of a Keithian than an O'Connorite. I would, therefore, use something in the 7 mm to .340 Magnum range with a twenty-four- to twenty-six-inch barrel that has not been contoured down to toothpick dimensions. (For proper balance in a rifle, the weight must be more over the forward hand to lend steadiness to the aiming.) I also like to hunt with a reliable "light-gathering" scope with good eye relief, for both dawn and dusk conditions and if I must take a shot at running game, which is easier to accomplish with a scope than it is with iron sights. A 4-power scope is sufficient for nearly all hunting needs, variable-power scopes going as high as 9- or 12-power being more for so-called varmint shooting (a form of pest control rather than genuine hunting) than for the taking of big game. It is far too hard to hold an inordinately high powered scope steady in most hunting situations; and any notion that such a scope might be useful in lieu of binoculars or as a spotting scope for scanning the countryside for game should be rejected out of hand: the scope atop a rifle is meant *only* to aid a hunter in aiming his rifle at what he wishes to kill.

Yes, a rifle should be capable of killing at long range, and a hunter should practice at ranges of two hundred and three hundred yards. Yet, he should also remember that hunters seldom miss *under* game at long ranges because, as Major Burrard writes, "nearly everyone overestimates distance"; and that most game is killed within a hundred yards—and most that is missed is missed within *sixty*. Realistic accuracy for a rifle hunter is being able to sprint a hundred yards and then hit a five-gallon bucket, offhand, at a hundred yards.

Concerns over trajectories and wind drift can also distract us from the larger question inherent in long-range shooting. We can

---

* For reasons that would take too long to explain fully here, a bullet fired over an uphill or downhill distance is actually affected by gravity for a shorter distance—like the base of a right triangle versus its hypotenuse—and so will have less "drop."

worry about geometry and wind speeds, turning ourselves into clerkly calculators of bullet drop and parallax and like punctilio; or we can choose to make them irrelevant by not taking extremely long shots. Burrard offers three hundred yards as a "maximum sporting range," and that is a fair figure, closer ranges being even more sporting. At distances significantly beyond that, hunting ceases to be hunting, becoming instead an exercise in remoteness. Hunting as an art requires us to use our senses and stealth to draw within killing range of our prey, not to wield our technology to detach ourselves from it and make it merely a target of opportunity.

As Burrard writes:

> if stalking is regarded as the craft of outwitting in its natural haunts an ever-alert quarry, whose senses of eyesight, hearing and scent are all developed to a degree far beyond human experience, what possible satisfaction there is to be derived from a sort of "barrage fire" is beyond my understanding.

O'Connor, for his part, sums up the predatory satisfaction he experienced in killing that elk at six hundred yards this way: "It was exactly like group-shooting from a bench rest on a rifle range."

Hunting deer one November in the breaks of the Missouri River in South Dakota, I was working my way up one of the long, rolling, bluestem— and buffalo grass—covered ridges in the cloudy late afternoon. Nearly to the top of the ridge, I saw a heavy three-point antler rising out of the grass, twenty yards away. If you hunt enough, such a sight reflexively causes the center of your body's gravity to be drawn down and your walk to transform into a slink. As I slipped forward, my heart fluttering against my ribs, my thumb lying against the safety of my rifle, the buck's body began to appear out of the grass, and I could see all the blood around it.

He had been dead only since yesterday, the night's frost settled on him and now melted to quicksilver dew; but his meat was already soured. The far bullet that had passed through his throat severed his jugular, and he had sprung off the crest of the ridge and spun in a circle, spraying a wide ring of blood, before stumbling down. But the one who had shot at him from the other ridge across the draw, 450, 500 yards away, had not seen that because the buck had died on the side of the ridge away from him; and when the buck did not drop instantly from the neck shot, as the shooter had wrongly assumed an animal always must from a shot there, but had run off, the hunter also assumed that he had shot poorly and did not have to bother with hiking across the draw to see whether the deer had been struck. Actually, for the range, it had been an accomplished piece of riflery, no more than two inches shy of breaking the buck's neck. It was also the most empty, mechanical sort of hunting: deer as object on a video screen; hunter as presser of buttons. *Zap.*

You will frequently hear it bandied about by those who hate hunting, or simply find it incomprehensible, that modern rifles and scopes give hunters an unfair advantage over the animals they pursue. This presupposes that the hunt was ever meant to be "fair," in the way that artificial notion is enshrined in such systematized pastimes as court games or other athletic competitions. Man is the most skilled predator the Earth has ever known and hunting is simply no contest between him and animals. There isn't even a referee. Whatever rules do exist in hunting, beyond government-imposed game laws, are those the hunter imposes on himself, and abides by. While his technology *is* nothing more than a natural component of his profound hunting skill, a hunter can, and does, act to limit it, to make his proximity to the game of higher essential value in the outcome of the hunt.

It is not terribly difficult to comprehend that our hearts will beat far differently within forty or fifty yards of a wild animal than they would some quarter mile off as we conduct the cool proceedings of plotting the arc of a bullet. To make hunting true, we must feel ourselves snared in the gravitational pull of the animal we pursue, having become a satellite of it. A rifle should never become (nor does it have to) a means for our standing back at an impersonal remove, dispensing a sanitized sort of death. When we choose to use our lethality, it is only the nearness to the animal that we achieve that can make us aware of the genuine gravity of the situation. When we make ourselves draw near enough to our prey that our weapon of choice becomes a matter of some indifference—as well a bow as a rifle, the long-range advantages of the rifle neutralized by our aboriginal predatory talents—then we have a far greater opportunity to learn all the lessons that hunting has to teach us about life and death and the wild and its occupants, and where even we may, and may always have, fit into that perhaps somewhat less than fearful symmetry.

6

EXOTICA

Rifles do hold enough of a fascination for me, though, that I will gladly travel from California to New Mexico during the snows of February to shoot a genuinely unique one. This particular rifle was a .416 Rigby Nitro Express owned by a friend, an old missionary of the Society of Jesus, who acquired it in India in the 1950s, after his '06 let him down and permitted a wounded sloth bear to chew on him moderately. The .416 is a classic caliber for the heavy game of the Indian subcontinent and Africa, but this day the good father and I were putting its 400-grain bullets to use merely to punch targets and explode, albeit *utterly,* water-filled white-plastic bleach bottles and wax-paper milk cartons set out at a range of two hundred yards from us across the rust-red soil and sagebrush of a rifle range on the outskirts of Santa Fe. Here, then, was an Elmer Keith brand of day: nothing seemed to please him more than persecuting pails of water and blocks of dried lodgepole pine with awesome firepower. As I fired this wonderfully large rifle, though, I would have given a great deal to be hunting Cape buffalo or gaur with it, instead of detonating semidecorative objects of plastic and paper into haloes of mist—even with the reverend father's exulting, "You *got* your eland!" Afterward, as I tried to find sleep in a cold New Mexico night, that day of target shooting had only succeeded in making the game of the Old World seem impossibly distant to me.

Yet within a hundred miles of here along the Canadian River there were aoudad, the wild sheep-goats of Barbary, and to the south, near White Sands, gemsbok, whose bloodlines ran back to the Kalahari Desert. And they were as wild and free-roaming as any elk or bighorn in the Rockies. Elsewhere, in American places sometimes not so wild, there were also black buck and nilgai and addax and other African and Indian animals to be found. So the distance to foreign game was not so immense as might at first have been suspected. The distance to real hunting, though, may not have been so easily reckoned.

Many hunters are content never to pursue game larger than rabbits or squirrels or birds. But for most there is a certain ineluctability to giving chase to big game. After we have hunted smaller game for a number of years, the allure, the challenge, the excitement tinged with unease, the powerful mystery large, warm-blooded wild animals hold can be overwhelming. There are usually more work, more risk, and from the standpoint of obtainable protein more reward in hunting big game. Hunters are drawn to big game as another step along the path of their education *as* hunters, their learning of the way. A question, though, is, Which animal should be our initiation into the hunting of big game?

If every one of us lived in prime deer or pronghorn country, the answer would be self-evident. But as in most matters of the hunt these days, it has become far more complicated than that. Although Theodore Roosevelt could shoot deer while standing on the porch of his Badlands ranch house, most of us are obliged to venture somewhat farther afield. For the majority of us, deer hunting has become nearly expeditionary in nature. We often need to apply for licenses and permits well in advance of opening day, travel at least some distance from home, search for land we will be allowed to hunt on, hunt during abbreviated seasons, and be prepared to share the hunting grounds with large numbers of other hunters. To hunt deer or pronghorns we must lay the groundwork so far ahead of time for so few days of actual hunting that it almost seems more prudent to *know* how to hunt big game before we ever set out to learn.

This is where the notion of *exotics*—non-native big game hunted in North America—can become so tempting. There are exotics on game ranches and preserves all across this country. One can shoot

Japanese sika deer in Missouri, Persian ibex in Texas, and Indian chital in Hawaii. One can *shoot* about anything one's heart desires on such demesnes, often without a closed season, bag limit, or license. This may seem an ideal way to learn the art of the hunter; but while we may learn how to shoot an animal on such game ranches, can we truly learn to *hunt* there?

Operators of many exotic-game emporiums will swear to us how difficult it can be to kill a game animal on their ranches or preserves. They will describe for us the half-day stalk and the three-hundred-yard shot, but neglect to mention animals killed beside the grain trough or shot by someone who could not be bothered with climbing out of the pickup. In an ultimate way, degree of difficulty may not even be relevant, because what seems most lacking to me in most exotic game is a genuine sense of place.

Exotics on private game ranches are private property, as much as a Guernsey or Ol' Shep. The attachments these specialized animals could have formed to the land they now occupy are usually no more than a generation or two old, at best, and therefore as tenuous as all get-out. Often these animals are fed like livestock; and their world is bounded, always, by a fence that cannot be leaped over or passed under—and no matter how vast the area encompassed by that fence, the most heavily used game trails will almost always run just inside the perimeter, the animals' having learned the limits of their enclosed world, yet still in search of a way out. They could not ramble off the ranch, however small or great, for love or money—at least not any money of their own.

There seems to me to be no way in which all of this would not conspire to dim and impair the natural instincts such animals will have gained from the millennia spent on their native grounds, those native grounds—and the climate, food, and predators found there—responsible for the very shape of the animal, from that of its hoof to the schematic of its nervous system, through the time-honored process of evolution it underwent there. The musk-ox would not be as it is had it evolved in the Malay montane rain forest instead of on Arctic tundra; and the Hill Country outside Austin is *not* the same as Uttar Pradesh for the barasingha deer (*Cervus duvaucelli*), even though it can be found, now, in both locales—the species, or rather that winding of DNA that forms it, exhibiting, perhaps, an even better chance for survival in the Lone Star State than in its native land. It's like those Beatles impersonators: not the real thing, but an incredible simulation. Only it is not even that, not really, a wild beast behind a fence in a land from which it never arose representing more of an amnesia victim in exile, the animal filled with a deep unknowable longing for someplace it has never seen. Trying to learn to hunt by pursuing exotics in such restricted and synthetic situations bears a considerable resemblance to a musician's studying music on a player piano. Or—let's say it—engaging in erotic love solely in a brothel.

This is not a moral argument, by the way. A player piano and, to be sure, a brothel can be quite entertaining under the proper circumstances and on the proper occasions. It is merely that what we experience with either is not authentic. We have an obligation to know what the real thing is like before indulging ourselves in artifice; and most exotic game survives in, for it, highly unnatural conditions and surroundings. In the hunting of most exotics the best we may hope to learn is how to become predators of illusions.

Some exotics *are*, by fiat of their natures, exempt from this rule, though. Those aoudad, with their caprid hardiness, have adapted to much open, craggy Southwest country, and fit in there as well as the indigenous cactus and piñons. The unfenced and fantastically wary nilgai of south Texas are an absolute delight. And then there is the wild pig.

The wild pig is the oldest and most primitive of the nonruminative Artiodactyla. Omnivorous and unspecialized, it, like that other unspecialized omnivore, man, has found its way—with and without the specific help of man—onto every continent on Earth except Antarctica. *Sus scrofa,* the native Eurasian wild boar and progenitor of modern domestic swine, can be hunted in Austria or Australia, Argentina or Arkansas. *Hunted,* not just shot.

Many of the wild pigs of North America are no more than Hampshires or Durocs gone feral; but when pigs *do* go feral, they do so in the biggest of ways. After only a very few generations of living without confinement, what used to be barnyard stock starts to have its wild genes dominate once more and begins carrying its ears erect, has its weight shift from the hams to the shoulders, begins to lose the curl in its tail, grows back an undercoat of woolly hair and a comb of long bristles along its neck, develops a more uniform coloration, and takes to moving about the country at the porcine equivalent of a lope. In many parts of this country—Tennessee and California, for example—pure wild blood from European boars has been added to the feral mélange, and a long-snouted, long-tusked, armor-plated—male pigs carrying a thickened layer of hide along their sides to shield

The wild boar has found its way into every continent except Antarctica. (*Photo: Durwood Hollis*)

their vital parts during the slashing, lateral combats they engage in with other males—*eminently* nasty piece of work has evolved. For this rooting animal no fence is a matter of any consequence as he expands his range from swamp to farmland to snowy mountainside.

So, one day in the late winter or early spring of the year out in California, when the waterfowl season is done and the fall, when we will want to hunt deer, lies ahead, we will be hungering both for wild meat and for giving chase to *something*. We will have a place we know, either a ranch or some forest land, in the Coast Ranges. It is country with canyons and oaks and chamiso and wallows and green fields of volunteer barley the pigs will be feeding in, and nowhere on this land will there be a fence composed of more than three strands of barbed wire. In summer the pigs will follow definite routes between water and shade, and along these routes is where we should hunt. But now in winter, the pigs are likely to be anywhere; yet it would be best to look for them at first light as they come out of the barley where they have been in the night.

Before dawn we will drive the pickup onto a ridge and shut it off. As the salmon light comes into the sky, we will shrug into our pack frames and feed rounds into the magazine of our rifle. We will have given some consideration to which rifle to take out after pigs, and concluded that we wanted one that would throw a 180-grain bullet with stunning velocity. This has led us today to a .300 Weatherby Magnum. No pig, we know, is less than rugged.

As we move out onto the ridge, there are cloven tracks all along its muddy spine. On a morning such as this the cold air will have all settled into the canyons running down on either side of us; and as it warms, the air will rise out of those canyons in anabatic fashion (while in the evening, in the katabatic way, the cooling air will begin draining back in, carrying scent down from above), so we will have the wind in our favor here in the morning. This is mandatory for hunting pigs, because it requires only a trace of man smell hundreds of yards away to send these animals packing.

There is a hump on this ridge from which we can glass a wide sweep of country. Along the higher ridge east of us trots a line of thirty or forty pigs, ant-black against the sunrise. To be honest, there are pigs everywhere here. Below us, half a mile away, there is a cluster— called a *sounder*—of four large pigs, doubtlessly boars, looking fat as ticks as they move up the grassy green ridge in our direction. These, we decide, will do.

We have to hurry because the boars are headed for the heavy cover at the head of the draw where they will spend the balance of their day. We slip below the ridge, onto the side away from the boars,

Boars: "When pigs *do* go feral, they do so in the biggest of ways." (*Photo: Durwood Hollis*)

and jog toward them. We need to maintain in our minds a reference map of where the moving boars are in relation to us, so we can anticipate where to find them when we head back over the ridge. When we think we have reached the right position, we pause to chamber a round and catch our breath—so we will be steady if we must shoot—before moving to the crest of the ridge in a low crouch to find the pigs.

We top out on hands and knees, careful to keep the rifle's muzzle clear of the ground to prevent dirt from obstructing it, and see the four boars fanned out 150 yards below us. One is a black devil whose lip curls over a good two to three inches of honed lower tusk. He is indeed a temptation, but is also likely to be old and tough, a prime candidate for sausage, and there will be just too much of him. Tender meat is the order of the day this morning.

One of the remaining three is a good-size, young, mixed-color boar standing broadside to us, and from our belly-down position on the ridge above, we decide to offer him the nomination. Prone, our elbows set firmly on the ground, we slide the cross hairs onto his shoulder and quickly tally the options.

The surest shot will be the shoulder, the partition bullet we are shooting, as we know, more than capable of breaking the near shoulder, topping the heart like a coconut hacked open, and breaking the off shoulder before expending the last of its energy in the shield on the far side as the boar rolls over like a beer keg kicked down a hill. As we have seen, though, that will pretty much be that for both shoulders as far as eating goes. We could try just *behind* the shoulder, putting the bullet into the lungs there, and at worst only lose a rib or two, but also risk having the pig run for daylight—as they are very wont to do when wounded—and maybe even be lost.

But because this is a pig destined to be spitted and salted and filled with garlic cloves as if they had been shot through the meat with a shotgun, and turned for ten hours or more over a white-hot mesquite fire till the shoulder blades and hipbones begin to break through the outer layer of blackened fat, we shift the cross hairs up to the long, tufted ear; get a solid rest for the rifle; ease the safety off; let out half our breath; and break the sear holding the firing pin with a steady, straight-back squeeze of the trigger with the tip of our trigger finger— that part of the fingertip between the first joint and the swirl of the fingerprint—the bullet striking a quarter-inch behind the ear and the boar somersaulting backward without so much as a squeal. It is not a shot to be tried ordinarily—the shoulder-heart-lung area is more

Boar hunting in the Coast
Ranges of central California.
(*Photo: Durwood Hollis*)

The author and boar in the
Coast Ranges. "It was not a shot
to be tried ordinarily, but this
time it succeeded." (*Photo: Durwood Hollis*)

reliable—but this time it seemed appropriate, and it has succeeded.

The other pigs, leaving trails through the dewy grass, have all vanished by the time we reach the dead boar and smell his sweet pig smell. If this happens to be our first big-game animal, there will probably be someone with us to shake our hand and tell us that we have done well. Unlike the way the hunting of other exotics may be, this hunting will have been real. We have only to feel the state our hearts are now in to know that. Now there is this boar, who will yield us over a hundred pounds of fine wild meat, to be dressed and gotten in from the field.

It is hard to know what all a morning like this will have taught us; but if we were sufficiently attentive to the lessons that were there for us to learn, it can only have been of help to us when we head out at last for deer and other native game.

7

DEER

When a hunter decides that the way has led him to deer—and more hunters are led to pursue the four main branches of the odocoilean deer than any other big-game animal in North America—he will discover that even in winter with, it seems, only pigs to hunt, deer season will have already commenced in his thoughts.

While downhill recreationists pore over the snow reports to gauge skiing conditions, and agribusinessmen concern themselves with mountain snowpacks to predict runoff for summer irrigation, the hunter of deer is watching the season to see whether it will be a harsh or an open one: the milder the weather the better the deciduous object of his desire is likely to have fared, and the greater its numbers when fall at last comes and he can give chase to it.

Deer, rest assured, are as deciduous as aspens and maples. Every year, bucks raise and shed a set of antlers in a cycle mirroring that of a tree that buds and leafs and falls. Antlers, unlike horns, are true bone, solid and marrowless, and a unique feature of the Cervidae—as all the deer are known collectively—though not of every one, musk deer and water deer, both small Asian representatives of the family, lacking them but possessing instead long sabered upper canines of nearly *Smilodon* proportions. Horns, on the other hand, are sheaths of *keratin*—the material from which claws and hooves are formed—set over cores of bone, and are carried by the Bovidae, all those ruminant mammals from the musk-oxen to bison to mountain goats to bighorns, and the Antilocapridae, populated solely by one species, the pronghorn antelope. Horn is permanent and unbranched (except in the case of the pronghorn where it is both branched—or "pronged"—*and* shed annually). Horn, in many species, is also carried by both sexes. Among the Cervidae normally only males are antlered, the single exception being caribou cows.

The antlers of a mature deer of several years of age are usually *multitined,* that is, carrying a number of points. On projections of the skull bones, called "pedicels," antlers, nourished by blood vessels and surrounded by a sensitive furry hide called "velvet," begin in the spring to sprout at an alarming rate. From nothing to a heavy, wide, copiously pointed rack representing a significant percentage of a deer's entire skeletal weight, a set of antlers may take no more than four or five months to grow. The factors determining such growth are an almost confounding equation of sunlight, the pituitary gland, growth hormones, genetics, nutrients, and minerals. (It is a myth—do I need to say?—that a deer's age can be calculated by the number of tines on his antlers: no exact correlation exists between antler points and a buck's years; that is, a two-year-old buck does not necessarily carry forked "horns," or a three-year-old, three points a side; extremely aged bucks, in fact, frequently develop retrograde racks that produce fewer tines with each season they survive into, not more.)

As a buck enters into the fall's breeding period, his testicles descend from inside his body and his testosterone level rises. This brings about a change in the development of the antlers, a pearled ring—called a "coronet" or "burr"—forming around the base, apparently cutting off the blood flow to the antlers and causing the velvet to dry up and begin to peel, the buck scraping his antlers against trees and limbs to clean off the tattered hide. At first the cleaned antler is white, but through an oxidized stain produced from the deer's rubbing his rack against brush and foliage—both to remove velvet and to strengthen his neck muscles for possible jousts with other bucks during the breeding period, or *rut*—and, it is believed by at least one authority, from blood seeping out from within, the hard antler is soon turned a polished oaken brown, the tips often ivoried.

When the buck has mated, testosterone declines and the bases of the antlers ossify, necrosis setting in. The connection between the bases and the pedicels remains solid right until the time the antlers are dropped: one day a buck can hook with reckless abandon at thick branches with his antlers; the next, merely bumping into a tree with one is enough to knock it off, leaving a naked, blood-stained pedicel.

Why, though, does a deer invest in such expensive contrivances as antlers in the first place? If they were defensive, why would they be shed in the winter when they could be of most benefit against predators? Deer seldom fight among themselves with their antlers, preferring to use their sharp hooves. They *will,* though, display them to intimidate bucks with smaller antlers and thwart a direct challenge to their sexual superiority, and to advertise to does their suitability as sires. Or perhaps antlers exist only to offer hunters something for their eyes to be drawn to, for their hearts to be pinned upon.

The root of the word *deer* derives from the broad notion of a breathing animal. The roots of other animal names are much more specific: *swine* comes from a root *meaning* swine, *goat,* from one meaning goat. But in the broadness of its name's origin, the deer would seem to have represented to the early northern European the archetypal wild creature. For such a hunter of the North, when the image of vast primeval woods and the animals moving through them was called to mind, the first animals to move through the mind were deer.

In North America we have two species of deer—as distinct from the elk (in fact, the truest of the deer, the deer of "deer") and moose and caribou who compose the rest of our Cervidae—the mule deer of the West and the white-tailed deer of the East, the West, the North, and the South as far as Peru. Both are of the genus *Odocoileus* that originated in the Old World before migrating to the New three and a half million years ago during the Pliocene epoch, over a million years before the jackrabbit's appearance on the scene, supplanting various aboriginal deerlike mammals, such as a long-pediceled Miocene semi-deer known, no less, as *dromomerycines!*

Nearly forty subspecies of whitetails, and almost a dozen of mule deer, are recognized by some experts, but from the standpoint of the hunter—in whose mind "deer" still fulfills that vision of the breathing animal—there are four deer to pursue in North America, depending on which, quite general, geographic zone one hunts in.

The black-tailed deer, a subspecies of the mule deer, hails from Pacific coastal hills and forests from Northern California through Oregon, Washington, British Columbia, and Alaska as far as Kodiak Island. The mule deer per se is an inhabitant of the more open high

Mule deer in the mountains. (*Photo: Robert Robb*)

ground between the western littoral and the western edge of the Great Plains. The whitetail can be found in mixed forests, bottomlands, swamps, and prairies from the Atlantic to the Pacific and points both north and south. And the diminutive whitetail subspecies, the Coues' deer (named in honor of the nineteenth-century American ornithologist and biologist Elliott Coues, and pronounced "cows"), dwells in the deserts of Arizona, New Mexico, and northwestern Mexico. East of the Mississippi there are no native deer but whitetails, whereas in the West the ranges of all these deer frequently overlap with one another's.

If you were to track all these deer through the entirety of the hunting season and across all that terrain, you could begin to hunt in midsummer along the California coast, giving chase to Columbia blacktails, called this for their solid-black tails fringed with white.* Midsummer is the hottest time of year in that coastal country, the heat of the day like that of a potter's kiln. At such a time in such a place, blacktails will be bedded in the cool shade of oaks, and a hunter learns to use that weapon he possessed even before the stone, his eyes, to find deer.

The human seems nearly unique among predators in his ability to recognize game that is not in motion. Other carnivores can sight an animal, can see its shape and know that *something* is there; but if it remains motionless, and unless they can smell it, these carnivores will be hard-pressed to say whether what is before them is a rock or an orangutan. This is why most prey species from the rabbit on up have developed the technique of "freezing" when they realize the eyes of a predator have fallen on them—I once spent a few still moments of eternity sitting in tall grass and looking, without daring to blink, into the eyes of a Kenyan leopard who was unable to tell what I was even at the distance two short leaps could cover in part of a second. It is only motion—most often flight—that appears to offer the final clue to a prey's identity, the telling gesture that confirms a hunting animal's suspicions and launches him into his final, lethal lunge.

But the human, even though he has allowed his sense of smell

---

* In contrast to black-tailed deer, most mule deer carry a short scut, brown at the top, then white and tipped in black. Another difference between blacktails and mule deer is to be found in the mule deer's metatarsal gland, located between the hock and the hoof on the hind leg, it being quite long, five inches or so, whereas the blacktail's runs between two and three inches, and the whitetail's is only about an inch.

to atrophy, *can* recognize the breathing animal even when it is motionless. He can scan with his unaided eyes, or, better yet, with binoculars, under oaks, looking for the deer. At first light he can look for them on ridgelines, that are covered in wild oats, where they will have spent the night, letting the wind pass over them and keep away biting insects.

Moving north in the blacktails' range, the hunter will come to perpetually rain-soaked evergreen timber. The first place to look for deer here is along the "edges," where the trees play out in meadows or, as aesthetically unspeakable as they may be, clear-cuts. On-the-edge is the manner in which a deer prefers to conduct his life, seeking food in the open, usually early or late in the day, and shelter in the woods or brush. The place for a hunter to seek him here is where he commutes between these habitats.

Later in the season, when their regular pattern of movement has been disrupted by the presence of hunters, deer will sink deep into heavy cover until relative calm is restored or hunger drives them out. Now a hunter can enter the dark forest and seek the deer's trails through the timber, lying in wait for them along these paths—the poet Gary Snyder, in an essay, describes, as well as anyone ever has, this sort of "stand" hunting, saying that the "feeling is that you are not hunting the deer, the deer is coming to you; you make yourself available to the deer that will present itself to you, that has given itself to you." Weather may also drive blacktails down from highlands and into more temperate country, as it does the Sitka blacktail on Kodiak Island, where the inclemency of November forces the deer down from the interior to the shore, and they stand alertly at the water's edge the way deer are normally only seen to do in the stirring illustrations from a boy's adventure story.

Perhaps en route to those island blacktails, though, the hunter will make a detour for the deer of October, the mule deer. The mule deer is for me the deer of that broken, elevated, sage-carpeted band of the continent that lies between the crest of the Sierras and that of the Rockies, and of that time of year when the leaves of aspens have turned and shimmer like sequins in the wind. Today's tall hot blue sky with clouds as thin as tissue in it can tomorrow settle around you in slowly drifting flakes as large as silver coins. This is when and where mule deer should be hunted.

At the season's outset, in the relatively warm fall weather, the deer will be high in their mountain territory, and it is to here that a hunter must climb to find them. As always, much depends on a hunter's eyes, and he must use them to look not merely at the distant places but at the near ones as well. There are times when a buck will be feeding almost a mile away across a wide draw, and others when he may be lying up in the mountain mahogany only forty yards from a hunter.

It is one of the most difficult lessons for any hunter to learn to wed experience to a freedom from preconceptions. Yes, in the early time the big bucks will be high, but this does not preclude their being low, too—conditions such as a dry summer and a lack of water above can drive deer down to lower levels early—and a hunter should be alert for them as he makes his way up to elevation. A true hunter *always* hunts, never allowing his mind to be only half-awake instead of fully alive and receptive. Eventually, for the truest of hunters, this attitude extends itself beyond the field and into all his life as he *hunts* knowledge, wisdom, purpose, and excellence in his work; a genuineness in his relationships with, and his treatment of, others; and the real spirit of his linkage to all of the wild and all its life. Eventually, for the truest of hunters, the hunt becomes not second nature but his original nature, the definition of his character. It becomes not something he does, but what at last he is.

In hunting mule deer, and all the deer—all *game*—a hunter must be prepared to spend a great deal of time looking and should not be afraid that, by taking time to stop moving and simply *to* look, he will be missing his only chance of seeing deer at some place farther on that he must be in a blind rush to reach. He will do himself no harm by finding a good vantage point and taking some time to glass with his binoculars or spotting scope from there, looking for the unexpected. He can search the surroundings with care and stand a good chance of sighting a buck that is intent on browsing or is bedded; and if the wind and the cover are in his favor, the hunter might even be able to mount a stalk after it.

At other times a hunter may move along the rims of brushy canyons, "rocking" them by hurling stones down into them to see whether he can put a buck out of his bed. When snows finally come to the high country, though, the mule deer can become the most migratory of our deer, sometimes moving a hundred miles to find wintering grounds. Now a hunter should look for them along their routes of travel or in the lower, milder areas. In snowbound country, though, and especially during the rut, when the deer will gather in large groups—the bucks contesting with each other over the does— the deer will often take to south-facing slopes that are more sheltered

The deer hunter should find a good vantage point and glass the surroundings with his binoculars or spotting scope. (*Author photo*)

from the cold winds and receive greater exposure to the sun. A hunter can find them, then, out in large open bowls on the mountainside, their minds occupied with other matters besides the possible threat a human may pose. A hunter should not assume that a mule deer—or any rutting deer—is oblivious to his presence at this time, though; he will flee as readily in the late snow time as in the time of yellow aspen leaves, bounding uphill, only to pause at the crest to look back once before topping over.

The mule deer, an animal of the open heights, plots his escape around flight, using his speed to put him above and away from a threat. The plan of escape a whitetail puts forth, on the other hand, revolves around his taking advantage of the mostly heavy, lowland cover he inhabits. A whitetail is more inclined to holing-up in concealment or ghosting away silently than he is to sprinting off in a crashing of brush. A whitetail is very keen on skulking.

Many whitetails, unlike wide-ranging mule deer, may live and die on a scant few acres of land. It would be a species of paradise for any hunter to have a tract of whitetail woods all to himself, to hunt in it every day of the season, to be able to inhabit it even afterward, throughout the year. A hunter could wander through its brakes and tiny clearings, come to recognize the trees on an individual basis, feel the changes the year's passage creates in it, see the deer's unique interplay with it, recall it on each return the way the scenes of a favored book are recalled when he is drawn to reread it. In his mind its tangled growth and contours—and breathing animals—could become something just as tangible as they are on the face of the Earth, and he could always carry his hunting grounds with him.

To hunt a whitetail in such habitat, a hunter may still-hunt: that seeping alertly through the woods, remembering the wind—keeping it in his face—letting every twig and branch and shape and smell and sound and the constant question of *What's that?* fill his senses, like water swelling a sponge. All deer can be hunted this way; and it is one of the most rewarding of hunting experiences as the human hunter becomes a glider among trees, the way a brush hawk or an owl is. He may also hunt this way through standing corn, a favored habitat for deer in farm country. Any whitetail that a still-hunter manages to spot, though, will probably be, as a Mississippian deer hunter named Faulkner said it, "already running, seen first as you always see the deer, in that split second after he has already seen you."

While there is hardly a dull moment in such still-hunting, it does not necessarily have the highest ratio of success—"success" in terms of deer seen and killed—of all the methods of hunting whitetail. That method would probably be from a stand, either on the ground or, preferably, in the air. A stand a dozen or so feet up in a tree or in a portable tower raises a hunter's scent off the ground and carries it over a deer's nose. Here the hunter's art lies in knowing where to take a stand, as it were. Along well-used trails is good, or at the margins of fields where the deer will come from the woods in the late afternoon and evening to feed.

During the rut—the peak of the breeding season that comes in November and December in most of the whitetail's range in North America—a hunter can look for round patches of bare earth, usually under the low overhanging branches of a bush or tree (a deer liking to nibble and to slash with his antlers at the foliage as he works) from which a buck has pawed all the leaves and other debris. These are called *scrapes,* and in the explicitly obvious violence of their creation they resemble the products of troubled minds, similar to the deranged paintings of lunatic sex offenders. They serve an as-yet-undetermined purpose in the breeding process, but do act to make a hunter aware of a buck's presence, and mark a spot to which the buck may return and where a stand may be placed nearby.

Hunting out of a stand, of course, can be a mentally enervating

Whitetail buck. (*Photo: Keith E. Benoist*)

Betty Wilson of Boise, Idaho, with a fine mule deer buck. (*Author photo*)

affair. A hunter must learn to sit motionless and silent, hunting with his ears as much as his eyes. A sound will come from behind him, and he will have to still his impulse to wheel on it, nostrils flared and eyes flashing whitely. Instead he must make his movements as contained and imperceptible as those of a clock's hands. Except for those times when a hunter tries to "rattle" in a buck by clacking together two antlers in imitation of bucks fighting, most hunting in a tree stand is like performing the slow-motion exercises the TV shows old Chinamen doing at dawn atop the Great Wall.

None of this makes stand hunting any less *actual* hunting, as a hunter must stay every bit as alert in the air as on foot as he waits for a deer to "present" itself to him. But in the air there is the opportunity for more contemplation. Hunting there amounts to long stretches of solitary meditation, on wind and light and cat squirrels and fluttering birds, combined with sudden bursts of adrenaline rage as a big buck drifts into view out of nowhere. If this kind of hunting sounds impossible to endure, take along a good book to read while you wait.

Or organize a drive. The communalness of hunting is brought back to mind with drives, as hunters divide themselves into posters and drivers. The posters wait, watching the expected escape routes of the deer, knowing that does and young bucks will come pell-mell; their long tails that give them their name—brown on top and white underneath—flagging as the moving drivers push the deer along. (I remember once seeing a whitetail doe dolphining out of a yellow stand of corn ahead of the drivers, holding motionless against the blue November sky for just a moment at the top of her spring as she looked around below her for a route out.) But the posters also know that the old, tall-antlered bucks will move with deliberateness and caution, tails down, giving a hunter, if they choose to put in an appearance before him, no more than a second or two to decide that it is safe to fire and that this deer is worth making the ultimate commitment a hunter can make to a game animal, to take its life and eat its meat. Those few acres of a whitetail's home, and the ways of surviving on them, are known to a buck far better than they can ever be to any human, no matter how well he may have learned them or how clearly they make up the landscape his mind holds. This knowledge of its habitat that a whitetail possesses is what makes many hunters consider a whitetail buck with a proud set of antlers the most difficult animal to capture in North America.

The Coues' deer's antlers at their proudest are far from astonishing, unless one knows his Cervidae. I have yet to hunt these tiny deer of the Southwest and Mexico. Of the two dozen or so other deer I have killed in two decades of hunting them, I have found them on the beaches of Kodiak or scrambling toward the top of a clear-cut ridge on the Queen Charlotte Islands of British Columbia, pawing the air as they went over backward, my bullet having passed through their heart. I have let arrows fly after them in the still, summer heat of a Monterey County evening. I have seen them spring up out of the Colorado sage twenty yards from me, their antlers shiny and hard, and move off in that floating bound of theirs as I raised my rifle. I have seen them in the South, inside the Levee, moving through honeysuckle, or in the North, drawing me through the snow in a stand of poplars when frost hung from my mustache. And someday I will see Coues' deer slipping between cacti. I have that to look forward to today, and all the rest to remember *and* to look forward to going after again. Those are good things to have in the winter when it is time to see about the fall and becoming a hunter of deer once more.

8

BONE, SKIN, MEAT

If we can accept the deer as our archetype for the game animal (and if we can recall our first sight of a wild deer—what a remarkable event it was to encounter without warning so large and complex an animal so adamantly *not* in the service of humans, one that did not wear a saddle or let down milk or fetch the Sunday paper or have any intention whatsoever of trying to please us, and obviously never would; how, if we were hunting him, that first sight filled us with such awe and terror and an excited trembling almost impossible to contain—we will have no choice but to accede to the fundamental power of this animal over us, this animal that teaches us to hunt big game most truly), then what is it about the deer that is most archetypical if not his antlers?

We have already looked at what antlers are in terms of a deer's biochemistry. Scientists classify them as "luxury tissue" because of the inordinate effort a deer expends in growing them, an effort far beyond their seeming practical worth. And from a hunter's viewpoint, antlers' strictly practical worth would seem pretty much null as well. They contain slim appetite appeal, except perhaps for gnawing rodents. Nor is there much call for them any longer to be used by us as digging tools or to be sliced and laminated into bows or used as buttons. Even when there was an everyday application for antlers as spoons or ladles or fishhooks, about any set would do, an exceptionally large rack not being required to manufacture such utensils.

Yet even the earliest of human hunters, as evidenced by the paintings they left behind on the vaults of caves, were drawn to deer with the largest of antlers. In their paintings—that represented, as best as can be surmised, either their image of the type of deer they wished most to kill or a pride-filled record of the fine deer they had killed—these early hunters would purposely emphasize the greatness of the deer's antlers by skewing the deer's head around at an unnatural angle to its body to display the antlers more prominently. But why should this matter to a hunter, then or now?

There is no question that it *does* matter, though. All those feelings a deer evokes in us are only heightened—exponentially, it often seems— when that deer carries magnificent antlers. In a sense there is no objective standard for categorizing such magnificence, just as there is none that can be applied to any work of art. Tolstoy, despite his sincerest efforts, George Orwell tells us, had no appreciation for Shake- speare. If Shakespeare's body of work can be calculated to be objec- tively great—if there is a scale someplace to weigh it on, or a tape to take its measure—then Tolstoy must have been a flaming natterwit and not a one of us should ever be moved by *Anna Karenina*. But art is as much luxury tissue of the human consciousness as antlers are of a deer's biology, and the magnificence of both is probably quite im- possible to put a figure on. All I know is that some deer antlers can move me every bit as much as *Lear*. Others are the *Macbeth* of antlers. And many may be no more than the *Timon of Athens*. There is beauty in all, but even beauty has its degrees.

I think that the beauty we see in antlers is our recognition of an enormous natural defiance, almost an animal arrogance, what the wild has always stood for. If a set greatly exceeds our normal expectations of what antlers should be, they will instantly draw attention to the deer carrying them; and because our predator's eyes are attracted to this deer, he is placed at particular risk. He will have to have eluded threats season after season, proving his "deerness" again and again, to have achieved such an advanced state of antler development.

Killing such a deer does not validate some sort of venal superi- ority in us, by the way. If anything, it is a humbling act. Ortega y Gasset describes the "hint of criminal suspicion" a hunter experiences when he has taken the life of an animal. All in all that is a healthy sentiment. It is necessary to keep the big picture in front of us, and killing should never be allowed to become simple or dispassionate. Before we kill a deer, we should determine that this is the right deer for us to kill by reading—as we can—the entire saga of his life in his antlers: his maturity, his ability to find food, the weather conditions he overcame, the sort of lineage he descends from. If his antlers are unquestionably grand, then we can rest fairly well assured that, more than just having been able to survive, he has been able to distribute his genomes around a good deal, ensuring the continuance of his breed. And although this will make the killing of such a deer an in no way casual affair, it *will* give a hunter an increased sense of satisfaction about his choice.

If, on the other hand, we kill a deer whose antlers are small and unprepossessing, his meat will be delicious and filling, but we will always have some question about how he might have turned out, if given another two or three years of growth. It is a little like walking out in the middle of a movie that might have turned out to be a classic had we stayed all the way through to the end—now we will just never know, and this can only add to the innate criminal suspicion we feel over the matter of animal death. (Choosing to kill deer with the largest antlers because this is an indication of a mature animal who has bred frequently and passed along his finer qualities is a theory applicable to all game animals, whose antler, horn, or body size is a sign of a life led to its fullest. For some hunters, though, wild meat is all, while there are many who are driven to acquire "trophy" animals for motives that are far from commendable, as we shall see in later chapters.)

Though the ultimate grandness of any set of antlers is as subjective an appraisal as our private feelings about any work of art, some general physical markers in a deer's antlers do exist that we can look for to help us decide whether an animal has reached his peak of maturity or not.

The mature mule deer buck carries the largest antlers of the North American odocoilean deer. These antlers are referred to as being *dichotomous*, forking evenly off the main branch, the forks usually forking again to create four tines on each side. Not all areas in the mule deer's geographic range produce deer with comparable antler size at full maturity; but where they reach their largest development, a rack with a width—measured on the outside span of the antlers—of at least twenty-eight inches is the sort a hunter, when he is seeking the kind of deer whose image would be painted gladly on the ceilings of caves, will look for.

Of the whitetail, blacktail, and mule deer, the mule deer buck carries the largest antlers. (*Author photo*)

A gauge a hunter can use for judging antler width is the mule deer's long ears. A mule deer, when he is standing alertly and is seen head-on, will display a span of between twenty and twenty-one inches from ear tip to ear tip. Using that, then, as a benchmark, a hunter can estimate how many inches of antler extend beyond the tip of each ear. If there is a minimum of three to four inches on either side of this span, this would represent a deer in that twenty-eight-inch category. If viewed only from behind, though, a mule deer's, and all deer's, antlers are harder to estimate because a hunter cannot so readily tell whether a deer is carrying his ears back—as he may do when he is feeding or trying to slip away from a danger he senses, making the antlers appear wider. A hunter, therefore, must try to see a buck from several angles before drawing any permanent conclusions (those likely to be accompanied by the sound of gunfire) about his antler size.

In addition to width, a hunter should look for good tine length. He can assess this by seeing whether the forks appear deep and the antlers rise tall. Usually it is better to judge the tine length on the basis of the front forks of the dichotomous antlers—because if the front ones are deep and long, then the back ones are likely to be as well, whereas the reverse is not always the case—if a decision must be reached quickly before a deer steals away. A hunter should also look for an overall thickness in the antler beams. In the most massively antlered deer there will be an unmistakable *Gestalt*—to slide, regrettably, into the jargon of Teutonic Psych 101—of bigness. Simply the way a large deer carries himself, the very manner in which he walks, can single him out. The largest of deer will be known on sight, but a thoroughly ingrained knowledge of the physical indicators helps verify the judgment of the passions.

A blacktail's antlers carry the same configuration as the mule deer's, only in a smaller format (though I have noticed in the most northern of blacktails a tendency for their antlers—and those of many three-point mule deer—while remaining dichotomous, to approximate the look of the whitetails', which will be described shortly). A twenty-inch spread marks a wide set of blacktail antlers; and a hunter can base his estimate of a rack's width on a span of approximately sixteen inches between a blacktail's ear tips, when the deer is viewed in the same head-on posture as a mule deer.

The whitetail carries the tips of his ears about sixteen inches apart, as well; and as with the blacktail's, antlers with a twenty-inch spread are those of a mature buck. Unlike the mule deer's and blacktails' antlers, the white-tailed deer's antlers are formed by an individual main branch with simple tines sprouting off it, usually four per side, but frequently more. The antlers of a whitetail may take on the look of a kind of crown over the head of a buck, like a spiky nimbus or an open basket made of bone.

Those Coues' deer I mean to give exuberant chase to one day (I met a good hunter recently who had spent winter weeks pursuing the little whitetails above Nogales, seeing excellent bucks each day, but having them always escape him in their desert territory, slipping away down the arroyos just like coyotes, leading him to declare, with sincere admiration, "I do not know that they are not the *king* of sport!") show full maturity with racks no more than fourteen or fifteen inches in width, but that can represent as much living as a mule deer's thirty-inch set of antlers.

And so from the outsize fresco of the mule deer's to the exquisitely executed miniature of the Coues' deer's, there is in all antlers a splendid wild beauty that calls up for us that time when untamed animals were at the heart and bone of our existence, and that draws us on to hunt deer still. There is such bestial pride exhibited by a set of great antlers that for a hunter to believe that by killing a deer carrying them he has achieved some form of vanquishment is pure vainglory. The best a hunter can do is to look on the deer's special accomplishment and wonder whether he could ever produce something of such natural elegance himself.

*   *   *

We no longer go in much for painting the images of deer upon walls of stone in red ocher and the blue juices of berries, yet there is a desire in us to preserve the animal after death, to keep him as a totem of our enduring bond to the ancient hunt and as homage to the spirit of the dead animal. The most elegant way of preserving a deer—or more to the point, the memory of him and the hunt, to remind us for years to come of a particular day afield on the unique native grounds of a wild animal, of its particular joys and sadnesses—is merely keeping his antlers. Europeans traditionally preserve their hunting trophies in this way, affixing those warm brown antlers,* on the stark whiteness of the skull, to their walls, making it more than a prize collected, but the essence of the objet trouvé—like those skulls and antlers, the "found objects," that when brought back to the cave and decorated became the human hunters' first works of art.

American hunters show a preference for "head mounts" that employ the deer's tanned headskin, or "cape," fitted over a form with the antlers attached. To *cape* a deer, or any animal—that is, to remove its headskin so it can be tanned and mounted—the only tools that are needed are a small knife (I use a paring knife with a high-carbon-steel blade just three inches long for caping, having used it to skin even caribou) and a sharpening stone or steel to keep the knife's edge keen as the animal is skinned (a small handsaw can also be added to this tool kit, useful for sawing off the top of the skull after the deer is caped, to detach the antlers, and for splitting the pelvic arch when dressing the animal).

The first decision in caping is who will put these tools to use. If the spot where you killed the deer is no more than an hour or two from a skilled taxidermist, the best method, to be frank, is to take the field-dressed carcass to him and pay him to do the job. He will have caped far more animals in his day than almost any ten of the most active hunters. He will know just how to carry out the task so the finished head will look most lifelike (a term not without some irony when used in connection with an animal that is undeniably defunct: how else do you explain its having seen its way clear to hang upon the wall?). Second to using the services of a taxidermist is, if you are hunting with a knowledgeable guide who has experience in caping, to let him handle it. You would, though, still do well to possess some

---

* Why is antler or horn or ivory, unlike marble and steel, never cold to the touch, even when the animal who grew it is long dead; is some heat of life retained?

A skilled taxidermist will make the head look lifelike. (*Photo: Daniel Hernandez*)

understanding about the proper process of caping so you can make sure the job is being performed correctly.

If you decide to cape a deer yourself, then you should know that the deer should be opened along the belly for dressing to a point no higher than the bottom of the sternum. After all the internal organs have been removed (to be explained in a moment), the carcass's hide should be circled with a cut running around the circumference of the body. This cut should be no less than a hand's width in back of the shoulders to give the taxidermist plenty of hide to work with. (At this stage or before, a hunter might consider taking several closeup photographs of the deer's head from several different angles to show the taxidermist how it looked in, more or less, life.) A hunter should try to make his cut through the hide only, and not down into the flesh below, because this exposes more meat to dirt and bacteria. He should also take care to keep his fingers out of the way of the blade, and *never* draw a knife toward himself—it can all too easily slip out and slash the hunter—but always *away*.

After this circular cut is made, the front legs can be detached at the knee joint and the hide split from there up the back of the leg to the "armpit"—for a lack on my part of knowing a more accurate term to describe a deer's nonhuman anatomy—and then down to the bottom of the sternum where the belly cut reached. Now, on clean dry grass or a tarp or a large wooden table, to prevent dirt from collecting on the meat, the deer's body can be positioned belly-down with the head and neck laid out straight. (The deer could also be hung by its hind legs; but when hanging, the carcass tends to twist around lazily and is awkward to work with.) From the back of the head, a little behind the antlers, a cut is made down the precise middle of the neck, following the line of the spine between the shoulder blades, to the circular body cut. This cut is made going *with* the grain of the hair, thus limiting the amount of shaved hairs that can find their way onto the meat and leave it with a strong flavor. (The inside of a deer is right tasty, the outside not nearly so.)

Now the hide can begin to be skinned away from the carcass. The skinning should be as close to the hide as possible without cutting through it, leaving as little meat and fat attached as can be managed. After a bit of skinning, much of the hide can be taken off simply by

Tools necessary for caping. *Left to right:* small, sharp knife; handsaw; and sharpening stone. (*Author photo*)

Packing out. (*Photo: Durwood Hollis*)

the hunter's pushing his fist between it and the carcass and flensing the skin away.

When the hide has been skinned back to the deer's head, the head can be detached—cut down and around through the meat of the neck to where the base of the skull joins the spine, and then the head can pretty much be twisted free. Now the head and cape can be bundled up to be packed out. (It is probably prudent to cover up the antlers, or mark them with some kind of blaze-orange cloth, before hoisting them onto your back to carry out of the field, or you run the risk of being mistaken for a deer yourself, with potential permanent consequences far too dire to contemplate. If nothing else, pack out the deer's head with the antlers pointing down.)

If the weather is cold enough—*well* below freezing, at least at night—or a hunter has access to a freezer large enough to hold the cape and head and antlers, he can keep them frozen until he can deliver them to a taxidermist and let him finish caping out the head.

If, however, the weather is warm and there is no freezer available, then a hunter who wishes to preserve the headskin of his deer in order to have it tanned and mounted must cape it out. *It is a good idea for a hunter to visit a taxidermist before going hunting to have the taxidermist show him the proper technique for doing this;* but as best as can be described in a book, what needs to be done is to make a Y incision across the scalp, each arm of this Y extending from the rear of the base of each antler to the top of the straight cut at the back of the head. Then the hide must be cut very carefully away from around the pedicels, leaving, ideally, no hide attached to the antlers. To do this, the knife blade should be kept as close to the bone of the pedicel as it can be. The hide is then skinned away from the face, the knife blade working close to the skull, with extreme care taken not to nick it here because cuts are very hard to conceal in the facial area.

When the skinning reaches the base of the ears, they should be detached so close to the skull that all that will be showing will be the small inner-ear canal, the cartilage of the exterior ear remaining intact (a hunter should not try to skin out the ears at this point; they will need to be "turned" later). Around the eyes, the best method is for the hunter to insert an index finger between the eyelids from the outside and pull the hide out as the knife, working slowly and near the bone, cuts around the membrane surrounding the eye, the index finger used as a guide to determine where the eyelid is so it will not be cut through—if a hunter cuts too fast or too deeply or too carelessly, he stands a chance of slicing-and-dicing himself up about like a food processor commercial. At the mouth, a finger is again inserted, at the corner, and pulls the hide away as it is detached along the line where the inside of the lips meets the gums. Now the headskin has been turned inside out and is attached to the skull only at the nose. The animal has been caped when the cartilage of the inner nose tip—care being exercised so the nostrils are not cut through—is severed and the hide comes free.

It remains for the lips to be "split," by cutting them open from the inside without slicing through the outer lips, so salt can be pushed up into them, then for the ears to be "turned." This is accomplished by separating the outer hide from the ear's cartilage, then, literally, turning the ear inside out, using tiny, shallow cuts as needed to separate the ear from the cartilage as the ear is turned. A variety of arcane taxidermic tools exist for separating the cartilage from the outer ear—generally some kind of blunt wooden stick—but I know of one skilled woman taxidermist in Saratoga, Wyoming, who finds the empty barrel of a ballpoint pen does a fine job, and even a lowly finger can make an adequate "turning stick." If done properly, a well-turned ear will look like some bizarre, wonderful, bluish puff pastry from a bakery out of the Villafranchian period.

(If this has, by the way, all sounded unsettling—and what will

follow on the subject of dressing a deer sounds no less so—it should
be noted that this is merely the way this is done, and that none of
these necessary procedures for caring for the carcass of a deer he has
killed is ever carried out by a true hunter with anything less than
reverence and a simple gaping marvel at the intricate workings of the
wild anatomy that are revealed to him through his knacker's chores.)

Caping requires no remarkable talents, merely patience—that
skill all good hunters need to have anyway—and care. A hunter, if he
means to preserve the skin of the animal he has killed, must take the
time and care to remove all the fat and meat from it that he can, so
that all that remains is the inner "blue hide" in which the web of
thready blue capillaries is visible. He may then either salt or freeze the
hide until he can reach the taxidermist or tannery with it.

Hunting musk-ox once in the High Arctic in March, I found
that freezing, whether one wanted it to be or not, was *the* means of
preservation, the hide turning as rigid as corrugated tin in the minus-
forty-degree sunshine, and taking two days to thaw out after I returned
south with it. Salting preserves a hide just as well, though, and is the
first step in tanning, whereas freezing is not. A large quantity of salt
is needed to protect the hide—five pounds at a minimum for just a
deer cape—and it must be rubbed thoroughly into all parts of the
inner-skin side. (It is more important in salting than in freezing to
remove *all* fat and meat so the salt can reach the actual hide.) The salt
brings to a halt the bacterial action that causes a hide to rot, and draws
the moisture out of the skin and locks the hair follicles in place. (For
this reason, if a hide cannot be gotten to a tannery for several days,
then the moisture-laden salt should be scraped off and replaced with
fresh dry salt every so often. The hide should also be unrolled periodically and let dry in the shade, though never in the sun because
this can cause any fats or oils still in the skin to liquefy and leak into
the hairs, the way oil leaks through a bag of french fries, "grease
burning" them.) If freezing a hide is good, and salting a hide is good,
then it must be that salting *and* freezing would be doubly good; but
this is not the case because the salt lowers the freezing point and a
hide in a freezer could remain wet, allowing the process of decay to
go on. Salt *or* freeze, never both.

The most fundamental thing to preserve from any deer whose life we
have chosen to take is, of course, his meat. His wild meat, that can
be obtained nowhere else but the hunting field, is at the primal root
of why we hunt. Wild-animal protein, that allowed our pip-squeak

primates' brains to burgeon to their current unwieldy, and undoubt-edly self-destructive, dimensions, can be fairly claimed as the very basis of our consciousness. Everything we know and see and sense and can tell each other about the world is the result of our having killed and eaten wild animals. That is why there is something absolutely sacra-mental about wild meat fairly gained. You can taste that in it.

I once tried farm-raised venison in a finer restaurant, and some-thing was amiss. It was not that the meat was bad: it was simply that it was no longer *game* meat. At best it could be described as bland; at worst, if you savored it, there was the unmistakable flavor of feed "pellets" and high fences and the narrow chute the deer had been prodded up to be slaughtered in confinement. I am arguably preju-diced—no, I'm *un*arguably prejudiced—but for the life of me I could not taste the mountain ridges that deer should have bounded across, the trees he should have slept under with ears cocked, last summer's grasses he should have pawed down through the snow to eat, the swift creek waters he should have drunk from, all those things I can taste in the meat of a wild deer I have killed.

The way a deer lives and what he feeds on are what also make venison, and all wild game meat from pure wild country, the healthiest animal flesh a human can consume, far, far lower in fats and cholesterol and chemicals than any domestically manufactured livestock. It is ironic that the lofty benefits many vegetarians ascribe to their diets of plant matter can be obtained through the basest carnivorous instinct: a taste for running beasts.

So when a hunter reaches a dead deer—or any game animal—his first obligation is to dress that deer to see to it that the meat is properly cared for. I suppose I should amend that, actually, to his *second* obligation. His very first is to make sure the deer is unques-tionably dead. If a deer's eyes are closed, he may very well be alive. This can be a dangerous situation for a hunter when he walks up on the animal—careful to approach him from the rear in case he should lunge forward—because a deer, wounded or otherwise, is fully capable of inflicting serious injury on a human. He can break a leg with a slashing kick of his hoof, or badly gore a hunter with his antlers. No, this is not an effort to portray deer hunting as a high-risk venture, the way it is sometimes shown in glaring headline type in sport-ing magazines—"ATTACKED BY ENRAGED DEER, I STRUGGLED FOR LIFE"—but merely to point out, again, that there *are* attendant hazards in hunting that need to be addressed, just as there are in all of real life, as we should know.

If you are unsure about whether a deer is dead or not, you can, if it can be done safely, shoot him again, in the neck or in the crease of hide behind his shoulder, about a third of the way up the width of his body. This shot should reach his heart.

If the deer's eyes are open, especially if they have begun to glaze over and take on an iridescent green film, then the deer is probably dead. A hunter can test this by touching the open eye with a long stick to see whether the deer reacts.

Of course, if the hunter made a good shot in the first place, one in that vital chest area, then the question of death will likely be settled before he even gets up on the animal. Such a shot also makes the task of dressing the deer a far easier one because the paunch and the intestines will not have been perforated and their contents spilled into the body cavity.

Making certain the deer is dead, a hunter unloads his rifle and sets it safely down, then fulfills his legal duties by tagging the carcass. If he can hang a deer while he is dressing it, this will make for a neater job; but at the least he should try to position the carcass so it is on its back with the rump pointed downhill, so gravity can assist him in the cleaning process.

The first step in dressing a deer is to cut completely around its anus, deeply enough to free the anal canal from any attachments. Then the hide of the belly is split from the sternum to the anus, again cutting *with* the hairs, the knife blade slid under the skin and inner muscle wall, but not so deeply that it punctures the stomach or intestines. The hunter can help hold open the cut with the index and middle fingers of his nonknife hand, spread in a V and moving along behind the *back* of the blade as it travels *away* from him down the deer's belly.

The blade will move around the genitals then back down the center line until it reaches the anus. The meat of the pelvis should be split down until the pelvic, or pubic, arch is reached. Now the hunter must return to the chest cavity and cut free the entire diaphragm from the chest wall. The hunter should then reach as far up into the throat as he can to sever the windpipe; and with one pull, the entire alimentary canal, with attendant heart and lights and liver and all the rest, can be removed, with only minor trimmings—such as cutting away the penis and urinary tract from the hide—required.

It is hardly more complicated than that; but it would still be better to have an old hunter show you how it is done, rather than to acquire all your knowledge of it only from reading. An old hunter could show you how best to hold the knife, how the pelvic arch should be split and the chest cavity held open with a stick and the carcass gotten up off the ground so the air can circulate around and through it and it can chill out and a dry pellicle form over the meat, sealing it against moisture and, therefore, retarding the action of bacteria.

An old hunter could show you how to take off the front legs at the knees and the hind ones at the hock, leaving the rear tendon attached so the deer can be hung by it. He can also teach you, if you must leave your deer in the field overnight, and there is a tree at hand, to hang it high so a wayward coyote—the only kind known—or badger or skunk cannot reach it and chew away on the fine hams or the tenderloins to its heart's content. (As a desperation measure, you can try leaving your T-shirt with the carcass, so your human scent remains around it, or sprinkle it with black pepper to keep animals off it if you are unable to hang it.)

If a deer can be gotten out of the field whole, that is the best way. In cold fall weather, I have more than once hung a dressed Colorado mule deer overnight, his meat getting down well below forty degrees Fahrenheit; then wrapping his and the similarly chilled carcasses of other hunters' deer together in tarps and sleeping bags, driven them a thousand miles home, and had the meat still be cold to the touch twenty-four hours and more later as I and the other hunters finished skinning them—the meat holding better if the carcass can travel with its hide on; then wiped them off, inside and out, to remove any loose hairs and other debris; and also cut away any blood-shot meat, before transporting them at once to the butcher's cooler, to have him hang the meat for a few days to age before cutting and wrapping it. If the carcass cannot be brought out whole, though, then it needs to be taken apart, first the quarters, then the body severed in two, in front of the tenderloins so they are not cut into, usually at about the third rib up from the bottom. This is something old hunters were put on this earth to show.

An old hunter can show and explain much to you beyond this, as well. He can tell you of the way of the hunter, maintaining the ancient tradition of oral teaching. The hardest thing for any hunter, old or young, to explain, though, is the biggest mystery the hunt contains, the one that while taxing his ability to make matters clear remains the one that he can never escape being asked, or asking himself.

Why kill animals? Why death?

9

MEDITATIONS

I declare I am a hunter, and the question is invariably the same: Why must you kill splendid animals when you hunt?

There is never any question of why I go in search of game, why I set out to try to create a special bond with wild animals. The motives for this are known implicitly, on an almost preconscious level. Pursuing animals is understood to be not only one of those so-called pastimes humans enthusiastically engage in, but, as well, a felt need to link the beating of our purportedly "civilized" hearts to that of wild hearts. But why must death be brought into it?

Death has always posed a problem for humans. The sudden death of someone we love can be the most painful, mystifying, and intimidating event we ever experience. And yet there are times when death is necessary—the death of a rabid dog; welcomed—the death of someone who has suffered for a prolonged period from an incurable and agonizing disease; and even celebratory—the religious slaughtering of animals to comply with dietary laws, not to mention the killing of the sought-after game animal. No wonder Ortega y Gasset tells us that "death is the least intelligible fact that man stumbles upon." What

Roe deer skull: classical European skull mount. (*Photo: Daniel Hernandez*)

kind of mind could possibly be capable of balancing the manifold contradictions presented by this ultimate phenomenon of life? The profoundly mature and wise one of the true hunter, would be my contention.

Finding a way of dealing with the inescapable conundrum of death has no minor relevance to the lives of all conscious beings. So one might be forgiven for supposing that, rather than questioning the component of death in hunting, any number of folks would be eager to look at this so-called diversion of millions of humans, which is made up of the most fundamental factors in life, to see what it is really all about.

Yet in "our time—which is a rather stupid time—hunting is not considered a serious matter." That quote, and most that will follow in this chapter, are from a lengthy essay by the one philosopher in this century to take the matter of hunting as seriously as it deserves. That philosopher is, of course, José Ortega y Gasset; his essay, published in book form, *Meditations on Hunting*. He takes hunting very, very seriously, yet not in the least solemnly, because what he is writing about is nothing so much as man's real happiness.

Ortega y Gasset was born in Madrid in 1883 and died there seventy-two years later. He studied philosophy in Spain and Germany, and held the chair of Metaphysics at the University of Madrid from 1910 to 1936. In Ortega y Gasset's philosophical view, the life of the individual is the basic reality humans have to contend with, vital reason supplanting absolute reason. He holds that the life we are given is without a preprogrammed plan, and that we have to choose the course of action we will follow in each of life's situations, unlike animals, who can rely on instinct. He is, also, an unhesitating champion of a particularly dynamic concept of privilege, to be earned, and continually re-earned, by an elite class who should be the natural leaders of a meritocratic society. Ortega y Gasset's is a nearly chivalric code of noblesse oblige.

It should not be surprising, then, to learn that in 1931 he became a delegate to Spain's Republican Chamber of Deputies, or that he exiled himself to Europe and Argentina from 1936 to 1945. It was while he was in Lisbon in 1942 that he wrote the prologue, to his friend Edward, Count Yebes's book of hunting stories *Veinte Años de Caza Mayor* ("Twenty Years a Big-Game Hunter"), that when published separately from the count's book became his own *Meditations on Hunting*.

Anyone who truly cares to understand the total "why" of the hunt, including the requisite presence of death in it, does not have to read this chapter. All he has to do is to pick up a copy of *Meditations on Hunting* and read *it*. No one else in the last half-century has explained the meaning of hunting better than Ortega y Gasset has in this essay, nor will anyone else in the next half. The chilling beauty of *Meditations on Hunting* is that Ortega y Gasset's words could as easily have been written five centuries ago, or ten or twenty—or twenty centuries from now—and he would still be speaking to the deepest emotions of all hunters, no matter how changed the conditions surrounding them. That is how timeless his words are, how close they come to being a "starry glimpse of eternity," as he describes the distance to which a genuine absorption in the occupation of hunting can carry us. His essay is a document on the changelessness of true hunters.

In *Meditations on Hunting,* Ortega y Gasset sets himself the formidable task of clarifying "what the devil kind of occupation . . . this business of hunting" is. Because humans, unlike more instinctual animals, do not have the option of "simply living," they must hand over their lives to specific occupations. Some of our occupations, such as work, are not a matter of happiness, but of pure survival. Yet there are other "felicitous occupations," as Ortega y Gasset calls them, that we choose to do only for the enjoyment we derive from them. (For some of us, such occupations even become our vocations.)

It is for enjoyment, not for mere pleasure—there being a real difference—then, that humans choose to take up the way of hunting. Hunting is far from plain ordinary fun, being, instead, a "vigorous discipline" to which the good hunter dedicates part of his existence, enduring the "innumerable annoyances" of the chase and meeting the demands it places upon him to "keep himself fit, face extreme fatigue, accept danger." For this reason it can be seen that true hunting transcends the notion of pastime—with all the drear connotations that tawdry word carries—and represents, instead, a "deep and permanent yearning in the human condition," something even those most obdurately opposed to the component of death in the hunt would have to acknowledge.

We engage in hunting, therefore, not for its pleasures, but for the happiness to be found in undertaking "an effort made completely freely, for the enjoyment of it," unlike all the other efforts we are forced to put forth on behalf of the bulk of our lives. Hunting, in spite of unpleasantnesses that can be associated with it, makes us happy, first of all, because we can *choose* to occupy ourselves with it.

Ortega y Gasset readily admits that hunting is a highly privileged occupation. He states that "the most appreciated, enjoyable occupation for the normal man has always been hunting," and for this reason has always been numbered among those favored by nobility, going back to that first class of noblemen, the Paleolithic hunter-gatherers. (The felicitous occupations Ortega y Gasset notes as being the ones normal men, even those of the apparently highest sophistication, have always wished to engage in when they were free to do whatever they pleased— namely "hunting, dancing, racing, conversing"—are precisely those that made up the entire *life* of "primitive" men.)

As I said, everyone seems more than capable of comprehending the impetus toward hunting, the longing to become, once again, a naturally functioning inhabitant of the wild from which the human arose. It is only the killing that gives some pause, or even causes them revulsion. I think much of this has to do with the perfectly understandable fear of death, that has the potential of developing into a somewhat childish petulance over the stubborn inevitability of the disagreeable event. People weaned on a sybaritic diet of empty amusements find it grossly unfair that death, of all things, should be part of the package of living. Not that hunters are what you would call *delighted* by this prospect themselves, but good hunters have never seen much percentage in turning their backs on death and trying to deny its ubiquity.

The known cost of all animal life—and a great deal of nonanimal—is, one way or another, the death of the representatives of some other species. There is almost no way for one form of life to exist *except* at the expense of another. An impala involved in seemingly peaceful grazing is as much a predator on a living blade of grass as the leopard who bellies silently toward him.

Even when some people can accept the universality of the killing that goes on ceaselessly around them, they want, to begin with, to disavow any responsibility for it themselves (an outrageous impossibility), or to insist that below the human level (*below* being a very operative preposition) it is conducted out of mindless need alone, that no enjoyment is ever taken in it. For this reason they will claim to tolerate the killing carried out by native "subsistence" hunters by consigning their hunting to rude necessity, and relegating such hunters not so subtly to a human status that should be considered not so enlightened as their own, in effect assuming these benighted creatures to be lacking in the full register of sincere feelings they themselves possess, and therefore unable to experience real happiness from any occupation, not just from hunting. They only *think*—to the limited extent that they can—that they are happy.

The unfortunate truth is that, not being exclusively carnivorous, *no* human is required to kill animals to survive; he can nourish himself just as well by killing only plants. Even the earliest, most primitive human had the choice of hunting or not. Having discovered hunting, though, the human carried on with it for the enjoyment it brought into his life. (How many farmers, or "ranchers," past and present, still choose to hunt when all their nutritional requirements can be met from their fields? Now, offhand, how many normal humans can we think of who would freely choose to dig for root crops for the sheer joy of it?)

Many who oppose the kill in the hunt suppose that the taking of a life is its sole purpose. But oddly enough, it is not even necessary for an animal to die to make hunting real. "*It is not essential to the hunt*," Ortega y Gasset italicizes, "*that it be successful*," only that the genuine possibility of success exist. Success in the hunt is the capturing, dead or alive, by a hunter of a free-roaming species other than his own—which is why even catch-and-release fishing, where the captured prey is turned loose alive, is a form, very much, of the hunt.

Whether or not the prey's blood *is* spilled in the course of the hunt, the *possibility* must still be present, because that is what, first, shaped the prey itself, gave it its swiftness and reclusiveness and wariness, living for the animal amounting to a state of "being perpetually alert for the hunter," even when he is not about. And because, ines-capably, the hunter is a "death dealer," as Ortega y Gasset rightly insists. The object of the hunter is not simply to move energetically across the hunting ground; "in the last analysis, he kills." Any attempt by the hunter to alibi his way out of this aspect of the hunt, such as by claiming that he "hunts" only with a camera, is "affected piety" and "a prudery of hideous moral style" that can only succeed in turning the hunt into a sham.

The killing of an animal is the "natural end of the hunt," by *all* predators, not just human ones; but for the human hunter all that leads up to the kill is not merely the means, but an end in itself. Death is necessary only to make hunting real, to enable man to reenact, completely, a ritual—of the chase—as ancient as the human. The hunt without the possibility of the kill is like sleep without the possibility of dreams. As Ortega y Gasset says in one of his most often quoted statements from *Meditations on Hunting,* "one does not hunt in order to kill; on the contrary, one kills in order to have hunted."

Hunting, Ortega y Gasset tells us, is a relationship imposed on us by certain animals—think of the sight of the deer—"to the point where not trying to hunt them demands the intervention of our de-liberate will." Those who wish to make a moral issue out of hunting—when it is absolutely beyond accepted, formal morality in the way, at essence, that other fundamental human activity, sex, is: sex can bring us pleasure or sadness, but the desire to join with another, whether or not acted on, remains basic and unalterable: by itself it is neither good nor evil; it only is—seem to have two profoundly contradictory bases for argument.

It is wrong, according to one tack the argument follows, to hunt and kill because by so doing—by feeling that he can rightfully attempt to take the lives of other animals—a human presumes himself superior to those animals without sufficient evidence for sustaining such a presumption. In effect, we are no better than any other beast.

The other direction from which this argument comes is that the modern human advanced long ago beyond his brutishly predatory inclinations, so that the urge to hunt is something degradingly ani-malistic. In short, we are *much* better than any other beast.

What's it going to be?

If it is wrong for a human to hunt and kill other animals, then it is no less wrong for a red-tailed hawk, for example, to hunt and kill other animals.

No? The redtail, it might be argued, *has* to hunt to eat; he, *certainly,* cannot enjoy it. Who says? A redtail is perfectly capable of scavenging to survive. But being a *hunter* is what made him the way he is, and it is only in order to continue being that that he hunts, and (for all any of us can know from our earthbound perspective) finds an enormous redtail sense of happiness *in* the hunt.

Being hunters is what has made humans what they are, too, from millions of years of a hunting past that shaped everything from our bodies to our brains to our social relationships. Ten thousand years of grubbing in the dirt is hardly an adequate period for the impulse to hunt to be extinguished in our lives. And so the real aberration is not that some humans still hunt and kill, but that some do not.

The fond hope of eliminating killing from the hunt—teach a wolf not to kill, if you can; create a monstrosity!—is an example of "man's supreme and devastating pride." Ortega y Gasset goes on to tell us, "If you believe that you can do whatever you like—even, for example, the supreme good, then you are, irretrievably, a villain."

Animal death will continue with or without man the hunter, so it is foolish for a human to believe he can somehow remove himself from it, or to discriminate between the killing carried out by human and nonhuman hunters. To those who still find the kill unspeakably repugnant, Ortega y Gasset, in what amounts very nearly to a challenge, offers "the fact that the greatest and most moral homage we can pay to certain animals on certain occasions is to kill them with certain means and rituals," as unpleasant as that may seem to some.

But why, finally, not be satisfied with occupations that do not involve any unpleasantnesses at all? What, ultimately, makes hunting so unique that humans pursue it at almost any cost?

It is the duty of the modern world to drive us every day further from all things natural and wild, to make us feel increasingly lost and isolated from our true, primitive natures. We need, desperately, to have a means of escaping such cold days as these and of revisiting the sunnier past when we had not yet been subjected to the barbarisms of civilization and were still genuinely human. We need to be able to do this, if only for brief periods, or go mad.

Of all the occupations we can choose to try to achieve this escape, the one that permits us to return most fully to an earlier day is hunting. By hunting, Ortega y Gasset says, "man succeeds, in effect, in annihilating all historical evolution, in separating himself from the present, and in renewing the primitive situation." Hunting is the "only occupation that permits [man] something like a vacation from his human condition."

But this must be *real* hunting, and it cannot be that without the possibility of real animal death. There must be a preservation of what Ortega y Gasset calls the "ferocious instinct" and "bitter impulse" that humans share with the other carnivores, the need, in the words of the "human ecologist" Paul Shepard, to "catch, kill, and dismember their prey." Shepard adds that the very measure of men's humanity is the extent to which they do this.

Hunting—the seeking, the chasing, the killing, the butchering, the "criminal suspicion" aroused by the confronting of death, the celebratory resolving of it all in the sacramental feast—which teaches us the total cost of meat, the price our lives and all lives exact from the world, is inextricably tied to our humanness. We learn this now from reading books like *Meditations on Hunting*. Ancient hunters, in a time before books, before even conscious thought, knew this in their very beings. The few remaining untamed human hunters—no more, now, than a generation or two away from becoming extinct or from being subdued into something far more tractable—who to this day set off from Arctic shores in skin boats or slip along a rain-forest path in Asia or Amazonia or jog across an African plain as yellow as the sun may still know hunting in this natural way. This is how the true hunter of the modern world strives to learn the way, too, so that it is no longer an occupation he must work at consciously, but has become as intimate a part of him as his own blood.

To give Ortega y Gasset a final word: "We must immerse ourselves wholly and heroically in an occupation in order to *be* it!" And so, eventually, we may find ourselves able to hunt our way off the page and truly into the wild.

10

HORSEFLESH

In finding our way into the wild, we may, as we have seen, join forces with other animals, albeit domesticated. Besides the dog, there is another, far more problematic beast we make an uneasy alliance with in the course of the hunt.

Perissodactylous, outsize, afraid of everything—including its own shadow—yet demonstrably refractory and certifiably dangerous, the horse was, after the dog, the second wild animal to be tamed by man, however tenuously, for use in the hunt. Evelyn Waugh, being as peripatetic as ever, once overheard a conversation between two Guianese horse owners that raised serious question about who, exactly, might have gotten the better of that particular transaction:

> "I tell you, Mr Bain [said one horseman to the other], that buckskin of mine was the finest mare bred in this district. You didn't have to use no spur or whip to her. Why before you was on her back, almost, she was off like the wind and *nothing* would stop her. And if she didn't want to go any particular way *nothing* would make her. Why I've

been carried six miles out of my course many a time, pulling at her with all my strength. *And* how she could rear."

"Yes, she *could rear*," said Mr Bain in wistful admiration. "It was lovely to see her."

"And if she got you down she'd roll on you. She wouldn't get up till she'd broken every bone in your body. She killed one of my boys that way."

"But what about my Tiger?"

"Ah, he was a good horse. You could see by the way he rolled his eyes."

"Did you ever see him *buck*? Why he'd buck all over the corral. And he was wicked too. He struck out at you if he got a chance."

"That was a *good* horse, Tiger. What became of him?"

"Broke his back. He bolted over some rocks into a creek with one of the boys riding him."

"Still you know I think that for *bucking* my Shark . . ."

And so it went on. Presently I asked in some apprehension, "And the horse I am to ride tomorrow. Is he a *good* horse too?"

"One of the strongest in the country," said Mr Bain. "It will be just like the English Grand National for you."

More than one hunter, when faced with the prospect of having to saddle up the next morning for his first horseback hunt into the high lonesome, has experienced "some apprehension" akin to Waugh's. *Some* apprehension? Blind panic is sometimes nearer the mark.

Prior to his first packstring hunt into the Canadian Rockies, an otherwise experienced, and normally rational, hunter friend of mine seriously argued—more to convince himself than anyone else—that he was in good enough physical condition that he had no need of a horse; in fact, he was certain that he could comfortably maintain, on foot, the fifteen-, sometimes twenty-five-mile-a-day pace the mountain horses would be setting. That is how desperate was his desire *not* to be on the back of a horse. The problem is that there is often simply no alternative for a hunter but to climb on, pull down the old Stetson, and call, "Let 'er buck!"

The necessity of hunting on horseback is not limited to preventing a certain wear and tear on a hunter's body. To begin with, a horse should never be considered an exemption from a hunter's meeting the demand hunting, as Ortega y Gasset tells us, places on him

Packhorses on an elk hunt. (*Photo: Robert Robb*)

to keep himself fit—although a sound riding animal can make it possible for a hunter with some physical limitation to reach hunting grounds that might otherwise be denied him.

The main advantage of hunting from horseback, aside from saving the legs, is that a hunter is provided with a mobile, elevated position from which to scout large areas of the country. Though he should pay attention to where his horse is walking, a hunter can pay far more attention to his surroundings than he could if he had to concern himself with where he had to place his own feet with each step. A horse is also in some situations essential in carrying in camp equipment and gear, and as a means of carrying heavy game animals out of the field. And last, wild animals are much more tolerant of the quiet approach of large quadrupeds than they are of the shuffling two-legged rush of erect primates, often to the extent that they will completely ignore that odd creature perched atop a horse. For these reasons, on horseback is in many circumstances the only way to hunt.

Once a hunter accepts the inevitability of this—and it need not be a completely cheerless acceptance, either—there are steps he should take to make his experience on horseback as pleasant as possible.

The initial step is to learn how to ride. This might appear so explicitly manifest a course to follow that my even bothering to mention it must seem gratuitous at best. As Americans, though, we share a legacy of belief in our all being the natural heirs to Roy and Dale, that we are all such Sons of the Pioneers that without our requiring the least little bit of training we can all spring nimbly into the saddle and gallop off into the sunset. We were born to ride.

Tout au contraire, a human on a horse is probably one of the most unnatural sights Nature has to offer for our entertainment, about like seeing a baboon astride a wapiti. Except that it's even worse than that. In the human's other hunting partnership with a domesticated animal, the dog, the two at least share a common interest: they both love meat. The only interests horse and human had that converged up till the time men decided to try to ride them were the human's interest in eating horses, and the horse's interest in running like hell at the sight of men. Such feelings die hard; so horsemanship is an art that flatly cries out to be learned.

One cold October morning at the foot of a southern Wyoming mountain, the bitter air carrying the mingled smells of sagebrush and horses, I watched a hunter from Miami, Florida, come west for his very first mule-deer hunt, hoist himself tentatively into the saddle on a small paint horse in the lantern light behind an old line shack. He mounted up not all that badly; but, as in a different context you could see by someone's outfit that he was a cowboy, you could see by the way this Greater Miamian held the reins that he might not have had what you would characterize as *extensive* equestrian experience.

"Uh, how, uh . . . ?"

" 'Make the horse *turn*'?" one of the chaps-clad guides standing beside the hitching rail queried.

"Yeah."

"Well, to make him go right, you put pressure against the left side of his neck with this rein and against his side with your left knee—by the way, instead of having them both on the same side, you might want to separate those reins and put one on *this* side of his neck, like this, and the *other* on the other side. And," the guide hastened to add, trying to give the *Reader's Digest* condensed version of equitation class, "you shouldn't hold those reins so loose that they drag on the ground like that; *you just might want,*" he was calling after him, now, as the hunter's guide rode out of camp and the hunter's horse sprang like a deer after him, the hunter lurching in the saddle like a bowling pin about to go down in a seven-ten split as his little pony swerved in and out of clumps of sage and cantered in a lively manner under the low-hanging boughs of evergreens, *"to tighten up on those reins a might."*

Somehow, the hunter stayed in the saddle long enough to ride up on a bedded, exceptionally good buck and to kill it outright with a single shot. That did nothing, though, to alter the fact that he could have saved himself a great deal of disconcertion if he had, a month or two before his horseback hunt, sought out a stable or riding school— of which there must be any number even in Miami—and taken his equitation lessons at a somewhat more leisurely pace.

Even a hunter who has gone to horse school, though, should not depend upon reencountering that same equanimity, gentleness, and ease of handling he found in the horse he trotted merrily around the riding ring upon in the mount he may draw from an outfitter's string—a string whose ridability quotient is frequently calculated on outfitting's harsh but necessary mathematics of "buy thirty, shoot ten," leaving the very real possibility that *eleven* would have been more in order. In other words, after learning on Flicka, a hunter gets to hunt on Fury.

Nonetheless, a hunter will have learned some valuable riding techniques from his lessons that he will be able to apply with good advantage to even the most cantankerous churn-head. He will learn the way to give the horse commands with his knees as well as the reins; the way to adjust the stirrups so that, standing in them, he will have a hand's width between his crotch and the saddle so he can ride comfortably all day without destroying either his knees or his seat; the way to ride with his heels down to take the strain off his calves, and with his feet in the stirrups no farther than their balls, both to maintain balance and to prevent his feet from getting hung up and to allow him to kick out of the stirrups quickly if his mount should suddenly bolt or fall and it becomes expedient for the hunter to part company with it. He will learn the way to let a horse pick its own route over rough ground or fallen timber—giving it just enough rein at such places so that it can look down to see the obstacle beneath its hooves—the way to persuade it calmly but firmly to go where the rider wants it to; despite the horse's innate inclination to return to the barn and nap; and the way to praise it when it has done right.

There is much a horse-mounted hunter needs to learn, and there is no substitute for his taking lessons to learn it. Yet, there are some specialized bits of information he can only gather on the trail, such as, pick a horse with high withers.

Horses, of course, are employed in hunting for carrying hunters and their gear through mountains; so, far more *up* and *down* is encountered on the trail than on your average bridle path. A hunter should soon learn that on the uphill passages it is best for him to lean forward over his horse's neck, while leaning slightly back on the down-hill side. This makes it easier for a hunter to hang on, as well as easier—and this is a far more important consideration—for the horse to pack his weight. Over a long stretch of downhill, with a horse without high withers, though, a hunter may notice that his saddle has begun to slip forward. Well before the pommel ends up over the horse's ears, the horse will have made its displeasure amply known—indeed, it will seem very much like "rodeo time" to the soon-to-be-dismounted hunter. A rider wants to check on where his saddle is situated on his horse; and if he sees that it has slid forward, he can adjust it quickly by riding his horse a short distance uphill. He should also check his cinch periodically, to make sure it is staying tight—although not so tight that it galls the horse—and he might also want to use a saddle with a breast band and crupper to help prevent the rig from sliding back and forth. The most prudent course of action, though, on any extremely rough piece of ground, downhill, uphill, or in between, is for a hunter to dismount and lead his horse down, up, or through it, *especially* on downhills, which are hard on a horse's legs to begin with, and are only made worse when he is carrying a rider.

Dismounting and walking every so often is a generally sound practice for both rider and horse along the trail. To the horseman it gives an opportunity to stretch his legs and work out any stiffness he may have gotten in the saddle. To the horse it gives a break from lugging that load of human around. A horse—Descartes aside—is not a machine that can be switched on and off at will. A horse, although it has the capacity for an exceptional amount of work, cannot go all day at a steady pace without any rest the way an automobile can. Pure horsepower is not unlimited, which is why many outfitters place a limit of between 220 and 225 pounds for the weight of the hunters they will allow their horses to carry. A hunter has to learn the capacities and the rhythms of the particular horse he rides—shifting his weight with the horse's gait so he is not beating constantly down against the horse's back, for instance, such pounding on the saddle capable of bruising the horse's kidneys the way a few rounds of boxing with a relentless kidney puncher would bruise a hunter's—learn that there is no standard-model horse, and that he and his horse must find a way of working together in order for the *two* of them to get where they are going.

As I have said, though, a horse is more than just a means of getting from here to there; he is an asset and a partner in the hunt the way a dog can be. That is the primary thing a hunter wants to

When hunting on horseback, there is no substitute for a good rifle scabbard. (*Photo: Daniel Hernandez*)

keep in mind when he is *hunting* from horseback. Unlike a sucker, a horse should always be given an even break; and a hunter will do well always to be slow and easy, but *unequivocal* with his horse from the very first moment he walks up to the animal till he dismounts the final time at the hunt's end.

A hunter will need a way of carrying his weapon on his horse, and there really is no substitute for a good scabbard. There are any number of ways of attaching a scabbard to a saddle, and it is largely a matter of personal preference. Hanging the scabbard horizontally along the horse's body, under the sweat leather, allows the rifle to be drawn from it quickly—assuming it is on the side the hunter dismounts on, which, though that is usually the left side, is not *always* that side: there may be times, on a sidehill or in a narrow draw or a timber thicket, when a hunter will have no choice but to dismount on the right, and the rifle will be on the other side.* But if the rifle is carried this way with the butt facing back, there is some chance of brush's catching in the sling or trigger guard and pulling the rifle out of the scabbard, and if facing forward, of brush's constantly being caught

---

* All else being equal, it is always easier to try to mount and dismount on the horse's uphill side; try turning him before mounting or dismounting so his left side is toward the uphill slope.

under it. And when carried under the fender, the rifle and scabbard tend to make the hunter's knee on that side sore.

The solution I have found is to hang my scabbard vertically on the right side, at the front of the saddle. From here I can draw my rifle out from either side of the horse. To make it even easier to draw out, I use a narrow sling on any scabbard-carried rifle, it being more difficult to pull a rifle from the scabbard if it is jammed in there with a thick, padded sling on it. I have also found that a scabbard should have a small opening at the toe to let twigs, leaves, and other debris fall out and not collect where the muzzle rests. And, of course, a rifle should always be carried unloaded while one is on horseback; *and* it is always a good idea, whenever you dismount—even if only for a few moments—to pull your rifle from the scabbard, in case your horse decides that this is the perfect spot for him to lie down and have a good roll.

Other gear that can be of benefit to the horseback hunter are saddlebags. In them can be carried a first-aid kit, binoculars, a paperback copy of *Riders of the Purple Sage,* a tuna-fish sandwich, or other vital matériel, though saddlebags should never be overloaded, again, to prevent their beating against the horse's kidneys. A hunter might want to buy his own set of bags, to make certain he will have some for himself on any guided hunting trip; and they do not have to be pricey, top-grade leather ones, either—sturdy canvas saddlebags with flaps that can be strapped closed are quite satisfactory.

A hunter should also carry his rain gear tied to his saddle, not stuck away under the manta-covered loads on the packhorses. Mountain weather can change violently and swiftly, and a rider setting out on a shirt-sleeve morning can find himself in a blizzard by noon. I also like a stout pair of leather gloves for riding, to keep my hands warm and to make, for me, holding the reins more comfortable. (The reins, by the way, should not be tied together at the ends for the simple reason that if, when game is spotted, a hunter has to "bail out" of the saddle and does not have time to tie his horse, he has only to let the reins drop to the ground and his horse will have difficulty in wandering very far away as it walks on the ends of them with every step or two.

(This also raises the matter of shooting game in the presence of horses. It goes without saying that a hunter should never attempt to fire a weapon from the back of a horse, or by using the horse for a rest, unless, of course, there is something intensely appealing to him in seeing a twelve-hundred-pound animal rise skyward like a Fourth of July fireworks display. First the hunter should, if at all possible, tie the horse—by the halter rope rather than the reins, so if the horse starts at the sound of the shot he will not injure his mouth—or have someone else hold the horse for him before he attempts to fire in the horse's vicinity. This can save a hunter a long and embarrassing hike back to camp.)

The final item of equipage no horseback hunter should do without is an honest-to-God cowboy hat. He should invest in a top-quality one, 3X Beaver or above, and let it grow old gracefully with accumulated sweat and trail dust and hard rain and bright sun. He should use it, by ducking his head, to protect his face from being lashed when he has to ride through heavy brush. In it he can even draw a drink of water up to his horse's lips.

After a long horseback hunt, a hunter will not feel in the least silly about wearing such a hat. After a long hunt, when he has come to know the rhythms of his horse, come to move across the far country upon him like a centaur moving through the mist—lifted above the ground but remaining tied to it by four animal legs—his apprehensions about steel-shod hooves and yellow teeth the size of walnuts and sunfishing widow makers and being dragged off by a runaway, will have, if not faded altogether, at least dimmed, and some pleasure may even begin to grow from having sat upon a horse's back. And despite his wariness he will have become something he may never have thought possible: a hunting horseman.

11

BEARS

It would be nearly impossible for a hunter not to feel that way about horses. Yet no matter how much horses fill our hunts with the romance of the Old West, there is simply no denying that when it comes to the subject of *bears,* what endears them so profoundly to us has at least *something* to do with the fact that they *eat* horses, don't they? The ancient human taste for horseflesh—that is not all that antiquated, considering the rather large amounts of horsemeat that are still consumed in the world, particularly in Europe—is only one of the many traits we have in common with bears.

Also linking us, as it sets us apart from most of the other animals, including many of the other predator species, is our mutual *plantigrade* stride, the full-soled print of the bear's hind foot (with the exception of the giant panda's, whose rear paw lacks a heel pad) being nearly identical to that our own bare foot leaves upon the trail. The bears share with us, as well, a separate tibia and fibula in the lower legs, and separate radius and ulna in their forearms, giving bears unusual rotation and mobility with those forearms—at least in comparison to many other mammals, no one's ever having heard of a "deer hug"—

permitting them a wide range of movement for digging, rooting, climbing, manipulating food, and hunting.

Our other similarities extend beyond the physical. Bears seem to mimic, in a fashion that is uncanny, our moods and habits of playfulness, curiosity, gluttony, sloth, sporadic bursts of industry, incendiary lust, aloneness, fierce maternal protectiveness, aggressiveness, and a potential for murderous rage—although bears direct such rages at members of their own species far less frequently than civilized humans do at theirs. Yet while it may be that bears mimic us, perhaps we have learned our own manners from our long, fascinated observation of them.

If the deer was the breathing animal, then the bear was the "brown animal." That is the meaning of *bear*'s Indo-European root. It could be, though, that the bear's name does not have its origin in the word *brown* as much as *brown* derives from *bear*, so that *brown* might literally mean the "color of the bear," or "bear color." With some somewhat creative linguistics, the bear can even be seen as the root of such words as *bright, barley, beer, berserk, feral, burden, burly, Bernard, Bridget, berth, bier, bury*, and *birth*. This is a fair mark of how deeply we bear in mind the bear. We even see bears (Ursa Major, Ursa Minor) turning in our night sky.

There are eight species of bears in the world—who are lumped in with the Carnivora, although this is a downright indiscriminate classification for animals whose thoroughly catholic appetite, dentition, and digestion allow them to be not only carnivorous, but insectivorous, frugivorous, herbivorous, cetivorous (being, as they are, terribly fond of eating the beached carcasses of whales), mellivorous, omnivorous—everything, in fact, short of photosynthetic.

This talent for eating *any*thing is what has enabled the bears to inhabit every continent on earth, save Australia and Antarctica. Big brown bears were once to be found from North Africa to Mexico—where Coronado and his retinue were very likely the first Europeans to encounter the great roan bears called "grizzlies"—and still inhabit Europe, northern Asia, and a fair chunk of North America; sloth bears (like the one who indulged upon the good .416-shooting father), sun bears, and moon bears are found across southern Asia from Malaysia to India to Japan; giant pandas (recent analyses of these pandas' blood chemistry showing a more pronounced similarity with the blood of bears than with that of raccoons) in China; black bears throughout North America; and the spectacled bears in South America; with the polar bears circling over them all on the pack ice of the Arctic Ocean.

In North America we hunt three species of the bears: the black (*Euarctos americanus*), the big brown-grizzly (*Ursus arctos* and *Ursus arctos horribilis*), and the polar (*Thalarctos maritimus*). The black is the most numerous bear, found, with the exception of a few plains and midwestern states, in every state of the continental United States, in Alaska, and in every Canadian province and territory—excluding Prince Edward Island—and in parts of northern Mexico. (I wonder what it must have been like for the first colonists, who had probably never before seen a bear outside a traveling tent show, when they came upon the black bears of New England? Did bears, and wolves and "catamounts," give a chill—or at least a significance—to the night in the New World that it had been lacking back in Plymouth? Here was a land having not only large ruminant quadrupeds roaming wild, but one with bears who had yet to learn to dance. What clandestinely delightful memories of ancient sacred animist caves, often shared by humans with bears, must this have evoked in the upright Puritan Fathers?)

Davy Crockett's early renown arose to a large extent from his tales—on occasion perhaps verging on the tall—of hunting black bears in the then-wilderness of Tennessee, claiming to have killed over one hundred in one year. Before this, Lewis and Clark's expeditioners had provisioned themselves with the meat of black bears. In literature, William Faulkner wrote incomparably of the black bear, Old Ben, in his novella *The Bear,* and the black bear has been the stuff of poets from Robert Frost to William Carlos Williams (who actually wrote about the polar bear, but what the hell!) to Delmore Schwartz to Gary Snyder to Lew Welch (who vanished into the California Sierras, and so, assuming he died there, may conceivably even have become *part* of a black bear) to Galway Kinnell.

The black bear, despite its name, is not always black. Its hide can be of any color from the icy blue of the Alaskan glacier bear to the white of the Kermode bear of British Columbia, to blond to brown to cinnamon or slate *or* even black, sometimes marked with a white blaze on the chest. The genetics involved in determining color are simply too complex to guarantee completely uniform coloration, even among littermates. Variations in color do seem to have geographical and climatic correlations, though, with *black* black bears predominant in wetter, eastern habitats, and the rainbow bears occurring chiefly in western and more arid ones.

Like all the bears, the black is praised for his hearing and his

A large trophy black bear. (*Photo © by Bill McRae*)

extraordinary sense of smell, whereas his eyesight is roundly dismissed as being on a par with that of most cavern-dwelling amphibians. His nose and ears *are* superb, but it is sheer folly for a hunter to write off a bear's eyes. I do not believe that there is any sound reason for assuming that a bear's vision is any worse than that of most dogs, and that his tendency to stand and stare, in seeming perplexity, at an animal or a person is not evidence of myopia in the least, but merely his efforts to confirm with his nose what his eyes have already shown him, demonstrating again the difficulty most nonhuman animals have in identifying a stationary creature. I think, in fact, that the black bear's senses *and* his not inconsequential predatory animal intelligence combine to make him—and the big brown bear and the polar—among the most challenging big-game animals on the continent.

Many (who can say what percentage?) of the black bears killed by hunters are killed incidentally to the hunting of other big game. A hunter buys a bear tag on the off chance of his seeing a bruin in the woods while chasing deer or elk or moose, and every so often he does just that. When black bears are pursued intentionally, though, three general methods are used.

The first, where legal, is to set out baits for them. There is no small amount of science involved in knowing where and when and with what to bait a black bear. In the spring hunting, when the black bears will have just arisen from the dens, they will be slow to come to meat until their digestive systems—literally sealed at the anus throughout hibernation with a several-inches-long plug of woody plant matter—have once again begun to function. So at first the bears will feed on what is essentially aquatic vegetation, such as skunk cabbage, found in muskeg swamps and marshes, which acts as a purgative.

When their taste for meat is revived, there is nothing that black bears like better than the meat of beaver. Bear hunters will collect beaver carcasses from trappers in the winter and "can" them in fifty-gallon drums. A week or two before the season, the hunters will set a barrel out beneath a hunting stand—the stand usually in a tree in a thicketed location, bears' being reluctant to approach food set out in the open—and cut a ragged-edged hole in the barrel, one just big enough for a bear to slip his head into.

By the time the season opens, the beaver meat will be a mass of squiggling maggots. These are to bears what Beluga is to a marchesa. When a bear does come to feed from the barrel—normally wired or chained to a tree to prevent the bear's rolling it away—he will catch a few strands of hair on the jagged steel of the drum; and when the hunter comes to check his bait, he will know which of the innumerable shades of black bear he is dealing with. By repeated checking, the hunter will also get some idea of when the bear is coming in to feed, early or late; and if the bear has left a track—or in the case of a sow with cubs, tracks, big set and small set, at which point the hunter should move that bait elsewhere because he will not (and legally cannot) hunt a female with young—the hunter can judge the size of the bear's hide from that print by measuring the width of the forepaw's front pad in inches, adding $1\frac{1}{2}$ to that figure, and converting it to feet (for example, the imprint of a front pad that measures 5 inches in width would normally translate into a bear with a hide squaring roughly $6\frac{1}{2}$ feet, the "square" measurement derived from the length of the skinned hide from the nose to the tail, when laid flat, added to the width across the front paws, then divided by 2 [see p. 119]. For brown-grizzly, only 1 is added to the pad's width before converting to feet.)

When the hunter concludes that a bear worth pursuing is coming to his bait, he can then set up in his stand and wait for him. Although it is not an absolute rule—*no* rules are ever absolute along the way of the hunter—bears seldom seem to come to a bait before late afternoon or early evening, particularly in the spring. In any case, it seems always to be last light when a bear presents the hunter with a shot, especially

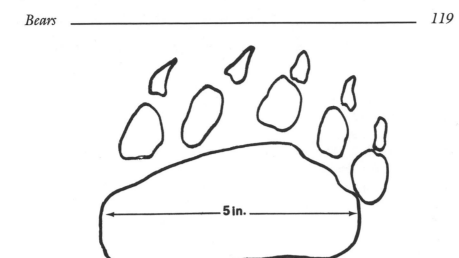

Print of a black bear's front paw, width about 5 inches.

if the hunter has chosen to hunt black bear with a bow and arrow, which is by far the most challenging and thrilling way to hunt black bears over a bait—although I do feel compelled to confess that, having been treed by a murderously enraged black bear sow once when I was armed only with my bow, *I* will never again climb into a bear stand without carrying a firearm, even when hunting with my bow.

From bait, a hunter may move on to finding bears with running dogs. This is where he will hear the big dionysiac symphony Ortega y Gasset described. In chasing large carnivores with hounds, the hunter has chosen to reduce his status in the hunt to that of a mere accomplice, one who simply aids and abets—quite happily—the true hunters, the dogs.

A hound man works for his dogs, not the other way around. The trailing breeds—Plotts, Triggs, Walkers, and the like—live for only one thing on this earth: to hunt and bay up big game. They do not do it because they are compelled to, but because they love to. The hound hunter does not, *cannot,* train his dogs to chase game; they know that from birth or not at all. The hound hunter can only train them *not* to chase certain animals, such as deer, and then sometimes only with the most strenuous of efforts.

A hound man's obligation in the hunt for black bears is to find a track, and then decide whether it is worth having his dogs pursue, on the basis of its size and freshness. He may do this with his own eyes or by using the nose of a strike dog—often an older, less fast, but far wiser hound, whom the hunter will let range freely ahead of him while he keeps the remainder of the pack confined in dog boxes, on a pickup truck, for instance, or held in check on leads. A strike dog, if extremely sensible, will sound out when he cuts a track, and then wait beside it until the hunter can come up and examine it. If the hunter chooses to follow this bear's trail, then he will turn his pack loose on it; and his part in the hunt will be, for all intents and purposes, completed.

The hunter, of course, will be permitted by the dogs to listen to their running voices in the timber as he follows after, sometimes for miles along ridges and down into cold shaded canyons, fording deep icy stony creeks, and up steep snowy slopes, his heart drumming against the curved staves of his ribs, his breath coming in sharp gasps of late-fall or early-spring air, until he hears the continuous, one-bark-per-breath "tree bark" of the hounds when they have bayed up the bear—all of it like squirrel hunting elevated to the level of the macrocosm. The bear he will kill when he reaches his dogs will be more theirs than his, because that is what is specified in the bargain he has struck with them: they will run their hearts out and tree the bear, and he will kill it, and the dogs will then rush in on the fallen bear (not that they would be afraid to confront a live bear on the ground, trail hounds highly capable of quixotic bravery in the face of a toothed-and-clawed animal four to five times, and more, their individual weights) and worry him, just enough to proclaim that this race is done, and that, no matter how long they have allied themselves with humans, they remain independent predators. Then the human will be responsible for removing the hide and quartering up the meat, letting the dogs feed on some of the intestines and the liver, and packing it all out of the timber, carrying the prize awarded for a race well run.

Whether treed or on the ground, a bear will possess certain characteristics that will assist a hunter in estimating how large it is. Before looking for any other characteristic, though, a hunter should see that the bear is alone. A bear accompanied by cubs is without fail a sow; and a hunter must remember that cubs can be anywhere within a hundred yards of the female, so he must look carefully before resolving to kill any bear.

Once a hunter has determined that a bear does not have cubs with it, he can then try to formulate an idea of the bear's size by seeing how it carries itself. If it looks gawky and long-legged, with large ears and a long snout, and tends to sit with its front paws in the air, it is probably a young bear. A large, *old* boar bear will look potbellied, his ears small—nubbed down by combat and frostbite—his muzzle short. He will walk with a pigeon-toed, rolling gait, and when he sits he will set his front paws on the ground. These are the things a hunter should look for when he strikes off to hunt black bears by the third method, spotting-stalking.

Bears incline toward reclusiveness, reticent to reveal themselves; but at certain times of the year, in certain habitats, they can be hunted without recourse to bait or dogs. In the early spring, when the bears are seeking vegetation to reopen their alimentary canals, they can be found on the hillsides, following the zone of greening grass and new leaf buds on the trees as that zone ascends steadily to the top. Such slopes can be glassed from the hill across the canyon, or, in country where a river runs through it, from the vantage point of a boat drifting in the current; and when a bear is sighted, a stalk can be mapped out and mounted.

In the fall, when the huckleberry and bearberry bushes are heavy with ripe fruit, the black bears will come to feed upon them; and if a hunter knows where patches of such berries are to be found, he can watch them, to see whether a bear appears there, and then go after it. In stalking a black bear a hunter wants to attend closely to the wind, and always approach quietly and from behind cover—the sun at his back, if possible—moving even more stealthily than he would when trying to draw within range of a deer because, he must remember, he is hunting an animal who is no less a hunter than he.

Big brown bears are hunted primarily by spotting and stalking. If any bear can be said to embody the essence of "bearness," then it is this bear. The bears go back twenty million years, but the big brown bear evolved only five hundred thousand years ago, making him the most *nouveau* bear of all. Yet he is the bear humans envision when the image of the "brown animal" shambles through their thoughts and dreams.

The big brown bear, in his annual cycle of disappearance and reappearance—submergence into, and emergence from, his winter den—acts out, or perhaps was the source of, one the most fundamental . . . "myths?" . . . "symbols?" . . . *truths* of human spiritual existence, that of rebirth after death—as the earth seasonally withers and then renews itself—a belief shared by both Indo-Europeans and North American Indians, by pagans and Christians, by humans almost anywhere the hibernation of bears could be observed. In the same Palearctic region, the big brown bear appears as prominently in the fables

Native Aleut guide glassing for bear on Kodiak Island, Alaska. (*Author photo*)

of Aesop and the fairy tales of the Brothers Grimm as he does in the stories of the Tlingit. The Norse, in their sagas, and the Chumash of native California, in their religion, both knew of "shape shifters" who could transform themselves into bearmen. *Beowulf* means "bee-wolf," or the bear; and the Inuit hold the bear to be left-handed, because that hand is the source of magical power, and the big brown bear is nothing if not magical.

The range of the big brown bear in North America begins at the far western tip of the Alaskan peninsula and fills the continental boundaries of the map from there throughout the state and east into the Yukon and Northwest Territories (NWT) to the western edge of Hudson Bay, southward through most of British Columbia and the Rockies of Alberta and down along that high range into Montana, Wyoming, and perhaps Colorado, with a very few bears still possibly to be found in the most inaccessible portions of Washington and Idaho. The coastal bears of southern Alaska, because of the easy availability to them of vast quantities of calories in the form of stream-running salmon, usually achieve a much greater size than the interior and northern bears (a tremendous brown bear from Kodiak Island could square-out eleven foot or better, while a grizzly of the barren grounds of the NWT would do well to reach seven—although even it can attain the nine-footer class, *and,* being the product of a blasted heath of a land where every berry or root or scrap of meat is the direct result of the most Herculean labors, such a bear undoubtedly represents an increased potential risk, over a well-fed Kodiak, to the exceedingly few humans he may ever encounter in his distant home, accounting *any* breathing creature as nothing more than just another item on that day's severely limited menu). The coastal bears of Alaska, then, are categorized as "browns," while the rest are known as grizzlies.

The most reliable gauge for determining the true size of any bear—black, brown-grizzly, or polar—at least in comparison to another of his species, is the size of his skull, found by adding the length—measured along the long axis—to the width—measured at the widest place at right angles to the long axis. Twenty-eight inches is a record-class brown, while for a grizzly the mark is twenty-four (and twenty-one for a black bear and twenty-seven for a polar).

Of the grizzlies, the largest of all were those of old California. Here was a silver-tipped bear whose own history embodied the cultural history of the Old West. He was called *Too-hah-̓give-dă,* "white and bad," by the Eastern Mono Indians, who along with the other tribes of California dreaded, worshiped, hunted, killed, and were killed by him. Then came Spanish explorers and mission priests whose endeavors were sustained by the meat of the grizzly. The *rancheros* followed with their penchant for bear-and-bull contests on Sundays and saints' days in the pueblo ring; but with their large herds of cattle and horses providing handy protein for the bear, they were responsible for the grizzly's population's doubling, from the five thousand estimated to be present upon their arrival, to ten thousand bears at large by the time the Yankees, drawn by gold, began in earnest to stream over the Sierras and sail into San Francisco Bay.

California's manifest destiny made no provision for the grizzly; so he was remorselessly destroyed—*not* hunted, not in any true sense, just forcibly evicted from the land the way all wild things, wild animals, wild people, eventually are when they occupy real estate wanted by men whose weather eye is most firmly on the bottom line. (Among those who enthusiastically shot and trapped California grizzlies was one James Capen Adams, a cobbler by trade from Medway, Massachusetts, who upon making his way to California in 1849, and becoming a hunter and a trapper of live grizzly bears, and establishing a menagerie on Clay and Kearny streets in San Francisco, was known

The author with an 8½-foot Kodiak bear taken by him, 1980. (*Author photo*)

Silver-tipped grizzly bear. Note size of hump and shape of face in comparison to the black bear. (*Photo © by Bill McRae*)

as Grizzly Adams. He departed California in 1860 and sailed 'round the Horn to New York City to exhibit his bears—one of whom weighed a verified fifteen hundred pounds—for Phineas Taylor Barnum, before dying of a skull fracture inflicted upon him by his bear General Fremont.) The way down for the California grizzly was precipitous after statehood, the last bear to be seen alive in the state sighted in 1924 in Sequoia National Park, sighted, it goes nearly without saying, by a crew cutting a road to bring the wilderness to the automobile. A time of "chawed up" men and "hairbreadth escapes" and the hunting of a monumental animal was gone from California, and we can all see only too clearly how California has turned out since.

Yet in those places where there are still grizzlies and brown bears to hunt, those places *with* big brown bears where, in the words of the essayist Ian Frazier, "big mysteries run close to the surface," the presence of bears drawing them up from some unfathomable depth, the dysfunctional paradise of California seems an unreal reality unnecessary to contemplate. Next to big brown bears, in fact, something as simplistic as California seems all too easy to ignore.

The principal occupation of the hunter in big brown bear country is, of course, the contemplation of, and the search for, big brown bears. For hunting browns and grizzlies, the most practical method is spotting-stalking because baiting is usually illegal, and running them with dogs would be tantamount to turning a pack of mice out on the trail of a twenty-pound house cat. Big brown bears are hunted in both the fall and the spring. In the fall, grizzly-brown bear hunting is usually conducted in conjunction with the hunting of the ruminant quadrupeds: moose and caribou and elk and sheep; and a grizzly-brown bear is often killed only because he has been happened onto. In the spring, though, a big brown bear hunt is a hunt for big brown bear alone.

A hunter enters grizzly-brown bear country looking for bears. His eyes are always searching for that great humped brown or blond or reddish or silver-tipped shape. Along the coast or on rivers the hunter can search from the water or the water's edge, glassing the high banks or hills or mountains rising to snow above him, looking for bears who have emerged from their dens. If he spots one, lying in the sun beside its den, trying to collect its half-awake thoughts before seeing what the—for it—new year may have in store, a hunter can try to estimate the size of the bear by such indicators as a face that is dish-shaped and a head that looks small compared to its body. It will have small ears, a long neck, a large hump, and a swayed back.

Its walk will be plodding and shambling, and in an old boar the claws will appear to be tipped with ivory.

In the interior country, a hunter can look for big brown bears on mountainsides and rock slides or engaged in deconstructing the tundra in a relentless search for a morsel of ground squirrel. For a hunter to stalk up on a bear for a shot, he will want its attention focused elsewhere, involved in excavating a rodent or digging up a root or sleeping. Unless a bear is thus engaged, or in motion toward the hunter, pursuit is for the most part futile, few, if any, hunters capable of overtaking a bear moving away from them. Even when a bear is bedded down, a hunter must still be prepared to walk long hard miles or climb into extremely rugged country, bears feeling perfectly at home in terrain that would give a bighorn vertigo.

A bear hunter will make extensive use of binoculars and a high-power spotting scope—20 power or above—to help him judge a grizzly-brown before he begins to stalk, then he should try to get as close as he possibly can to a bear before trying to kill it: closer than one hundred yards if there is any human way of getting there. At that proximity he should be able to judge the bear's size accurately, and tell the condition of the bear's pelt, looking for patches of discolored or lighter colored hide that can show that the bear has rubbed off the long guard hairs there and exposed the woolly underfur, giving the hide a ratty appearance. But that is not the primary reason for a hunter's drawing as near as he can. The primary reason is to make certain that he can kill his bear dead.

Some big brown bears will die easy; others die hard. And there is absolutely no way of knowing beforehand. A brown or a grizzly *can* be killed with a well-placed broadhead arrow or 50-caliber black powder ball, or a 150-grain bullet from a .270 W.C.F. or a 160- from a 7mm Remington Magnum or a 180-grain from a .300 Winchester or Weatherby Magnum *or* a 220-grain from a .30-06; *but* a 250-grain bullet from a .338 Winchester Magnum or a .340 Weatherby Magnum, or a 270-grainer out of a .375 H&H Magnum, aimed at the center of the shoulder, will do a far more certain job of putting a bear down as quickly and unambiguously as possible, which for the sake of both the animal and the hunter should be the main objective whenever a rifle is fired at a bear. Yet even if the bear collapses instantaneously with the first shot, a hunter must be ready to fire again, at once, if the bear should try to regain its feet, as they are so very wont to do. (If a hunter needs to shoot any wounded animal a second time, clearly the best time is *before* that animal gets to its feet again. This is not cold-blooded in any way, but is the most humane course of action, when compared with the possibility of letting an injured animal run off.)

The aggressiveness and the peril posed by a bear in the wild have without question been grossly exaggerated over the years by tales that do far more than just *verge* on the tall; but there is coming forth these days an even more pernicious brand of *bumph* about the supposed timidity and total innocuousness of big brown, black, and even *polar* bears—the most carnivorous and predatory of *all* the bears. This is nothing less than mawkish fantasy: *every* bear carries within him the capacity for danger.

Consider a mature Alaskan coastal brown bear boar. This is an animal of upward of one thousand pounds, a half-*ton* in weight, who can dash one hundred yards in 6.8 seconds flat—if you are fifty feet from such a bear, this means that it can cover the ground lying between you, uphill, sidehill, *down*hill, over brush, under brush, *through* brush, in a second. *One-Mississippi.* This is an animal who can kill a horse or a steer with a single blow of its pie-plate-size paw, and then carry that horse or steer away without leaving a drag mark. He can turn a backcountry log cabin into kindling; a light plane into shattered metal and plastic, pathetic bits of black rubber, and tattered canvas flapping in the north wind; and a human into leftovers. The *likelihood* of his committing any of the above acts is admittedly slim—though not unheard-of—but his *ability* to commit them is undeniable. To deny the bear's majestic power is to mock his fierce bestial spirit in the service of imposing an agenda of false sentimentality upon the wild. Bears are not Teddy's bear.

I do not know whether the polar bear is the most magnificent of North America's bears; but it is the one that holds an overpowering allure for so many hunters, whether they will ever have a chance to hunt it, old Nanook, or not. I am one who would like to hunt the polar bear, to strike off one day across a sea frozen green as polished jade, dry snow drifting across it like ribbons of sand across a desert, with an Inuit hunter and his sledge and his team of sixteen huskies. I want to wear a suit of caribou skins that still smell of caribou meat and fat, sleep beneath the ice dome of an igloo in the Arctic spring's night while the large bear and the small bear turn above me in the sky, hunt along the open leads where the ivory-colored bears—crawling across the ice with their paws hiding the telltale black spot of their noses—go to hunt seals, and with luck see a great bear walking on the whiteness, and give chase. Because the bear is not only the brown animal, but the ivory one and the black one and a part of all the animals of all the colors of the game that inhabits the hunter's red heart.

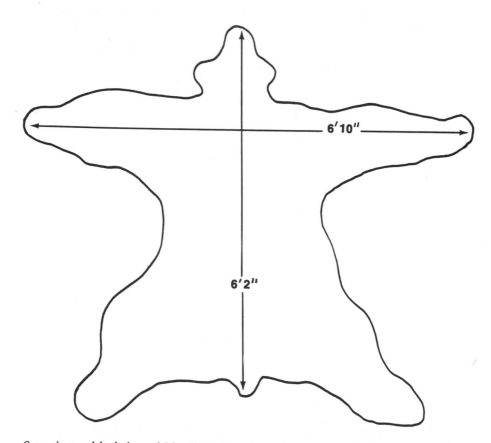

Squaring a black bear hide. Width at front legs, approximately 6 feet, 10 inches; length approximately 6 feet, 2 inches.

12

ELK

And aside from the horse's value as emergency rations for bear and human hunter alike, the other important role he has to play in the hunt is to carry us into the country of the elk. Hunters, horses, pack strings, and elk do seem inextricable; and the sharpest memories that may be retained from the hunting of elk often have to do with the nights spent lying out on the trail: saddle pads for mattresses; mantas stained with old blood wrapped around down sleeping bags; the clang-ing in the dark of the hobbled pack mule, as he makes his way to the spring creek, like the sound of Marley's ghost; and the sting of the first snowflake as it sears a sleeping cheek.

It is not memory, though, that draws most of us into elk country for the first time, but imagination. The attraction the hunting of elk holds for many hunters when they first hear the stories of it, then begin to *listen* to those stories, then to consider going out to hunt the subject of those stories, then become *obsessed* with the entire idea, has in undoubtedly no small measure to do with the country elk are envisioned inhabiting. In its classic, idealized form in the hunter's heart, elk country is always lush meadows that are the enclaves of black timber through which stands of yellow aspens streak like veins of ore, all of it surrounded by tall snowy mountains. It is crisp clean morning air, and evenings rushing headlong toward cold. It is the predawn chugging of the fire in the cook-tent stove as the iron starts to glow red. It is the sound of running streams; and it is lying on a ridge, glassing a thousand yards across a bowl a burn opened up a dozen years before, seeing elk begin to drift out of the trees: cows and calves first, the big bull last. Imagine a hunter's delight when after years of riding and slinking through such country in his mind, he enters it in the flesh and finds it just as he had pictured it, echoing with the hoarse squeals of bugling bulls.

Often, particularly in the early season, that is precisely the way some elk country will be. Other elk country may be far different; but just as it is—as we shall see—with the wild sheep of North America, there is no country in which elk are to be found that is ever *truly* ugly.

Where elk were found aboriginally on this continent was almost everywhere except the harsh deserts of the far West and the swampy South. Many contend that the elk was, to begin with, an animal primarily of the Great Plains—when that expanse of grassland represented the American Serengeti, and the elk its eland—and that he was driven into the mountains. But in the shameful saga of the last century's slaughter of the elk—from an estimated ten million animals here to greet Columbus to fewer than a hundred thousand by the 1920s, that figure now grown again, primarily through the conservation efforts and money of hunters, to over half a million—the open prairies were merely among the most accessible and conspicuous places from which the elk could be eliminated by a consortium of forces, from commercial meat hunters and collectors of ivories—the elk's rounded, thumb-size upper canines, especially the larger, darker-stained ones of the bulls, also called "buglers" and "tusks," that were held in great esteem by both the Plains Indians (the price of a good Indian pony being a hundred ivories) and members of an eponymous fraternal order (who dangled them from their watch chains)—to the railroads and farms and overgrazing.

The Eastern elk was early on exterminated from those mixed conifer-hardwood forests—through the tops of which that squirrel was making his earnest way from the Atlantic to the Mississippi. Then at the start of this century the Merriam's elk, of mountainous Arizona, New Mexico, Texas, and northern Mexico, was shown the way to the Big Exit, and we lost what was probably our largest subspecies of elk. And it was only by the slimmest of margins that we today still have

Glassing for elk in British Columbia. Note elk bugle tube in belt. (*Photo: Robert Robb*)

our smallest subspecies, the Tule elk, that once ranged in herds of up to two thousand across the bottom of California's San Joaquin Valley, up into the foothills, and out onto the central California coast.

The Tule elk was rescued by the efforts of a California rancher named, of all things, Henry Miller, who in the mid-1870s gave some of the remnant herd refuge on his land. The three other remaining subspecies of elk survive today because their native ranges contained remote, rugged, and thinly populated islands in which they could remain, undisturbed.

The Manitoba elk, who when he mingled with the buffalo *was* the true eland of the Americas, once spread from the shores of Lake Winnipeg down over the prairies to the Texas panhandle; but this habitat was reduced by the progressive breaking of the wild soil until he was to be found only in what are now national and provincial parks in Canada.

The Roosevelt's elk had the good fortune to live in the dark rain forests of the Pacific Northwest, and so was never seriously threatened by humans. He was found from San Francisco Bay, north along the coast to Vancouver Island, and was a main staple of the Lewis and Clark Expedition when it wintered at Fort Clatsop south of the Columbia River, the party killing 129 elk between December 1, 1805, and March 23, 1806, when they began their homeward journey. The Roosevelt's elk, although his antlers do not grow as large as those of the Rocky Mountain elk, is now our largest subspecies.

Traditionally, the Rocky Mountain elk roamed through the Rockies from northern New Mexico into upper British Columbia and Alberta, before having his range shrunk down into only what would fit within the Yellowstone–Jackson Hole area, where he weathered the nineteenth century's unregulated killing. From the corps of animals found there—at one time numbering only in the thirty thousands—the elk was reintroduced to his old haunts and transplanted to new ones, so that today he covers most of his old territory and may be found in places he never was before.

The Rocky Mountain elk's antlers are the largest of the North American wapitis'—as the Shawnee called him, *wapiti,* said to mean "white rump," referring to the light patch of fur, surrounding his tail, that is most distinct in his long winter coat—and when he and the other subspecies of wapiti are taken all together, they comprise our greatest deer.

"Our greatest deer?" When a moose is much larger and a whitetail buck probably much wilier? Theodore Roosevelt thought so, going so far as to declare in his unweasling way, "The wapiti is the . . . stateliest deer in the world." The American elk is of the genus *Cervus,* the marrow of the deer family. Members of this genus are to be found worldwide; and if one accepts the elk as being of the species *Cervus elaphus* (some authorities do not, preferring to place him in his own species, *Cervus canadensis*), then he is the same "red deer" that is hunted in Scotland and Spain and Poland and Afghanistan and Tibet and Mongolia, and the red deer is the most *deer* of the deer, *the* breathing animal. And the American elk is the final vision of what the red deer ought to be. Were one to construct a red deer with an eye exclusively on aesthetics, then he would look exactly like an elk, with his white rump and honey-colored body and chocolaty neck and head. He is the only member of his genus found in North America; and he, of course, lives on ground that "is most favorable to the hunter, and the most attractive in which to hunt," to quote Roosevelt once again.

And the wapiti's antlers are the largest of all his species'. In a record set, the main beams may exceed five feet in length, be up to a foot in circumference, and be spread nearly four feet wide. Unlike the mule deer's, an elk's antlers are not dichotomous, but grow tines off the main beams, usually branching at the terminal points. A bull's first set of antlers is generally a pair of long spikes (though he may grow multitined sets of antlers from his very first year: I once killed a decent six-by-five bull who aged out at only three-and-a-half years), his second set being called "raghorns." In configuration, an elk's antler begins with a *coronet*—the pearled ring around the base—advancing upward through the brow tine, the bez, the trez, the dagger point, the fifth, then ending in a sixth point in a "royal" elk, a seventh in an "imperial," and an eighth in a "monarch," with even more points possible.

Every elk hunter is hunting for one perfect royal elk. When, and if, he ever sees one, there are several keys he can use for judging the size of the antlers. He should first take note of the depth of the fork, or "cradle," between the fifth and sixth points—after carefully counting the points to make sure there *are* six, and that the cradle he is looking at does not lie between the *fourth* and a terminal fifth point. He will be looking for a fork seven to ten inches deep here, as an indication of a good-quality head. Then he will want to see, if the bull will lift that head, how far back the antlers reach; if they reach the hip, or nearly so, then a hunter knows that they have good beam length. He then wants to see that the tines are long. This can be ascertained by seeing whether the brow tine is almost the length of the muzzle, and whether the dagger point is a long one. Putting all these together usually means an exceptional set of elk antlers. Add to those antlers the fact that the elk will have had to have given the hunter *time* to make such an evaluation—when any hunter who sees a bull standing long enough for him just to get a shot at it, before it takes off running, can assume he has done quite well for himself—and the statistic that most hunters require five seasons of pursuing elk before they kill *any* bull; that *all* bull elk die hard*; and that once that bull is killed it will take every bit of strength that horse, who carried the hunter into elk country to begin with, has (and more than one trip) to pack that elk out—reminding the hunter, as he should be reminded with all game, that if he cannot pack it out, he should not kill it—*then* the elk's claim to being our greatest deer seems more than secure.

The principal art of hunting elk lies in finding elk. Gregarious animals, they tend to be located in scattered gangs, rather than spread out in ones and twos over wide areas, the way deer can be. In the early fall, in the rutting, or "bugling," season, they may be found by the signs they leave on trees—rubs made by their scraping the velvet from their antlers and polishing them to a high luster—and the muddy wallows where they rolled to cool themselves, to protect themselves against biting insects, and to let off sexual steam.

Elk usually follow a pattern of feeding from before dawn till a little after, then lying up in their bedding cover to ruminate, before coming out to feed again late in the day. In the early fall they are likely still to be up in the open high country, the bulls assembling their harems; but as the weather cools and the grassland feed lignifies, the elk will be using the meadows less and feeding more upon the shrubs of the sheltering forest. This is the time, though, when the bulls will be bugling, announcing their intentions, and presences, with a rising squeal, ending in a series of deep grunts, a call that can never

---

* Elk will fall to .270 W.C.F.s and .30-'06s, but in elk hunting there is a genuine place for the use of Magnum rifles of probably no less than 7 mm in caliber, with a Magnum .30 caliber better, and something in the big .338 range excellent (whereas the lightest-weight bow hunters should consider, for releasing a broadhead arrow at an elk, is one with a draw weight of no less than fifty pounds, and muzzle-loader hunters will want to shoot a black-powder rifle of at least .50 caliber; .54's being better yet). An elk hunter should, as well, not let himself be shaken by the sight of a bull *not* dropping in his tracks with the first well-placed shot to the shoulder. An elk, remember, may weigh nearly half a ton, and will often seem to react hardly at all to being hit by a single bullet. An elk hunter must be prepared, therefore, to keep on shooting, at the *same* bull, *until* it goes down, never allowing himself to assume he has missed and to begin shooting at *another* bull, resulting in *two* wounded bulls.

Elk bugling. (*Photo: Robert Robb*)

fail to send a tremor through an elk hunter's being. A hunter who has closely studied this call—and the several variations made by bulls, as well as the sounds produced by the cows and calves—and learned to imitate it, just might be able to call himself in a bull. But if nothing else, the bull's calls *will* help a hunter to pinpoint it. *And* at this time of the season, as he still-hunts cautiously toward a bull in heavy cover— mindful of the fact that if he "spooks" a herd of elk, they are likely to take off on a run that may carry them miles farther on into the timber—a hunter will smell the bull long before he sees it, the strong rutty odor of the bull marking it as clearly as do its bugles.

Once the hunting season begins, though, elk will push farther into the timber of their own accord, shifting their feeding periods more toward the nighttime hours. This is the hard time of elk hunting, when an elk hunter may spend five or seven or ten ever-shortening days, as the dark heart of fall draws in and the light of the low sun filters through cold clouds—reminding him of the duck-hunting light he first saw so many years ago—traveling through the noisy understory of the timbered slopes, looking for any sign of the now mostly silent bulls. He will travel, out of necessity, and not infrequently desperation, the high ground and the low. He will try to be on ridges above the old burns well before dawn, to be hunting around them as the sun

Bull elk. (*Photo: Robert Robb*)

rises. Or he may follow out the creek bottoms, to see whether the elk have gone to hide down there. He may take to reading every omen and portent that comes to hand, looking even to the flights of birds, like ravens or magpies, to show him where the elk may be, the birds seeming to like being around the big deer. Then when he does find them, it may be by sheerest accident when he stumbles onto a herd, the wary old cows, the sentries of the gang, spotting him first, the sight of him sending them loping off to run a full dozen miles deeper into the trees.

An elk hunter will hope for snow, then, to drive the elk down, to push them out onto the south-facing, snow-free slopes. He will have fresh tracks to follow, then, and his own steps will be muffled. He will try to hunt down onto the elk from off the high ridges, the animals, as most animals are, more concerned with down-slope threats than with the possibilities of death from above. And more often than not, the elk hunter, like all hunters in all times, will fail. To "fail" at hunting, of course, is the best sort of failure there is; and failing at elk hunting is among the most splendid brands of failure to be found in hunting.

A trophy bull elk is one of the most unpredictable animals for any hunter to have success at capturing; but when he does succeed, it is often with the most deceptive of ease. I was, naturally, riding a horse on my second hunt for elk when I killed my first royal bull. I was also one-quarter mile from the ranch house, heading for the timbered slopes out yonder. It was opening day of the season, and from glassing at dawn the day before, I knew that the elk fed until just daylight in the hayfield I was now riding across in the semidarkness. The rancher riding beside me reined up suddenly and pointed away to the edge of the field where the yellowish smudges of elk were just visible against the stand of spruce and poplars that flowed down off the hillside.

We kept riding—the cold northern air of the Rockies a bitter caress upon our faces—until we could put some of those trees between the elk and us. Then we dismounted and tied the horses, and I pulled my .375 H&H Magnum from the scabbard and we crept back to where we could see the elk, but where none of the elk, especially the cows, could see us, and I picked out the big herd bull, and I killed him.

That is as easy as elk hunting gets. And I have never had it so easy since. But in any way that a hunter gets to have elk hunting, it is a gift.

An elk hunters' camp in the Rocky Mountains. (*Photo: Robert Robb*)

13

THE BESTIARY

After the gift of elk, what else would we ever possibly be tempted to hunt on this continent? As it happens, an entire *world* of wild animals.

To begin with—in point of fact, few hunters probably ever *begin* with this animal, but all the same—there is the moose. Next to the bison, the moose(*Alces alces*) is the largest self-propelled, trackless, and wheelless vehicle to navigate upon the landmass of North America: several ill-starred attempts at breaking moose to the halter have been recorded, some, even, that were not without momentary flashes of bizarre success, there being reliable reports of matched pairs of spirited moose drawing open sleighs across the ice of frozen lakes, before their wild natures reasserted themselves and the moose plunged off into the first open water to freshen up, sleigh and shrieking passengers still in tow.

The largest of all the deer family—as large as any of the hooved mammals of Africa—the moose ranges across the northern tier of the United States, throughout Alaska, and across the southern two-thirds of Canada. Despite his impressive size, though, the moose does seem to suffer from something of an image problem.

A good many hunters, to be honest, consider the moose to look plainly goofy. His long, light-colored legs appear out of all proportion to his short, heavy, dark-brown body. With those long legs and a back that slopes down from high-humped withers to a muscled rump, there is something vaguely giraffid about his profile—until one comes to that *head*.

Mule-eared and bulbous-nosed, the lips endowed with clever prehensility, the eyes practically Martian in their bugginess, a "bell" of hide dangling below the chin (shorter and wider in old bulls, perhaps because it has been frozen away over the seasons), and topped by multipointed, bipartite, palmed antlers that can spread out over six feet in width and weigh up to eighty pounds, the moose's head is, at the very least, the most extraordinary head of any big-game animal on Earth. There is nothing even slightly uncomplicated or minimalist about it; it unreservedly sets out to overwhelm the beholder with absolute excess. It would be necessary to turn to something extinct or from a previous geologic age (the Irish "elk" or the bush-antlered deer of the Villafranchian come to mind) to rival the moose's outlandishness. There are even said to be some who actually find the moose *handsome,* and I am one of them.

The definition of a *large* set of moose antlers varies from area to area in the giant deer's range. A Shiras moose—the type found in the western continental United States—who carries a rack fifty inches wide is a large Shiras moose. A Canada moose of sixty inches would be a large one of that type, whereas seventy inches would be large for the spread of an Alaska-Yukon type's antlers. Width of spread is not the sole criterion of a big set of moose antlers, though, and a hunter should also look for wide main palms—like large concave shields carried high—and deep brow palms—like big hollowed-out wooden bowls—to give an overall substantialness to the rack.

As well as being an amazing sight to see, the moose is also a fascinating animal to hunt. He is thought by many to be only a lumbering strider through bogs and marshes, and he does display an affinity for dark wet timber; but he will also be found in the low willow brush along creeks and rivers and at the edges of lakes, *and* on hill- and mountainsides. Along the high ground beside watercourses is good terrain from which to hunt for moose, and floating down rivers in a raft or canoe can also produce the big cervids.

Indians in the upper Yukon had a technique for hunting moose that depended on the moose's sticking to a pattern of feeding early and late, and bedding during the day. The Indians would find a track;

Alaska-Yukon bull moose. Moose antlers can spread out to 6 feet and weigh up to 80 pounds. (*Photo © by Bill McRae*)

and if they thought it fresh enough, they would follow in a series of wide half-loops, keeping to the downwind side of the track line. They knew that when the moose bedded, he would first double back on his track and scent the wind for the smell of any trailing predator; so the Indians continued to make their half-loops until they did not cut the moose's track again. This told them that the moose had lain down; and they would then backtrack toward him in another series of small half-loops until they came into sight of him and could get a shot. Or found his tracks where he had gotten clean away.

A moose seldom stands around like some kind of a billboard, and many hunters actually rank his intelligence above the elk's. Despite his appearance, and the unfortunate associations some have with him and the likes of Bullwinkle, the moose can be as canny a herbivore as a hunter could ever wish to pursue. I have hunted him just enough to know that he is perfectly adept at disappearing into cover so sparse as to suggest the talents of a burrowing animal.

Yet like elk, the moose can also be called during the rut, hunters referring to moose-calling as "grunting." Traditionally, a moose hunter uses a cone of birch bark to amplify the low grunts that imitate the call of a cow moose, or that can be made to sound like the angry challenge of another bull (the rhythm similar to a bull elk's call, only in a lower register). Other sounds used to attract a moose can be made by raking a stick against the limbs of a tree or bush, or by striking a tree trunk to simulate the noise of males fighting, and draw in a bull moose in the same way a whitetail buck may be rattled in. A hunter afloat can also try to seduce a bull by slapping his canoe paddle against the water to re-create the sound of a cow's walking, or by dipping up water in a hat or other container and pouring it out to make a bull think that there is a cow nearby, micturating. (With all these sounds that he can produce to attract game, though, whether moose or elk or deer, a hunter must be careful that he does not become so infatuated with them that his overuse makes them begin to sound unnatural and only manages to drive the animals off. To learn what is "enough" sound, a hunter must listen to the game.)

Moose, whether called in or stalked up on, should be considered as hard to kill as elk, and a .338 or .375 is in no way "too much" gun for them. A moose can "lock up" when hit well; and though a hunter may believe that he has killed the animal, and that it will be only a moment before it topples, he would be well advised to continue shoot-ing, aiming for the shoulder, until the bull *does* go down. And, all else being equal, a hunter should see whether he can arrange for that moose

An especially large barren-ground caribou bull. (*Photo © by Bill McRae*)

to go down near (*but not in*) water, or where packhorses can be gotten to him, because carrying out all the parts of a moose over long distances *on* his back will make even the sternest man weep.

A properly placed bullet from high-powered 7 mm, or even a .270, caliber rifle, on the other hand, is quite often enough to bring down a caribou bull, the most wintry of our deer. If any animal's antlers rival the moose's, then the caribou's come closest of all. With those antlers, with forward-curving main beams of fifty inches in length and more, crowned by pointed palms, a long lone point growing off the back of each main beam, palmated bez tines, and wide brow tines known as "shovels"—although they are not used as such, the caribou digging down through the snow with his wide-splaying hooves so his fur-covered muzzle can reach the tundra below—a big, white-caped bull caribou is as striking and exotic-looking a big-game animal as one may hope to hunt on native ground.

In the entire world from Lapland to Greenland, there is only a single species of caribou, *Rangifer tarandus;* but five types, based on the relative size of their antlers, are recognized as inhabiting the north of this continent. Those that have, in general, the largest racks are the barren-ground caribou of Alaska, followed by the mountain caribou of British Columbia, the southern Yukon Territory, and the McKenzie Mountains of the Northwest Territories; the Quebec-Labrador caribou; the central-barren-ground caribou of the Northwest Territories; and the woodland caribou of Newfoundland.

Caribou are found on the rolling tundra of the Arctic and sub-Arctic, always in motion, their hooves making a fabled clicking sound. They are a migratory herd animal, and the prime art of hunting *them* consists of discovering what country they are moving through or into. (As little as a generation ago, Indians of northern Canada starved to death when the caribou they counted on for their fall meat failed to follow the anticipated migration routes and swept out of reach of the landbound hunters.)

A hunter may often search for caribou by moving along the edges of lakes or up and down rivers in a boat or canoe—glassing as he travels—or by lying in wait at expected crossing points or by climbing to the high ground to look over the bowls and barrens below. When he sights a moving herd, a hunter must try to get ahead of the animals so he can intercept them, because trying to overtake walking caribou, even ones slowing to feed, is pure beau geste, caribou seeming to glide across the rough, green ground—that humans can find nearly impassable—the way the planchette seems to glide across a ouija board. Caribou country does not often grant the hunter good cover to use for stalking up on a bull who has stopped to feed or bed down; but a hunter, if the wind is right and the herd is not so large that his approach will be picked up by the eyes of outrider caribou before he is within range—and if he is at all skilled in "putting a sneak" on an animal, staying low and moving only when the animal's eyes are turned away—should be able to move through the tangled birch and the wild bearberry, red as flame, and close to within two hundred yards or so of a bull. Then, at that range with a flat-shooting rifle, he can hold on the center of the bull's shoulder and touch one off.

The meat of elk and moose is superb—*no* game meat, of course, is ever less than excellent—but there is almost nothing on Earth better than the meat of a caribou bull killed in late August or early September, just before the rut, and hung up to let age for a week in the cold air of the north. It is among the finest meat of all the deer.

Before leaving the deer, we should speak of the one predator in North America whose appetite for venison surpasses even our own, the cougar—*cougar* derived from *suasuarana,* the name given the great cat by the Tupi Indians of Amazonia, meaning, curiously enough, "like a deer," in reference to his coloration. Also called mountain lion, puma, or panther, the cougar (*Felis concolor*) is simply the most splendid eater of deer to be found from British Columbia to Patagonia, killing up to a deer per week in some places. He is also the truest object of the hound hunter's pursuit. To try to hunt lions without dogs is like trying to catch smoke in your hands. A hunter may pass a thousand days afield in cougar country and never once glimpse a lion—a big tom at dusk, perhaps, belly-heavy with deer meat, his thick tail swishing.* Yet there may have been a dozen times and more when a cougar saw him.

A cougar is first seen by the large, round clawless (he retracts his claws when he walks), four-toed tracks he leaves, running in a staggering line down the trail he has been hunting slowly along. In fresh snow is a good place to look for the tracks of a big lion—one set, alone, no tracks of any young accompanying a male's—but it may take weeks to find such a set, and then they must be fresh enough for the dogs to follow and catch the cat and tree him, which after the tracks are found may be a matter of hours or days, and is an exercise that is successful far less often than may be imagined by many who have never hunted the American lion. Once treed, a cougar can be killed with a rifle in a caliber suitable for deer; with a black-powder rifle; a bow and arrow; or with a handgun in at least .357 Magnum caliber or heavier. Whatever his weapon of choice, a hunter wants to be sure that he can kill the lion dead with it, a wounded cougar who comes down out of the tree into the dogs and man is a far from laughing matter.

A .357 Magnum revolver with a 6½-inch barrel is what I used to kill my eight-foot, 180-pound male lion on a day after Christmas Day along the border between the state of Washington and the Dominion of Canada. It was almost dark when the hound man and I at last reached the steep, snow-covered hill where the Walkers were baying madly around the tall fir tree, high up in which the big cat perched.

"When you fire," the hound man urged as he snapped the chain leads to the dogs' collars and pulled them away from under the tree, "run like hell!" I knew, though, that if you are thinking that when you are trying to kill an animal, you will begin to run *before* you fire, and will risk only wounding him. So I realized that I could not run

---

* A record cougar, like a record bear, is determined by his skull size, 15 inches representing the sum of a big cat.

Cougar—the American lion. (*Photo © by Bill McRae*)

after I fired, but would have to wait for the lion when he came down, ready to shoot him again before he reached me.

I stood on the white slope directly beneath the cougar and thumbed back the hammer of the heavy Smith & Wesson and lined up the iron sights—the way my father had shown me to line up the sights of that old .22 rifle all those years ago—on the tiny patch of the cougar's calmly breathing chest, showing far up through the boughs. If I stopped to think how this qualified as "fair," it was only to decide that it was no *less* fair than this cougar had been to the deer he had just leaped upon and killed, or than a red-tailed hawk is when he drives his talons into a crouching rabbit; no less fair than any predator is to his prey. What is "fair" can be highly arbitrary, situational, and subjective— and is usually couched in terms of "You are not being fair to *me*"— and this was something more important than fair. This "game" was not being played on artificial turf or under the lights; far more than fair, this was *real*.

In the dim light the yellow tongue of flame licked skyward and then there was the sound of limbs crashing down as something heavy came down out of the dark tree and I could not see the lion anymore and something hit the ground hard off to my downhill side and when I wheeled on the sound my boot slipped out from under me and as I sat down heavily in the snow I thumbed the hammer back again. But there, thirty feet from me—his warm gray fur deep as my knuckles, and with the dried blood of deer still on it, his meat (as it would prove to be when eaten), like the meat of all the great cats, some of the finest of wild flesh, as pale as the palest milk-fed veal—lay the big tom cougar, dead.

Although the moose and the caribou are relatively new arrivals in the New World, the cougar is endemic to it, as is the pronghorn antelope (*Antilocapra americana*), next to the peccaries, our only native artio- dactyl.

The 'lope arose on the North American continent and never strayed from here. He is small, at 120 pounds or so one-third the size of a caribou, a *tenth* the size of the moose, and delicate in appearance— though he is far hardier than he might appear, a Wyoming rancher once telling me how he had witnessed a herd chase and surround a coyote who had just killed a pronghorn fawn, the antelopes stamping the little wolf to death with their sharp hooves. His body is banded in buff and white, his face black, with a black blaze on the jaw of the bucks. He is also our swiftest land animal, perhaps even the world's,

The pronghorn is one of the swiftest land animals a hunter can give chase
to. (*Photo: Daniel Hernandez*)

capable of speeds well above fifty miles per hour over the open yellow
prairies and deserts that stretch from Alberta to Mexico, having gone
so far, in the interests of increased velocity, as to sacrifice even the
dewclaws other artiodactyls carry. In flight across those wide-open
spaces, in bands that veer in unison like flocks of birds, the pronghorns
almost seem to make the Earth's rotation visible, as if nothing could
move that fast over the land without the land's moving to meet it.

The pronghorn is the longest-range game a rifleman gives chase
to. His oversize eyes are exceptionally good, and he situates himself
in good vantage points, ready to make a run for it at the first sight
of humans. By using the normal contour of the land for concealment,
though, a hunter who is willing to get down on hands and knees can
draw well within Major Burrard's maximum "sporting" range of three
hundred yards of a "speed goat"—as some westerners call them. At
that range a rifle in the fast .257 Roberts to .270 W.C.F. category is
quite sufficient for antelope.

Both bucks and does carry horns, but the female's are seldom
very large. The pronghorn's inward-hooking horns are the only ones
in the world that are forked, and the only ones that are shed annually,
the black, keratinized, outer horn sheath splitting open and coming
off each year. A hunter will want to kill a buck with the biggest of

horns, of course; and the size of a buck antelope's horns can be judged by looking at the length of the ear and figuring that to be between five-and-a-half and six inches. If the hunter will mentally superimpose that ear length onto the antelope's horn when he is studying it—remembering that the base of the ear sits on the pronghorn's head below the base of the horn—and can place at least two ear lengths onto the horn up to the hook, and the hook turns down deeply, then he is probably looking at a horn in the fourteen- to fifteen-inch range, the head of a respectable buck—a hunter may also try to estimate horn length by comparing it to the length of the buck's face, which will be between twelve and thirteen inches. If the horn is even longer, the prongs, or "paddles," thick and long, the horn itself heavy and *black*-black, the antelope the hunter is looking at is something far *more* than respectable.

The horn length of the mountain goat (*Oreamnos americanus*) is something that is very hard to judge, as is trying to tell a billy from a nanny. The large—three hundred pounds and more—rupicaprid, a New World relative of the Old World serow and chamois, inhabits rugged mountainous country from Alaska and the Yukon, south through British Columbia and Alberta, and into Washington, Idaho, and Montana, and as far south as Wyoming and Colorado, and in transplanted bands in other states as well. He survives, in part, because he lives and gambols about on earth that is tilted at angles more extreme than almost any other animal can tolerate. (There is a maxim among mountain hunters that a man can make his way securely in sheep country by watching the sheep and just doing what they do; try this with goats, the maxim concludes, and you will die.) Yet to hunt the white goats, a hunter must find a way, somehow, to get above them. Mountain goats are known to "die hard," so a .270 should be viewed as a bare minimum caliber for them.

A goat with horns of ten inches or more is a big goat, although it takes a *very* experienced eye to judge the length while the animal is on the hoof. Just being able to make his way up into goat country and to return with a billy, though, may be trophy enough for any hunter.

It is only in the farthest of North American reaches that the musk-ox (*Ovibos moschatus*) is to be found. Vaguely related to the mountain goat, the heavy, yet surprisingly nimble, oxlike animal—known to the Inuit as *omingmak*, "the bearded one"—abides on the white winter

Mountain goats are surefooted on the sheerest of slopes. (*Photo © by Bill McRae*)

The author with a musk-ox in the High Arctic of the Northwest Territories of Canada. (*Author photo*)

tundra of the High Arctic of Alaska and Canada, his shaggy coat of long guard hair and *qiviut* underfur—the finest wool on the planet—enabling him to endure minus-forty-degree Fahrenheit weather in comfort. In that essentially flat country, the brown steaming hillocks of the herded musk-ox are the most distinctive geographical feature on the landscape. The musk-ox bull's horns are marked by a wide, tightly fitted boss and horns that go straight down, then turn back up: in the biggest of the bulls the black tips reach back up to the eye level. Musk-ox are not overly difficult to find or kill—although they do possess a goatlike stamina, and so a .30-'06 would be about as light a caliber as I would choose to hunt musk-ox, after having a gunsmith strip away the oil from the action and replace it with a dry lubricant to prevent the rifle's freezing up on me in the subzero air—but the art of hunting the musk-ox, like that of hunting the mountain goat, lies in surviving the antagonisms of the alien terrain that is his home.

The distant Arctic is by no means the final destination to which the hunter's way leads. There are yet upland birds and wild turkeys and the wild sheep and the farther continent of Africa that a hunter will want to see. And there is at least one additional big-game animal in this bestiary that a hunter will want to see, too, an animal who at one time was, if for nothing other than his sheer, astonishing numbers, the greatest object of the American chase.

The American buffalo (*Bison bison*)—or bison—came to this continent, as did all the other Artiodactyla except the pronghorns and peccaries, from the Old World, crowding across the snow-free plain of Beringia. Some of the now-extinct species that he came in carried horns that spread nearly seven feet across, whereas the modern buffalo's are seldom more than two feet in tip-to-tip width. In his wild millions he ran upon the Great Plains with a sound like thunder, supplying the Indian hunters, who had followed him from Asia, with not only meat but nearly *all* their worldly goods, from tepees and canoe covers to spoons and cups, to the horned medicine hats of the medicine men and robes against the winter wind, to scores of other household items. No need to explain here what became of all the buffalo's wild millions, and the Indian hunters who followed in their

The American bison, or "buffalo," supplied the Plains Indian with most of his needs. (*Photo: Robert Robb*)

wake, except to say that the five-bottom plow and the railroad right of way contributed as much or more to their diminishment as the .50-caliber rifle of Christian Sharps ever did.

Buffalo can be hunted today, behind fences, in frequently highly straitened circumstances that shabbily attempt to reenact the aura of the Old West. But in some places—the Henry Mountains of Utah, parts of Wyoming, Montana, Alaska, and northwestern Canada and others—small numbers of buffalo still run as freely as the twentieth century permits anything to run, and a hunter can still go in honest pursuit of them. Can still load up a .338 or .375 rifle, or maybe one of those old Sharpses, and try to track the largest land mammal in the hemisphere, the strongest link left us to that time before America was America, being a continent, then, exclusively of wild hunters and the wild hunted.

14

UPLANDERS

A hunter who pursues the animals of that bestiary, the postgraduate school of big-game hunting, has probably already served his apprenticeship with deer. Although there may be no more challenging animal to hunt than deer—especially big deer—they do seem to be, because of their ubiquity, the logical place for any big-game hunter to commence, just as the migratory birds are the first winged animals a shooting-flying hunter is likely to raise and point and swing a shotgun on. When he begins, the shooting-flying hunter may not know, yet, where or how to find other birds; and the joy of hunting the migrants—the "sport," if you must, of it—particularly with waterfowl, lies in not having to chase the birds, but in luring them, through the arts of decoy placement and calling, into range. It is the bird who presents himself to the hunter. When a hunter decides to step out of the blind, though, to go in serious quest of upland birds—often at the same time in his progress as a hunter when he begins to wander farther afield from the deer in search of big game, without ever abandoning the deer altogether—he discovers that it is *he* who must present himself to the bird.

Excluding woodcock and snipe, who are tiny, *migratory* upland birds who represent the doctoral theses of wing shooting, the upland birds of North America are all those ground-nesting, nonmigratory, chickenlike, or gallinaceous, fowl of the Family Phasianidae who must be flushed to make fly. Unlike doves and waterfowl, whose arrival we anxiously await in the grain field or on the pothole's edge, like friends and relatives crouching behind the furniture in a darkened house, ready to jump up and shout, "Surprise!" when the birthday guest steps through the door, upland birds do not make flight their life's work, do not utilize air for transport so much as for a means of escape—fleeing agilely into a dimension we have always longed to have access to.

The escape of the ring-necked pheasant is as spectacular as that of any uplander. A native of Asia, the large cock birds feathered in iridescent purples and olives and golds, with barred tails up to two feet long and a white collar encircling the neck, the imported pheasant has lived on this continent for a century. He has found a fertile new home in the "pheasant belt" states of South Dakota, Iowa, Nebraska, and Kansas—and in many, many others—where he depends on the farmers' leaving him enough cover on the field edges to shelter him against predators and weather, and in which his hens can raise their broods, having become in those areas something of an agrestial crop. A hunted pheasant may "hold tight"—allowing the hunter to draw well within shotgun range before taking flight—or "flush wild," far ahead of the hunter. In any case, when he does flush underfoot or at some distance, it is as explosive as the last starburst mortar concluding tonight's fireworks display, often leaving a dazzled hunter to wonder how he could have failed to hit a bird of such generous, pyrotechnic proportions.

Pheasant hunters classically pursue the birds—almost always the roosters only—in drives, working strips of harvested grain crops or weed patches and tall grass. In these drives the posters become known as "standers" or "blockers" and will take up positions capping and flanking the end of the strip, cupping it to prevent the birds' flying out beyond the range of at least one of the hunters' guns. The drivers will also shape themselves into a U, to contain the pheasants, as they move slowly down the strip, ideally into the wind, both to facilitate the gun dogs' picking up the scent of the birds and to force the pheasants up against the wind to slow their flight. The drivers, preferably no more than five yards apart (to prevent cool-headed birds from sneaking back on the ground through a gap in the line), will

The pheasant soars up like a fireworks display. (*Photo: Robert Robb*)

move forward in a leisurely but deliberate zigzag to cover more ground, pausing every so often—the stillness of a hunter frequently making a bird, who would sit firmly while booted feet passed closely by, too nervous to stay put, driving it in desperation out of cover—the drivers calling out "Hen!" or "No bird!" when a female flushes, and holding their fire. But when a male rises in a towering flush, the hunters will call out "Cock bird!" or "Rooster!" and they will fire only at birds who are in their direct zone of fire, and only at those who are high enough so that the No. 6 or 4 shot from their modified- or improved-barreled 12- or 20-gauge shotguns will not sting the blockers standing at the end of the field.

The blockers' job, by the way, besides entailing the risk of catching a peppery string of lead—and once again, the indispensability of wearing protective shooting glasses when using firearms should be noted—is one of the more major chicanes of all hunting. The novice and the easily gulled are often sold a rather ripe bill of goods that, as backstops, they cannot *fail* to get the most shooting when a flurry of birds is beaten their way, when in almost every actual circumstance it will be the drivers who will get much more of what's to be had. Nonetheless, blocking is simply part and parcel of the bargain members of the community of hunters strike among themselves. There is something of an obligation to it, a sense that, "by my troth," a hunter owes the hunt his turn at blocking; and he that blocks on this drive is quit for the next.

Driving and blocking require a substantial contingent of hunters, one or two hunters, even with a dog, seldom able to do justice to the hunting out of thirty rows of dryland corn or a wide plot of brittle weeds. Two or three hunters, then, should concentrate their attentions on brushy fence lines, or work their way up narrow draws whose bottoms hold rushes and thistles and whose slopes are topped by thickets of low scrub, or find a slough or water hole where the pheasants have come to drink. In warm pleasant weather the birds may be far-flung, scattered out to feed; but in cold or snow or high wind, such sanctuaries will always be a fair bet for finding pheasants.

The gun dog, while useful for flushing pheasants—wild pheasants generally not holding well enough for a pointer to be of real use—is close to essential for quail. The smallest of our native phasianids, the quail are most naturally beheld off the end of a dog's nose, or erupting in flight just over his head. Like all the other upland birds, save the pheasant and the sage grouse, those flushed quail can be killed cleanly with not only No. 6 shot, but with No. 7½s or 8s—which are often preferable at the close ranges at which most quail are shot. Because of those close ranges, and the relatively small size of the quail, they are among the few birds that can sensibly be hunted with the 28-gauge—an exquisite little kestrel-swift weapon—or even, in *highly* skilled hands, the .410, shotguns that are far from the wisest choices for birds much larger than these.

The several native species of quail range widely across North America; and the quail hunter, with his fast-handling, open-choked 28-gauge and his Elhew pointer, may hunt bobwhite—a small brown joy buzzer of a bird—on southern farmlands and in open timber, the birds coveyed up in clumps of honeysuckle and beggar-lice. If the hunter and his dog can find a covey, then they should try to break it apart, to send the birds in many different directions, the smaller divisions holding better than a single large flock—a rule that holds true for all the upland birds.

In the West, along the southerly portions of the Divide, the slightly larger scaled, or blue, quail is to be found, flushed from cover beneath the sagebrush by the passing hooves of flying pronghorns, sending the birds sailing stiff-winged out over dry grasses and cactus. In the nearby canyons and among the juniper stands on the mountain slopes, the rare, clown-faced harlequin quail may be found. In the Western deserts, the Gambel's quail, the male's head topped by a black comma of feather, may be located near the few sites of water; while in the foothills and broken chaparral country of the far West, the

California quail. (*Photo: Robert Robb*)

practically identical California quail makes his home. Above him, in the high country of the Sierras and Cascades and the other tall ranges of the Pacific Northwest, the mountain quail dwells, the male sporting a long straight plume, like a stroke of calligraphic black.

The hunting of each quail species bears more similarity than dissimilarity to the hunting of the others. In brush, near water, is always a good place to begin the search for quail; and with Gambel's, California, and mountain quail, the hunt may begin with calling to the birds to see if they will identify their whereabouts by calling back. The flush of quail, even when you know the birds to be there, can be, because of the unknown quantity of birds that may burst forth, even more astonishing than the detonation of a pheasant. No matter how the terrain may alter and the shape of the birds change, quail remain quail.

It is in the terrain of the mountain quail that a hunter might see the forest grouse: the ruffed grouse, and in the densest of the black timber, the slatey spruce grouse and the duskier, heavier blue grouse, both species marked by small red combs above the eyes.

The "ruff"—the male of which possesses a ring of black feathers around his neck that can, during courtship displays when he is also strutting around drumming like a damned fool, be fluffed out like an opened umbrella—is the most widespread of all the American grouse. He is found in mixed and deciduous forests from northern Georgia, up through New England and the Great Lakes states, and throughout Canada and Alaska. Though not a bird possessed of blinding speed, when flushed he will take the utmost advantage of the available cover, putting as many trees and as much brush as he can find between himself and a hunter. His intelligence, as perceived by humans, seems to swell with his proximity to civilization. A bird who may be viewed in the remote Omineca Mountains of British Columbia as a pathetic simpleton, blossoms into a rocket scientist when spotted in a blur of wings in New Hampshire. As for the artful blue grouse, found in the forests of the Pacific Northwest from Alaska well down into California, and the spruce grouse, living among the balsams and the lodgepole and jack pines across the breadth of the North American north, it is probably all for the best that they inhabit *the* most remote of habitats. They simply are *never* going to land a job at NASA.

In even farther removes, the most northern of the grouse, the ptarmigan, are to be found, the willow ptarmigan in the willow and tangled birch brush and muskeg that disrupt the tundra of the Arctic. The rock and the white-tailed ptarmigan (the most southerly of the ptarmigan, found in New Mexican heights) make their homes above timberline on the slopes of mountains, the rock ptarmigan primarily in the north. The birds will be as two-toned as Italian wingtips in the early season, cackling as they flush from patches of brush the color of a housefire. By late season, the now-white birds may fling themselves out of the snow at a startled hunter's snowshoed feet. They are quite a delicacy to wolves, I have heard, which seems high culinary praise, indeed.

In their open way the tundra lands of the ptarmigan are not unlike the bluestem and buffalo grass prairies of the Great Plains where the sharp-tailed grouse and the prairie chicken abide. Here on hillsides and in sandhills and on grassy plains and in brushy draws and among abandoned farm buildings the brownish birds (a little smaller than a hen pheasant) huddle, then flare up and sail off at the approach of hunters, passing above old bison horns and skulls. Farther to the west on the high sage plateaus, the grayish sage grouse, the largest of our grouse—sometimes the size of a small turkey—struts and displays in the spring; and in the fall, when hunted, he lifts up with every bit of the swiftness of a pterodactyl, and yet, for all his apparent oafishness—compared with the immigrant cunning of the pheasant—remains a magnificent obsolescence, the Great Pyramid of the upland birds.

The inescapable conclusion to all the upland birds is the genuinely swift immigrants, the gray, or Hungarian, and the chukar partridges. "Huns" are often found in the same habitat as pheasants, particularly in the rough cover around the edges of fields. They range across southern Canada and the northern United States from the Midwest to the West. They flush like quail, but are somewhat larger, marked with a rusty face and a patch of the same color on the chest. They will roost on the ground in a circle, tails together, leaving in snow an imprint like a wagon wheel, with the dry pellets of their droppings at the hub. They, too, are best hunted by scattering the covey, then hunting out the individual birds. Huns are a highly adaptable and hardy bird and show great promise of being a major species for the upland-bird hunters of the future.

The essence of hunting upland birds, as opposed to the migrants, of course, is walking to find the game. A hunter must be willing to cover miles of often fruitless ground before he puts up even a single bird. For this reason it is not always easy to persuade a young hunter of the joys of pursuing upland birds—especially at a stage where all he craves is maximum action for the least investment of effort. But the older hunter may with time come to see the effort *as* the action, and the game rising up in front of his gun as the pleasant surprise, the prize at the bottom of the Crackerjack. It is a wonderful event to experience, it was certainly hoped for and sought after, but it was not entirely necessary to make the day afoot worthwhile.

If the walking is the point, then the most heroic walking in upland-bird hunting is in pursuit of chukar.

Those granite-colored birds, red-billed and -footed, black-masked, and barred with black along the sides of their bodies, who came originally from the deserts of India, are the most upland of our upland birds. This is not strictly a matter of the elevations at which chukar are found—the forest grouse can be found as high or higher—but of the nature of the terrain they inhabit.

I was hunting elk once at seven thousand feet in the mountains of central Idaho. At noon I hiked out to the point where the land all fell straight away to a creek far below me. Across the canyon rose a tall cliff I hoped to see bighorn sheep ambling across. It was a November day too warm for elk, and in no time I was lying on a flat rock, dozing in the sun. The quiet *chuk-chuk-chuk* sound, like the muted

The sage-grouse hunter. (*Author photo*)

barking of some small dog, came from below, and in a minute the four tall-stationed birds, heads flicking nervously from side to side, climbed up through the rocks ten feet from me, then walked out of sight, moving through this country of wild sheep that was now their home.

Even in the lower country where the chukar can be found—their range covering rocky and arid places throughout the Far West—the birds are almost never seen on level ground, although they can sometimes be put up out of the sage on the plateaus at the rims of back-country canyons. Almost always, though, the hunt for chukar means climbing the steep slopes the birds have walked up, only to turn around to descend when the birds bust and sail back down. How to describe a day of it: taking the stairs in the Empire State Building, street level to observation deck, over and over, the stairwell either too warm or much too cold, the air thin as Tibet's, *with* the Muzak on the fritz, nearly captures it.

In such hunting a pointer who will work close and hold staunch when he is on a covey of chukar trying to conceal themselves in a jumbled pile of naked stones will do much to help a hunter locate the birds. And when the birds will hold, and the dog stands there, locked solid but trembling with anticipation, it is like that symphony all over again, human and dog doing together what they did to begin with when they first "domesticated" each other: hunting well.

A big-running dog, on the other hand, who crashes with loony élan into the birds an eighth of a mile ahead of the hunter, and goes on crashing into them despite the hunter's frantic efforts to call him in, until he feels like reaching for an '06—either for the birds or for the dog, whichever seems the more appropriate response—is not a great deal of assistance, but is often the kind of dog a hunter finds himself helplessly hunting behind. Not all symphonies are masterpieces, of course; and this can only go to remind hunters that their true purpose in walking around out here is to put birds to flight. The migrants will fly on with or without hunters; but the gressorial hunter's presence transforms the upland birds from mere ground-scratchers into plumed trajectories. At a hunter's feet, which are so inexorably tied to the earth, these birds launch themselves skyward, seeking in the medium of air a freedom that a hunter can only envision in his dreams, or at the sight of them.

15

"TURKIE COCKE"

There must always be one who is largest of all. In his capacity as the largest of North America's native gallinaceous fowl, the wild turkey is regularly referred to as the "king" of upland birds. This is, in its fashion, the equivalent of saying that the African elephant is the king of the land mammals. That is true, but only as far as it goes. Lost, somehow, is the genuine magnitude of the situation. Take Elvis: Elvis was, and remains, the king of rock 'n' roll. The elephant is the Elvis of the land mammals. The wild turkey is the elephant of the upland birds.

To put it less syllogistically, think of those iridesced wild birds of the Phasianidae as a rainbow, and at that rainbow's ever-elusive end in North America there will be, along with *Agriocharis ocellata*—the closely related ocellated turkey of the Yucatán—*Meleagris gallopavo*, whose taxonomic name is a train of Latin words all clacking along to evoke the collective notion of the guinea hen, the rooster cock, and the peacock. However, the wild turkey is none of the above.

The first of the birds brought to Europe by Hernán Cortés were from stock the Aztecs had domesticated long before the Spaniard's hungry gaze fell upon rich Tenochtitlán. They were named "turkeys" after that Middle Eastern nation's barnyard guinea fowl. The wild turkeys the sober Pilgrims encountered in New England, though, stoutly resisted almost all efforts at such domestication; but they were so numerous at that time as to make the farm raising of them hardly cost-effective anyway. William Wood of Massachusetts, writing in the 1600s, reports that "the price of a good Turkie cocke is foure shillings; and he is well worth it, for he may be in weight forty pound." John James Audubon writes, "At the time when I moved to Kentucky in 1807, Turkeys were so abundant that one weighing twenty-five to thirty pounds brought a quarter of a dollar." William Clark, on the Missouri near what is now Leavenworth, Kansas, at about this same time, records, "Deer and turkeys in great quantities on the bank."* And it was not uncommon for the early Great Plains homesteaders to mistake the dusty cloud of a large flock of turkeys, going in search of mast, for a herd of bison stampeding down upon their sod-roofed dugouts.

The wild turkey's fatal flaw, though, was that he could be shot on his roost at night with little complaint. This the old-time market hunters did in "great quantities," as well as trapping him most efficiently; and when these persecutions were combined with the widespread clearing of the virgin woods, the wild turkey's numbers began to swoon.

In 1850 Massachusetts' last wild bird was killed—it would not be until the 1980s that the restoration of the birds would allow the hunting of wild turkeys to be resumed in that state. By that midcentury mark, the turkey was considered as rare in the eastern United States as the heath hen, who in three-quarters of a century would gain the distinction of permanent extinguishment. In 1931 the curmudgeonly William T. Hornaday, apostate hunter and director of the New York Zoological Park, was predicting the imminent total disappearance of the wild turkey from the North American scene; and he was almost proved right. From the bounty of the pre-Columbian era—when the "millions" the turkeys numbered would have been somewhere in the

---

* The tendency of those two species to be found together is still evident today, the deer perhaps finding security in the acuity of the turkeys' astounding senses of sight and hearing, while the turkeys rely on the deer's sense of smell: what threat one misses the other may detect.

Rio Grande wild turkeys. (*Photo: Robert Robb*)

"untold" category—the bird's population shrank steadily until in the 1930s or 1940s there were—what?—forty thousand? Thirty thousand? Twenty thousand?

Man-reared turkeys would not adapt to the wild circumstance, and it was not until the methods of transporting live-trapped wild birds to release sites in suitable habitats were perfected—once more the overwhelming majority of the money and effort behind this restoration, as it has been with the restoration of almost every wild animal of this nation who was once threatened, coming directly from hunters through government fish and wildlife departments and through private hunters' organizations—that the wild gobbler's call was heard again in many areas of his native range, as well as in Rocky Mountain and Pacific coastal locales where it had never been heard before. By the middle of the 1980s there were upward of three million of the birds in North America. Once again they are here for the hunter to pursue.

And the wild turkey is pursued unlike any other upland bird. In fact, the wild turkey is so outside the other upland birds in almost every respect that even granting him sovereignty over them is something of a non sequitur. The wild turkey is actually the king of nothing, nor does he desire to be. The wild turkey is the the wild turkey, and that is far more than enough.

The pursuit of the wild turkey is tied to the earth, as the pursuit of wild mammals is. The wild turkey is hunted and killed on the ground; and although he is quite capable of powerful bursts of flight, the air seems as foreign a medium to him as it would be to a bear or an elk.

Wild turkeys are hunted in both fall and spring. In the fall, the hunter seeks out the flocks of hens and one-year-old toms, called "jakes." His object, upon finding a flock (which may take up to days or a week of hard hunting), is to scatter the birds in every direction, often by running at them, yelling and waving his arms—there is slim hope of a hunter's sneaking undetected within shotgun range of a flock of wild turkeys. Then at the spot where he flushed them he will fashion a blind, that he can see 360 degrees out of without being seen, and wait for the gregarious turkeys to re-form their flock there. If he knows how, a hunter may try to entice birds back by producing a shrill *kee-kee-run* whistle or by clucking. But as in calling waterfowl or elk, or anything at large in the Out There, inept calling is worse than none at all; and to learn how to call turkeys correctly a hunter must listen to an experienced caller or one of the many instructional tapes or phonograph records that are available, and to practice faithfully in order to reproduce the proper rhythms and tones.

Dogs are often used in the fall hunt to scatter the flocks. Audubon used a well-trained dog that would scent the birds and run silently until he sighted the turkeys. The dog would then rush barking into the flock, the birds marking all the points on the compass rose as they flew, affording the hunter a greater chance of having the turkeys reassemble at the same spot than he would have if they had all taken off in one direction. Theodore Roosevelt employed dogs as well in his hunts for turkeys in Texas, his packed greyhounds flushing a bird and then chasing it as its escape flights grew ever shorter and shorter in duration, until the dogs could catch it.

Hunters who truly love to hunt the wild turkey, though, know that as enjoyable as the fall hunting for him may be, there is really only one time of the year for hunting turkeys, and that is the spring. "In the spring," says Audubon, "the hunter *calls* the Turkeys," though it is more along the lines of the *Turkeys'* calling the hunter. Calling is *the* way to hunt them, especially when the turkey a hunter will be calling will be a big gobbler, *the* game of springtime.

A day of spring hunting will begin, then, the evening before when the turkey hunter will be in an area he knows to hold birds, looking for the roost trees the birds will fly up into as the darkness settles. He will position himself to hear the big birds flying up to their perches, making sure that they do not see him; then he will withdraw quietly to return in the morning.

"Morning" for the turkey hunter will have arrived by 3:00 A.M. because he must be in position well before the first traces of daylight, awaiting the gobbler's descent. As he dresses in his camouflage clothes, the hunter will be reminded of those first black mornings of dove hunting that so perplexed him as a boy, and he will smile at the thought of how familiar this still hour has now become to him as he steps out the door and into the night, like someone shrugging a comfortable old coat of darkness over his shoulders. The morning will be crisp, even cold; but the smell of the mild spring day to come will be in the air. As he walks quietly and quickly to the place from which he will call the birds, he may pause on some high point to listen and to give the *"who-cooks-for-you, who-cooks-for-you-all"* hoot of the barred owl, or the howl of a coyote, and in a moment receive back that sound that confirms someone as a lifelong hunter of turkeys: the lusty gobble of a male bird, flashing through the blackness like sheet lightning.

Now the hunter hurries to set up in a place he can call from. This may be at an elevation above the bird's or below, depending on his belief as to which direction the gobbler will approach from; but he will not want to be too close to the bird for fear of frightening him off, perhaps no closer than two or three hundred yards, depending on the cover.

A hunter may set up merely by sitting with his back to a tree, or he may find a deadfall to lie behind—mindful of the fact that in warm spring weather it is not unheard-of to discover venomous serpents out and about in much of the wild turkey's range, particularly in the south. The turkey hunter may go so far as to construct a blind from brush or cut cane or camouflage netting; but whatever the nature of his redoubt, he will have made certain that he is completely camouflaged himself, from shirt and pants, to cap and face—either masked with greasepaint or covered with a mesh hood, the hood's having the advantage of hiding a hunter's shifty, white-flashing eyes—to camouflage gloves on his hands. He might even have covered his shotgun, or bow, with camouflage tape or spray-painted it in a camouflage pattern, all so he can be as one with his surroundings. He will have taken such seemingly extraordinary measures because he knows that the wild turkey—who is, let's face it, a *bird,* the proud possessor of all the awesome brainpower *of* a bird—does have, nonetheless, a bird's eyes and a bird's reflexes: at the least sign of anything abnormal or threatening, a turkey does not indulge in indecisive Hamletic brooding—he gives a frightened *"putt-putt-putt"* call of alarm and makes tracks. He *will* often run to escape, but he can also become airborne with the explosive speed of a quail (imagine a quail the size of a spaniel, erupting from cover), leaving the hunter to wonder what in the world he could have done wrong.

At the first hints of light, the hunter may try a few soft clucks. He will produce these on one of the various types of turkey calls, from friction calls such as a cedar box in which a pivoted arm, usually chalked, is scraped across the top of a sound chamber, or a slate call in which the tip of a wooden striker, with a corncob handle, is drawn across a small disk of slate—or some other glasslike material—that is held in the palm. There are other calling devices that are wind instruments, from horseshoe-shaped mouth diaphragms that lie against the roof of the mouth; to "tube" calls, some of the most effective I have ever encountered crafted by an Arkansas friend of mine from an old tin Scotch snuff can with a half-moon snipped into the lid and a Trojans stretched across the opening, the caller's lower lip pressed against the tin half and air forced through the narrow slit between latex and metal; to the second joint of a turkey's wing bone that is sucked upon with a kissing action; to, finally, among the very best hunters, nothing more than the hunter's own voice.

After the hunter gives his clucks, the gobbler will answer eagerly. The hunter knows to wait motionlessly now. He may even have brought along a cushion, not as some sort of self-indulgence, but to make it easier for him to sit without the discomfort that can cause him to fidget. He will be hunting with his ears now.

Perhaps a quarter-hour after his clucks, the hunter will yelp, and the gobbler will answer, maybe even start to draw near. This is a complete reversal of the natural order of these affairs, because the male gobbles to bring the hen to *him,* but now in his ardor *he* is going to her.

The hunter may even hear the turkey's strutting toward him, now, the bird in the hunter's imagination coming with his wings cupped and his tail fanned, his brightly colored wattles swelling out, a drummed note sounding from his puffed-out breast. If the hunter has ever heard a big buck approaching his stand, or been lucky enough to be in a blind of sisal leaves and acacia branches when the sound of a leopard feeding on the hanging bait came from a nearby tree, he

A hunter of wild turkeys. (*Author photo*)

will recognize the same mounting excitement here, having to struggle to hush his breathing and control his movements as a *bird*, of all things, draws closer.

When the bird is within range—forty yards or less to be certain—and he has clearly seen that this bird carries the male's beard that grows from his breast, growing up to eleven or twelve inches in length, the hunter will wait until the gobbler's head is behind a tree, or the turkey has turned away from him, before lifting his shotgun and easing off the safety, or pulling his bow back to full draw. The shotgun hunter will be using either a 12- or a 10-gauge, with No. 4—as a minimum—or No. 2 or BB shot in Magnum loads. The hunter will aim for the turkey's head, *only,* knowing that the heavy birds can escape after being wounded only in the body. The gobbler will halt in his strutting and fluff out his feathers so he appears fully twice his enormous size, and will give one final call. Then there will be the hollow boom of the big gun and the dry, already-dead flapping of the twenty-pound gobbler's big wings on the forest duff as the hunter runs toward him and the morning light begins to slash down through the tall wild trees.

That, of course, is the ideal of the turkey hunt; and for every morning that turns out that way there have been dozens of others when the roosting places remained undiscovered the night before—not even a loose feather on the ground or droppings (round, popcorn-shaped ones left by hens, J-shaped ones left by gobblers) to show where the turkeys had been; when the gobblers would not answer the owl hoot or would not come to the clucks and yelps, hanging up a hundred fifty, two hundred yards away, their gobbles running through the hunter like surges of electricity, mingling joy and frustration in him. Other times, a bird—especially true of the young jake—may have come in silently behind the hunter and stood watching until the hunter, unaware, tried to shoo away a buzzing mosquito with the slightest flick of his head, that hint of movement igniting the turkey like a rocket. Or maybe a gobbler saw the weapon's being raised, or the hunter tried to get too close or call too often, or called not authentically enough, or sneezed or yawned at the wrong instant, or suffered any one of a maddening assortment of mishaps that can befall the turkey hunter in the cold and wet or the cool and damp or the warm and humid area where he goes to pursue a gobbler in the spring.

That *is* what makes the spring hunting for the wild turkey unique from the hunt for the other upland birds, though. The turkey hunter goes out, unconcerned with covey rises or the chance of making a right-left double, and hunts a single turkey the way the large mammals are hunted. In the hunt for a large male wild turkey in the spring all the same fatigues, dangers, and "innumerable annoyances" of hunting big game in the fall are to be found. The wild turkey is, in effect, big game adorned with plumage. Within a turkey hunter the wild turkey lingers in full feather, strutting before him no matter what the season in that clearing the way of the hunter always winds through, that clearing where we ultimately meet all the living objects of our pursuit, that glade of the hunter's soul.

16

RAMIFICATIONS

In one of the most extreme places to which the way of the hunter can lead, the white ram, his heavy black horns circling back in a mathematically definable spiral—that is shared by the shell of the nautilus and the nails of our own fingers, if we let them grow long enough— those horns circling around behind his ears and below his jaw and then up past his eyes, the flaring "lamb tips" reaching above the broken and scarred bridge of his nose, rests upon the rocky chine of the mountaintop that is held in the glass of the spotting scope set on the river-valley floor below. From where I now sit, leaning against my pack frame set among gray stones tumbled smooth, the ram is a thousand feet and more above, shimmering in the lens, secure.

A way *can* be found to climb to him, to get above him where the mountain reaches even higher, and to slip down through the piled rocks and drop onto him. There are two other big rams with him, two more sets of incomparable eyes to be concerned with; but I would be dressed in white, carrying my .340 Weatherby Magnum; and if they saw a flash of me as I scrambled over a rock, there is a chance that they would take me for just another sheep in such a high place,

A Dall's sheep ram, Alaska. Judging by the growth rings around his horns, this sheep is probably at least ten years old. (*Photo © by Bill McRae*)

and not even bother to stand. Or they might be up in an instant and away on their concave hooves more swiftly than any man could hope to follow. With sheep there is just no telling. But for this sheep it would be worth the effort to find a way to him. Nonetheless, he is secure.

I have already killed a white ram a few days earlier, having climbed in the rain up a snow slide, and then up a chimney of rock, six hundred, seven hundred, a thousand feet from the valley floor, running across the steep shale slides because there was no way to walk across them without falling, until I could belly up a grassy slope and look over to find my own full-curl ram feeding toward me as I eased the cross hairs onto him.

So I will not be climbing for this other wild mountain sheep now, but just go on watching him. He is a magnificent ram, though, who would be well worth making a fair climb after, even if he could never be reached. Though for some hunters, even those who fancy themselves "sheep hunters," he might not be, no matter how magnificent, unless a kill were a certainty, and perhaps not even then.

If wild turkeys breed hunting fanatics, wild sheep breed lunatics. There are hunters who divide the world into two clear-cut categories: the hunters of sheep and everybody else. For some hunters the only true hunting country is sheep country, whether the glacial mountain valleys of Alaska, the rolling tundra mountains of the Yukon Arctic, the timbered mountains of the Rockies, or the desert mountains of the Southwest and Mexico. For such hunters the only way is the way of the wild sheep.

The wild sheep of the world—the mouflons, urials, argalis, Asiatic bighorns, the Dalli, and American bighorns—inhabit what has been called the "great arc" of the wild sheep, that sweeping curve of mountainous country that runs out of the Mediterranean's western end, where the wild mouflon are native to Corsica and Sardinia, then eastward through Asia Minor, the Hindu Kush, the Pamirs, the Himalayas, and the other mountains of Central Asia, through Mongolia and Siberia—where the largest of the wild sheep (some approaching four hundred pounds), the argalis, are found—to Alaska and the Yukon and the western Northwest Territories, down through British Columbia and Alberta, and along the Rockies and the Cascades and the Sierras into Mexico. In North America there are two species of wild sheep, *Ovis dalli* and *Ovis canadensis*.

The Dalli are considered "thinhorn" sheep, and are categorized as being of two types, the Dall's and the Stone's. The Dall's sheep are pure white, found in Alaska and the Yukon and the NWT, while the Stone's, of northern British Columbia, reaching as far south as the Peace River, are of a grayish blue-black color. They both will weigh in the neighborhood of one hundred eighty to two hundred pounds, and while for exceptional rams the horns may reach over forty inches in length, the bases will seldom exceed fourteen and a half inches in circumference. (The horns also record the ram's age when horn growth halts each year during the rut and a deep, dark annular ring is formed.)

Ovis canadensis', or the bighorns', horns can carry circumferences from fifteen up to sixteen or seventeen inches, and a ram may weigh three hundred pounds. The bighorns are considered to be of two types, bighorns and desert sheep. The bighorn sheep are found in craggy country in British Columbia, Alberta, Montana, Wyoming, Washington, Oregon, Idaho, California, Nevada, Utah, Colorado, and New Mexico, with the desert races, *Ovis canadensis nelsoni* and the

The author with a trophy desert bighorn. (*Author photo*)

like—who weigh about what the thinhorn sheep do—supplanting the bighorn races in the hot, dry southern lands of California, Nevada, Utah, and New Mexico, and in Arizona, the Sonora Desert of Mexico, and Baja California almost all the way to the peninsula's tip.

A hunter who kills all four types of North America's wild sheep is said to have taken the "Grand Slam," a lop-headed concept of what goes into making distinguished big-game hunting if there ever was one, the gimmick dreamed up in the late 1940s by the late wildlife photographer, writer, and hunter Grancel Fitz. The distinction of having chalked up a Grand Slam—some hunters priding themselves on how few *days* it takes them to collect theirs (about like seeing how few days it takes you to enjoy living)—and the widely read writings of Jack O'Connor did much to popularize the hunting of wild sheep in this country over the last forty years. What the *exact* allure of hunting sheep is, though, is rather more mysterious.

A bear is probably a more difficult animal to stalk than a wild sheep, and a goat often inhabits more treacherous terrain. Nonetheless, whereas bighorns will sometimes take shelter in black timber when pressured, the usual survival technique of all the wild sheep is to seek the highest, roughest ground their habitat has to offer, and to stay up in it as much as possible. In this way, the hunting of Dall's sheep in August amid the lunar geography of a far northern drainage, and that of hunting desert bighorns amid the moonscape of naked rocks and cactus and dry arroyos in December, when the sounds of rutting rams fighting—the banging together of their horned heads like the distant reports of gunfire—will echo in the cold desert air, are much alike. Any sheep, in order to be hunted, must be seen—usually from some distance through a spotting scope—then a way must be found to stalk up on him so that a hunter can get within range for a shot. A .338 caliber would certainly be at the upper end of sheep rifles, with anything in the fast, flat-shooting .270 Winchester Center Fire (W.C.F.) or Weatherby Magnum, 7mm Magnum, or .300 Magnum class being more than sufficient. And whether or not there are harder animals to hunt, sheep hunting, because of sheep country and sheep weather—both of which conditions humans may find incredibly hostile, whereas sheep merely find them middling—will always be hard enough, an experienced sheep hunter I know able to assure us that one thing that can always be counted on on any mountain hunt is at least "three days of bad weather or mass confusion."

One has only to note, though, how quickly a group of hunters, who have been nodding only politely at someone's tale of the imperial elk he killed, will give their rapt attention to another hunter, when he tells them of the forty-two-inch Stone's ram he killed after an eight-hour climb in the mountains above the Muskwa River, to see that the allure of sheep hunting is *palpable*. *Big* rams *are* sometimes taken by flukes or lucky accidents; but it is almost *never* easy to kill one honestly without having to go up into places where humans were never really meant to go, but where sheep were born to be.

This allure, then, creates among sheep hunters two other categories: those who hunt rams because they love to, and those who hunt them because they believe they are required to. The first, as long as they are in sheep country—arguably the most dramatic, strikingly beautiful, and certainly breathtaking of all hunting country, which may also have much to do with sheep hunting's allure—or en route to it, even if only inside their minds, are always happy, no matter how the hunt may turn out. The second are never happy. At best, if they do manage to kill a big ram, they feel a momentary relief: this is an animal I do not have to hunt again, they think, a dismal obligation having been fulfilled.

Such hunters may fear the mountains, or fear failure ("failure" by their own lights) even more, and so go after sheep solely out of vainglory or a desire to acquire status among other hunters, to gain the cachet that they believe the hunting of wild sheep imparts. Every step up the mountain is hateful to them, and what should be a joy becomes a duty. *Real* hunters, they think, kill sheep; and only by killing sheep can they class themselves among the real hunters. The novelist Thomas McGuane, in an essay on fly-fishing, touches on what lies at the root of this attitude quite aptly when he writes:

> one must show purpose. American shame at leisure has produced the latest no-nonesense stance in sport . . . the "headhunter" being [one of] the most appalling instances that come[s] readily to mind. No longer sufficiently human to contemplate the relationship of life to eternity, the glandular modern sport worries whether or not he is wasting time.

But, as we know, at the true heart of hunting must always lie the possibility of failure. A true hunter is always prepared to fail, and fail with good grace. It is always a no-lose proposition for the true hunter, anyway, because even if the game eludes him or outwits him, he has still had his free days in the wild, doing what the genus *Homo* was designed to do, pursuing wild animals, following the way. If he is lucky enough to kill an animal, then he is just that much ahead of the game *of* the game.

But some hunters, often rich and powerful men outside the world of the sheep (who does not know or care about how rich or powerful the men may be, and like all wild animals, will never accede willingly to their wishes), never see it quite that way. For them the head on the wall means everything. They will not be made a laughingstock by any herbivore, or admit to anyone—not even themselves—that a mountain could take their measure. If they cannot climb to the sheep, then perhaps their young guide *can,* for the proper valuable consideration. Perhaps a particularly grand sheep might be discreetly spotted from the air and a nearby place found to land and stalk him from. Perhaps someone else has a very good ram's head he could be persuaded to part with, or maybe the taxidermist could be able to add an inch or two of epoxy and fiberglass to the horn, because, after all, this ram's horns by rights really ought to be about, say, forty-four or forty-five inches long, shouldn't they? And then when he is gathered with other hunters, other men who may be so equal in wealth and power that they use their hunting as the only means they have to compete with one another, and the others begin to tell of the brown bear or the exceptional white-tailed deer they killed last season, *he* can nod politely, his stomach eased comfortably out against his belt, a quality cigar smoldering between fingers that are ringed in gold, the ice rattling pleasantly in his glass of excellent scotch, and offer his story of the record-book Dall's ram he took this year, telling the story of his hunt with such understated verve that in time even he will come to believe it himself and will honestly no longer remember what the truth actually was. And, of course, why shouldn't he tell his story the way he wishes—after all, he did pay good money for it.

What this has to do with hunting—not just sheep hunting, but *any* hunting—is utterly beyond me. Hunting is in every sense *non*competitive. When a man begins to see game strictly in terms of inches on a steel tape or a ranking on the page of a record book; when the animal is no longer eyes and ears and nose and brain and agile hooves and a wild grace, but is reduced to an arithmetic problem; when a man hunts with a calculator in place of his heart, the game, the *true* game is over, and the way is lost.

And it doesn't have to be like that at all.

I visited the home of an avid sheep hunter once. His comfortable house was on a lake near a large city, a floatplane tied to the small dock in front. He led me downstairs, past the bright Miró hanging in the hallway, to the small basement trophy room where there were the heads of two dozen or so sheep and ibex from his mountain hunts around the world. On one wall alone were three Grand Slams— though I doubt he would have called them that—a fourth one at his other home in another state.

The rules of hunting etiquette, when being shown a wallful of sheep, call for one to ask what this one measured, what that one scored. More than politesse, though, prompted my asking him these questions. I was curious to see what his feelings were toward all these most impressive animals.

He smiled at me, somewhat embarrassed, and admitted that he had never bothered about putting a tape on any of these spiraling horns. He hunted sheep simply because he loved to hunt sheep. What other reason could there possibly be?

There will always be men, and women, driven to hunt sheep, or any animal, for the wrong reasons, but more and more their days seem numbered. Regulations against illegal methods of hunting are more rigidly enforced; the records keepers demand more documentary substantiation of the animal's size and how it was hunted; and those who once hunted for strictly social reasons find that hunting is perhaps not so socially esteemed in their circle as it once was—better to take up golf or polish their backhand.

Now, more than ever, the only reason to hunt wild sheep, to hunt at *all*, is one's love of, and passion for, the wild and hunting. It is the only true reason to run twelve miles every week, to do pull-ups to strengthen the arms, and sit-ups to toughen the stomach, all so a mountain can be climbed and a big ram reached. It is the only reason for a hunter to travel the long way to sheep country, to lace on stout mountaineering boots and to carry his raingear and insulated clothing and a good spotting scope in a pack on his back—carrying, as well, binoculars, a small emergency medical kit, matches, a flashlight to show the trail down when he must take it in the darkness, and, oddly, a canteen, because at the tops of the mountains where the sheep live, even in the north, water is scarce, and it may be many hours up and many dry hours back down. It is only for the love of it that anyone should be prepared to go into places where every step could send him three hundred feet down a chute of jagged shale; where rockfalls may come down on him with a roar like the pealing of thunder; where the sun may become rain, the rain, snow, in less than an hour; and where a hunter must be prepared to spend the night clinging to the mountain, having dug himself a bed into its side just the way a sheep digs his own bed—although unlike the sheep, a hunter will probably not sleep. Because he loves it, is the only reason for a hunter to go up in search of big rams—marked out by their heavy-based horns, the mass carrying deeply into the curl, the horns perhaps curling fully, or broomed far back, nearly to the bone core, big-horned rams not only a sign of healthy, thriving herds, but also of male sheep who are usually past their breeding primes—looking for them in that high country above the trees where at every latitude (except in the country of the desert sheep) it is the Arctic every bit as much as any land above the Circle is.

So I go on sitting here among the rounded stones in this glacier-scoured valley, watching the great ram a mile in the air, wondering where and when I will be able to climb again after another wild mountain sheep (knowing that I must, the love for it now so strong), and hoping that it will always be for the right reason.

17

"MUNICIPAL PALEOLITHIC MAN"

Tonight hunters gather to feast in the great hall of the great museum in the great city. Outside in the falling snow, astride his granite horse, sits the image of the last president any of these men can think of with unalloyed admiration. He, too, was a hunter, the epitome of the kind these men strive to be, a naturalist-conservationist hunter—one who knows the true wild and works to protect it. He founded the organization to which these hunters belong, and their banquet is as much to honor and reaffirm his ideals as it is to renew fellowships.

These men, who will soon be seated at long tables arranged between bull moose fixed in combat and a bison herd in permanent migration across a painted prairie, might be looked upon as the elite of hunting. Wealth, circumstance, and much good luck have allowed them to hunt further and more intensely than millions of other hunters. By rights, the sight of big-game animals, particularly dead ones, should have lost much of its power to amaze them. But as they drift past the mounted specimens in the exhibit hall's glass cases—animals that were chosen to be not merely representative of their species, but among the very largest and most spectacular to be found—it can be seen

unmistakably that they are filled with the very same thrill-delight-awe
that overcame them when they were small boys and their fathers,
smelling of woodsmoke and sweat, had appeared out of the fall evenings, bringing home the still-warm bodies of dead bucks, or when,
unobserved and without permission, they had crept like the hunters
they imagined themselves one day to be into their grandfathers' dens
to feel the coarse hair of the bear hides spread out on the varnished
floors there. Why the sensation comes is still a mystery to them, but
come it does; and as they always do, the animals succeed in humbling
them.

Even hunters like these—perhaps *especially* hunters like these—
understand the innate superiority of the animal. The grace, the strength,
the cunning, the perfect fit it achieves in nature is the animal's birthright, while the hunters must struggle for even a vague approximation
of these gifts. They realize that in the hunt, although they may be
amateurs of the best kind—who go in pursuit of game only because
this is their great passion—they are also amateurs of the rankest sort.
Such hunters, who have seen so much of the world, have all seen, or
know of, the real human hunters, the genuine elite of the hunt.

In the Arctic and those rain forests and across the plains of Africa
the pure hunting peoples still manage to cling tenuously to the existence we all enjoyed ten thousand years ago, before agriculture and
the domestication of wild animals altered and distorted human life.
In the early 1970s the late anthropologist Carleton S. Coon estimated
these peoples' remaining numbers in all the world at a bare quarter-
million, and by now that figure must assuredly be far lower. The ones
who endure do so in what is, however harsh and brutal the environ-
ments may on occasion be, not just a species of paradise, but the very
definition of it, roaming, as all our ancestors did, the "most favored
parts of the world" (as Coon called them), the as-yet uncleared and
unbroken game lands. They remain what we all once were, wild peoples in wild places.

Such people in such places deserve sanctuary every bit as much
as any endangered bird or mammal or fish. They are untamed, yet
remarkably gentle humans who hunt without recourse to reasons or
vainglory, who hunt only because that is what humans have always
done, as naturally as pronghorns have always run. Whether or not
there is hope for their final survival is beyond the scope of this book.
But what continues to survive, even in people in places far removed
from the last wild game lands, is their hunter's heart. This heart can
still be found, even outside the shrinking domains of the untouched

hunting peoples, in that exile from Eden who has made the way his life, not merely his pastime.

Ortega y Gasset called such an expatriate hunter "municipal Paleolithic man." He is the kind of hunter who is never really out of the woods, having wisely chosen to ignore the last ten millennia or so. He knows the score, but he is the kind of man who will work all day in a mill so he can chase animals all night. His hunting grounds are his real home, and he will know them and their inhabitants almost as well as they know themselves. There is always a skin drying in the shed of such a man, and a cut of wild meat always on his table.

The hands of a hunter such as this will be older than his face, and there will be nothing younger than his eyes. I have looked into eyes like that at least three times. All belonged to old hunters, old masters.

One was a purported poacher in Cuba, a man, it was said, who despite the grave risks he ran of imprisonment and worse continued to stalk deer in the island's swamps, elegantly and good-humoredly eluding and outwitting the formidable armed pursuers the government sent after him, while maintaining the most absolutely sunny disposition any man could possess. Another was an old Inuit who appeared one sleeting day around a bend of the Noatak River, far above the Circle, hunting winter meat. He was with a group of younger men, traveling in two open boats with caribou carcasses and antlered heads, like figureheads on Norse ships, lashed across the bows. They came ashore; and while the young men asked me about animals and weather, he stood quietly off to one side, his hands in the pockets of his wolf-trimmed parka, no questions to ask because his eyes and senses and experience were telling him all. The third was a white-haired African I was introduced to at a game department office in the Kenyan highlands. He had been an official killer of elephants all his life, a man whose job it had been to live with the herds, to know their actions and intentions, and when they went where other humans did not want them to—trampling crops or destroying plantations—to shoot them. He had stopped shooting elephants by the time I met him; and released from the mixed blessing of his occupation (no other could have been more exciting, and none harder, both emotionally and physically), he was now content to spend his afternoons in the shade of the tin-roofed veranda of the whitewashed office building, standing in the motionless way an old elephant bull will beneath the shade of a savanna's single fever tree, seeming to do no more than watch the rain, left by a sudden noon cloudburst, steam from the grass and leaves. When I took this old hunter's hand to shake it, the gravity I felt in it could have sunk an iceberg to the ocean floor, if its warmth did not melt it first.

His, and the others', eyes were those of authentic predators at ease, eyes alert and bright and so calm they were unnerving. They were eyes filled with tender lethalness. They took your full measure without threatening. They saw things as they actually were, free of preconceptions, prepared to view the unexpected, showing the universal receptiveness that in the martial arts is known as *ki*. They were the exact kind of eyes I hoped, and still do hope, to see one day in the mirror.

Men with eyes like that adamantly refuse to fit the neat, popular images many wish to assign to hunters to make them comprehensible to an age so badly out of touch with the wild—images of comic, ineffectual Fudds, sexually frustrated psychopaths, or gun-toting, motor-homing louts eagerly adhering to McKinley's law (said to have been formulated by a hunter named McKinley who held that the only sure means of not running out of booze on a hunting trip was to pack one quart of liquor and half a case of beer per man per day into camp). Such men cannot be stereotyped because they are like nothing most of us have ever seen before—at least not in the last ten thousand years. Like some whitetails, these men may inhabit a world no bigger around than the few miles of hills and woods surrounding the spot where they were born. But because of their intimate, intense relationship with that small circle of wild earth—their full-time absorption in it and the native skills they demonstrate there—they are the hunters that other hunters, no matter how supposedly elite their station, truly envy.

These eternal troglodytes, as Ortega y Gasset also styles them, are often practitioners of the most extreme modes of the hunt. Because of the closeness they feel to animals, they frequently join forces *with* animals in the hunt, acting as accessories to their hot-blooded weapons' carrying out of their instinctive predatory actions.

They may hunt with birds of prey, a hunting technique that goes back as much as four thousand years and seems to have arisen independently in cultures as diverse and separated as the Scandinavian and the Japanese. Hawking, or falconry, is a "rage," as T. H. White called it, that has been, and is, shared by both municipal Paleolithic men and princes (the true hunter's heart cuts across all social and class statuses). With these birds there are essentially two types of hunting that are carried out.

The first, and possibly the more dramatic, is that done with the

Tom Cullen, falconer, with
an African hawk eagle.
(*Author photo*)

true falcons, birds such as prairie falcons, peregrines, and the large,
sometimes snow-colored gyrfalcons. In a highly simplified description
of how these "longwings," as they are known, are hunted, the falcon
is let fly from the fist and allowed to soar far above open country
where he "waits on," hovering while his human retainer, assisted often
by bird dogs, goes about his obligation of flushing a bird—usually
one of the upland variety, up to the size of sage grouse, but also ducks
and pigeons. The falcon then dives, or "stoops," headfirst onto his
prey at speeds approaching those of Indy cars on the straightaways,
the rushing air whistling through the bells tied to his legs, flattening
out his dive at its bottom to strike a powerful, glancing, open-taloned
blow. When he is lucky enough to connect—even falcons miss—the
feathers of his prey will seem to explode, as if the bird has been hit
by a load of No. 6s. If the bird is able to struggle on, the falcon may
strike again, perhaps even "binding" to it, sinking in his talons to ride
his quarry to the ground. Then the human hunter approaches the
falcon, now mantling his prize with his wings, and draws him off it
by presenting the lure, the cloth or leather "bird" the human has used
to train him, and slips the dead bird into his game pouch and offers
his gloved fist for the falcon once more to perch upon.

The other type of hawking is that involving the true hawks—or
accipiters—the buteos, and the eagles. This group includes such birds
as the goshawk; the Cooper's and Harris' hawks; the venerable work-
horse—in Steve Bodio's phrase—of this class of raptors, the redtail;

such foreign birds as the African hawk eagle; and even the golden eagle. These birds hunt mostly in closed country, weaving their ways under the forest canopy, picking up rabbits and hares, but also sometimes game birds. Sometimes the hawk or buteo or eagle will fly ahead of the hunter and sit on the limb of a tree and stare balefully down on the human as he works his way to him, beating the brush and driving out the prey. The raptor will then swoop down on the running or flapping animal; and if he can catch it he will kill by "footing" it, driving his talons with enormous pressure into lungs or heart or brain. Some Harris' hawkers will carry their birds on their fists, and at the sight of game actually take the bird in their hand and hurl it like a spear. There is little ceremony connected with hawking of this sort.

There is almost no ceremony at all connected to the type of hunting with animals other municipal Paleolithic men do, that carried out with coursing hounds. Also known as gazehounds, sight hounds, or long dogs, these are hare-footed dogs who hunt by speed and sight—instead of scent—killing the game themselves, unlike gun dogs—who use their noses to flush game for the hunter—and even unlike trail, or scent, hounds, who after they bay the animal up the tree let the hunter kill it. The gazehounds don't even allow the hunter *that*.

    The coursing-hound breeds are pureblooded greyhounds, whippets, salukis, Russian wolfhounds or "borzois," Scottish deerhounds, Afghans, and Irish wolfhounds, along with hybrid or mixed-blood variations on them. The origins of coursing go back to the hunting of rabbits and gazelles in the open country of ancient Egypt, the Middle East, and that of the Asian steppes where the nomad tribes wandered, probably to a time even before falconry.

    In modern "free coursing," the hunter and his unchecked dogs walk the open land, hoping to put up a cottontail or a jackrabbit or a fox. If a rabbit breaks from cover—the hunters crying "Hare up! Hare up!" to notify the dogs if they cannot immediately spot it—then the race is on, the greyhounds, the swiftest of the long dogs, being carried to speeds up to fifty miles per hour by their "double-suspension gallop," the powerful stride of their hindquarters driving their forelegs into the air twice before their rear feet touch the ground again. What possible chance could a jackrabbit have of escaping such *engines*? *Every*, as it happens, as he cuts and sprints and turns and feints and yaws through the sage, heading for the nearest barbed-wire fence to duck beneath the bottom strand, leading the dogs on for sometimes a mile or more, more often than *not* escaping. To complement his speed

A hound man, Floyd Mansell, with his coursing dogs. (*Author photo*)

merchants, a coursing-hound hunter will often add dogs with good staying power, such as salukis, to his pack to continue the chase when the rabbit has winded his balls-to-the-wall greyhounds. The greyhounds will run on, though, however winded, because like all the long dogs they demonstrate in the field the poise of conditioned athletes, seeming to tell the humans that they are only in it for the sport, for the all-out joy of the run, just as the hunter's primary aim is to *see* how they run. A missed rabbit does not seem to perturb the dogs overly as they trot back to the hunter; they will look forward to the next race just as eagerly. Yet though their elongated physiques appear to be built almost exclusively for speed, they can, and do, kill—a jackrabbit at the "catch" dying as swiftly and painlessly in the jaws of a gazehound as he would from a well-placed bullet—and the hunter *will* have rabbit stew.

Coursing hounds are even used to take animals up to the size of coyotes. Coyote dogs are often hybrids or mixed-breed "staghounds," who still carry the rough coat of their deerhound ancestors, or are "coldblood" sight hounds, or "grade hounds"—purebreds without registration papers, as opposed to "hotbloods," the officially registered sight hounds. They all qualify as working western dogs; and while human hunters may conduct their pursuit of the little wolves from horseback, it does not seem inappropriate that they more often use stripped-down ranch pickups equipped with quick-release dog boxes. But even in this seemingly unsentimental brand of the chase, municipal Paleolithic man sides with honor, choosing not to use the truck to run the coyote ragged, but only to bring his dogs within range for them to make a "good run," the coyote always having a far better than average chance at escape. Without the good run there would be no hunting, for dog or for man.

Even in locales where there seems no possibility of hunting *anything* anymore, municipal Paleolithic man hunts on. In trash dumps, abandoned warehouses, and "maggot factories," maniac English "ratters" hunt rodents with terriers akin to the southerners' fice dogs. Or they may send ferrets down warrens to drive out rabbits, or hunt almost anything that moves with their *lurchers,* the indispensable dogs of poachers, frequently a crossbreed of the greyhound and the collie, basically a gazehound with a nose and brains. And sometimes they *may* poach, not necessarily for profit, but often for the purest of motives: because they cannot *not* hunt, despite what any of civilization's laws may say.

The true human hunter is incorrigible. Even while functioning in the civilized world, he remains outside it. Ignore the question of whether anyone should really *want* to see the end of all hunting and the loss, forever, of this art that was most instrumental in the million-year rise and survival of our species—and may still be necessary to it. Far more fundamental is the question of exactly *how* the ending is supposed to be accomplished.

Let me describe the last place I went hunting with a hawker and his hawk eagle. It was between a dry riverbed and the railroad tracks, beyond the chain-link fence encircling the three-par golf course of a mobile-home park, just down the hill from the Unocal station, and within sight of the freeway. We did find cottontails and California quail there; but even if we had not, how can it be expected that hunting can be driven from the fibers of humans when they are willing to resort to places like *that* on the hope that there will be game there to pursue? In the last bomb-cratered city, someone will fly a bird of prey over the wreckage, or turn his dog out after game in the vacant lots among the rubble.

It would be a mistake to assume that municipal Paleolithic man is a mere relict. It has been only four hundred generations since we were *all* hunters, far too few to permit genetic changes of any consequence. We are still made in the likeness of hunters, and it must be remembered that the favorite activity of hunters is *hunting*. More than gathering plants or stealing honey or building shelters or singing songs, more, perhaps, even than loving, hunters love to hunt. And they will do so for as long as they are able.

Municipal Paleolithic man, and the elite hunters, know that the end is not yet here, though. And in their own ways they labor to see that the hunt will continue, that the traditions and the wild and the wild things in it will be maintained.

Something they both share, as well, is a longing for a far place they may never see. If they retraced the hunter's way, back through those four hundred squandered generations and one hundred centuries, back a million years, they would find themselves in the heart of the place where the way began. Africa is the heart of the hunter's heart, and every hunter longs to see it once. Though few, having once seen it, are content never to see it again.

18

THE NITRO EXPRESS

By a river in southern Kenya, in a twilighted warm savanna place—where there wasn't a hint of even a lonesome dirt road—I shot a lion once. I shot him three times with my .375 H&H Magnum, the first 300-grain soft-nosed bullet breaking his spine, rolling him with a roar, the second two anchoring him in the chest. He was a huge cat and as assuredly dead as a lion could be. I started to run toward him, full of adrenaline and elation, but the professional hunter, the "PH," grabbed me by the collar and yanked me back. He got right into my face, then, his blue eyes cold and furious above his crooked, many-times-broken nose.

"*Never* run up on a dead lion," he rasped at me. "It's the dead ones that kill you."

So we walked the rest of the way up to the great cat, very slowly. We poked him a bit, keeping our guns on him, and when we saw that there was no longer any question of his still being of this world, I extracted the round from my rifle's chamber and pushed it down into the magazine. Closing the bolt, I handed the rifle to one of the Samburu trackers, all of whom were now crowding around me, laughing and shaking my hand, admiring this lion who would yield much good medicinal fat for them to carry home to their families. Which was the precise moment the lion chose to lift his enormous shaggy head from the ground and roar one last roar at us.

The sequence of events that followed this was blurred then and remains even more blurred today, but somehow I did find myself once again in possession of my rifle, once again with a 300-grainer "up the spout," with the trackers all standing sensibly off in a knot—which looked suspiciously like a job action—fifteen yards away and pointing at the lion, silently admonishing us to *deal* with this matter, as the PH crouched and prodded the cat with the muzzle of his .375, finding, at last, no life left there. Three lethal hits from a .375—900 grains of jacketed lead—and it is still the "dead ones that kill you." The trackers returned slowly, and we all stared at this lion in a far more serious light, as around us in the rising evening darkness the remaining members of his pride began to roar.

Moments such as that, or when a Cape buffalo refuses to go down after you have hit him a half-dozen times or when a duiker antelope runs a hundred fifty yards before giving in to the .300 Magnum wound in his thirty-pound body or when an elephant bull charges you and if you have to shoot him all that he will be showing you for a target is the extremely hard-to-hit frontal brain shot as your mouth goes dry and papery and you realize how far out of hand your longing to see this continent has gotten, make you wonder, exactly, just how big a gun you should have in Africa. What constitutes "enough gun" in this place you have always dreamed of hunting; what is too little; what, if anything, is too much?

Africa is where that first gun, that boy's Christmas of so many years before, has brought us at last. Roosevelt always knew he would come here someday, to this last remnant of the Pleistocene; and every other hunter knows he will, or would like to, too. It is as much a logical conclusion to the hunter's way as the chukar is to the pursuit of upland birds. It is also where it all began. This makes it too complex to understand in any sort of abstract terms. Something actual, of steel and wood, is required to make it explicable. Something like guns. Africa must be seen in terms of a hunter's weapons of choice.

Guns, to be sure, are always a most spirited topic of noontime conversation in safari camps all across the African continent, PHs and their clients gathering under the thatched shade out of the midday sun, the still air bearing the urgent calling of a dove and the drone of insects and sometimes the grunting of hippos, debating over a lunch

"It's the dead lions that kill you." (*Photo: George H. Harrison*)

of wild game what the best rifle of all might be. In no other game field that I am familiar with is the talk of rifled long guns fraught with such romance, true-life adventure, superstition, technical jargon, and fervently held opinon. Here all the twinkling numbers take on a life of their own.

Part of the explanation for this is that in Africa, as in no other locale, there is a genuine call for such a wide variety of calibers. Whereas in North America a hunter could use nothing but one of the reliable modern .30-caliber rifles to hunt, quite handily, all of those big-game animals to be found from Mexico to Alaska, the much wider variety of game available across the African continent could conceivably require a battery of guns starting with the .22 Long Rifle and ending with the .600 Nitro Express—that burns 110 grains of cordite (nitroglycerin) powder and steams a 900-grain (over two-ounce) bullet out its yawning muzzle about like a speeding train exiting a tunnel (the name *Express,* in fact, harking back to Purdey's introduction of the "Express Train" rifle in the 1850s, the gloriously evocative phrase coined to publicize those weapons' heavy caliber, high velocity, and a striking power approximating that of a coal-fired locomotive). The nineteenth edition of *Rowland Ward's African Records of Big Game* lists some 170 species and subspecies of game animals for which they maintain records so that if one wished to hunt every animal in Africa one would have to commence with the seven-pound royal antelope (world's record horn length, one and three-eighths inches) and conclude with the elephant, who can stand fourteen feet or better at the shoulder, not *one* of these animals, as another PH once put it to me, willing to die gladly with the first shot, however accurate. Obviously, what the *right* weapon is for one animal is certainly not going to be *right* in every other instance for another.

If a hunter is contemplating his first safari to Africa, though—as all hunters who have not yet been there are doing—he will want to have at least an inkling of what to bring with him and will like to be able with some confidence to get by with something less than six or seven different rifles. All right, let's see whether anything can be done to clarify this even a little.

Traditionally, back about the time when people smoked with cigarette holders and set sail on the *Normandie,* hunters making a long, mixed-bag safari took three rifles with them—and often threw in a shotgun on top of those. These rifles were usually classified as a "light," a "medium," and a "heavy" caliber. Numerous definitions exist for differentiating these classes of guns, but the one I like best is the one

Rifles used for hunting in Africa can be varied. (*Author photo*)

the widely experienced big-game hunter Walter H. White postulated while we were on safari together a few years back. To his way of thinking, having owned and shot about everything from a .577 on down, a light caliber for Africa would be any gun firing a bullet weighing 249 grains or less; a medium would fire a bullet of between 250 and 399 grains; and a heavy would fire a bullet of 400 grains in weight or more. His other qualification would be that these rifles would all propel their bullets out the muzzle at a minimum of 2,000 feet per second (thus eliminating some of the old large-caliber black powder rounds; yet even though the .600 Nitro Express can only manage a muzzle velocity of 1,950 feet per second, it would still be allowed in among the heavies because its *eighth of a pound* of lead-and-steel bullet is perfectly lethal on anything that walks, even at that "pokey" speed), and *my* added stricture would be that no caliber below .24 be used, as it has no place in the hunting of African big game, except maybe royal antelope.

The light calibers have always been considered the choice for use on the so-called thin-skinned game of Africa, such as gazelles and lesser antelopes—all the deer-size or smaller animals. In fact, any of the rounds suitable for whitetails or mule deer would be a good pick for these animals. The .30-'06, the .270 W.C.F., or even the .257 Roberts is most acceptable for this type of game. An advantage of the light calibers, not often mentioned, I believe, is that the rifle usually does not weigh a great deal; and when out for a stroll in search of game, the hunter is more likely to be carrying it himself, rather than letting his gun bearer do so, as he might be inclined to do with a much heavier gun, and so is at all times armed. Because no one ever knows what may be lying up behind the next termite hill during a stroll through Africa—this uncertainty one of the continent's more fatal attractions—being armed is a state one should consistently aspire to.

I *have* heard of the lights being used on larger game with some success. A young woman I know flipped a six-hundred-pound greater kudu bull onto its back, stone dead, with a single shot to the chest from her .243; the legendary elephant hunter W. D. M. "Karamojo" Bell did kill hundreds of giant tuskers with a relatively minuscule 173-grain full-metal-jacket "solid" from his 7 × 57 (Bell was, though, an expert in elephant anatomy and could locate the vital spots with surgical precision, and it is also believed that he wounded and lost far more bulls than he was willing to let on to), and the late hunting writer John Jobson proved the worthiness of his .270 in Zambia two decades ago (but, then, few hunters shot quite like Jobson), as did O'Connor on his numerous safaris. These remain, though, borderline rounds at best for the heavier game of Africa, lacking that extra margin of power the mediums possess. I once witnessed one of that "glandular" class of sports tumble a Lelwel hartebeest with a single .270 shot placed high in the withers, only to see the animal, while this shooter dawdled over putting in another round, spring to its feet and stagger off into the trees. Had it been a medium bullet, I believe that animal would not have gotten up, at least not for several minutes.

On the cusp between the lights and the mediums come the .270, 7 mm, and .300 Magnum cartridges. In this category the .300 can normally be loaded with a bullet up to 220 grains—less than the 250-grain minimum for a true medium, although there are custom-made 250-grain .30-caliber bullets available for hand loaders. Nonetheless, when the .300 Weatherby Magnum, for example, is loaded with a 180-grain partition bullet in factory ammunition it delivers a factory-listed 4,210 foot-pounds of muzzle energy, which compares favorably with the 4,470 foot-pounds of energy a 300-grain bullet produces at the muzzle of a .375 H&H Magnum (based on the ballistics information contained in the forty-fifth edition of the *Lyman Reloading Handbook*), though the .30-caliber bullet does lack the heavier one's momentum. These calibers should, though, stop game. Sometimes decidedly so.

Hunter and sable antelope. (*Photo: Daniel Hernandez*)

I once saw a hunter rake a good roan antelope bull through both shoulders at nearly two hundred fifty yards with a 160-grain partition bullet out of a 7 mm Remington Magnum, and the seven-hundred-pound animal clattered off a mere twenty yards before collapsing with a shudder. My father's old friend, Roy, has in years past used a .300 Weatherby Magnum to take everything from leopard to kudu to sable to eland to Cape buffalo to *elephant* with little problem—though he had to place his shots always very carefully—and on my last trip to Africa I found that my .270 Weatherby Magnum shot fine on many larger animals. While I would not recommend, though, that most hunters use any of these, let us call them "welterweight," calibers for either elephant or buffalo or white rhino (the black rhino being now too endangered by commercial poaching to be hunted)—some African nations even have laws designating certain calibers, usually .375 H&H and above, as a minimum for use on "dangerous game"—or even eland, I think that for any animal up to the five- or six-hundred-pound class they are far from a bad choice. A concern one might have about their extremely fleet bullets, though, is the possibility that in brush or heavy grass they could get tipped aside or broken up before hitting the target, although not even the heaviest of bullets will shoot well through brush.

The true medium calibers include the .338 Winchester, .340

Weatherby, and .375 H&H Magnums. No hunter traveling to Africa could go far astray packing one of these as his one and only gun. On one of my African safaris (that sounds far more insouciant than it actually is—I have been to Africa only three times, or, rather, only had the great good fortune to be there three times, although for a total of over seventy days of hunting and in some rather interesting places) we would be on foot and so I took only one rifle, a .375 H&H Magnum, and killed six head of game with it, going from an exceptionally long-horned central African giant eland, the size of a Brahman bull, to what was apparently an even *more* exceptionally, for its species, long-horned western bush duiker, who was every bit as large as a dog someone would name Skippy, whom I killed in order to have something to eat. Altogether the .375 H&H caliber has taken a score of head of African game for me with absolutely no complaints on my part whatsoever.

The .375 is now over seventy years old, having been introduced by the English gun makers Holland & Holland back at the zenith of the Empire in 1911. Whether it would be accurate to say that the .375 has killed more large African game in that span than any other single caliber would be hard to know, but it certainly does *seem* that way. The other mediums, of course, also work very well for the heavier nondangerous game; but the one advantage the .375 seems to have over the .338 or .340 is that it will fire a heavier bullet than they. For African game especially, I am of the belief that the heavier the bullet, within reason, the better. Extremely long range is not a major factor in African shooting, and the .375 shoots quite flat well out to the three-hundred-yard range we always want to try to stalk within, so being able to hit something as hard as I can seems the most sensible course to me. In Africa it is the power to *stop,* not simply to kill, that should be most highly prized in any firearm. The game there is *that* tough.

The .378 Weatherby Magnum hits hardest of all the mediums, so hard that it marks a clear demarcation between the mediums and the heavies, only its inability to fire a 400-grain bullet keeping it from the ranks of the heavies. It does have thoroughly devastating ballistics, although a friend of mine has told me, on the basis of personal experience, that shooting one does tend to "take you out from under your hat," recoilwise. I cannot say, never having had the pleasure of touching one off; but if you want the ultimate medium, this is without a doubt it.

The heavies commence with the various .400 calibers (the .404

Jeffery, .411 K.D.F., and the .416s Rigby, Taylor, and Hoffman, and the like) that can throw a 400-plus-grain bullet, and advance upward through the .458 Winchester Magnum, the old and seemingly obsolete Nitro Express calibers (.450, .470, .475, .476, .500, .577, .600, and so on, though there is these days—particularly in the case of the .470— a resurgence in popularity of the double rifles, perhaps out of a certain nostalgia, and a renaissance of interest in these cartridges), and the relatively recent, though hardly brand-new, and most powerful addition, the .460 Weatherby Magnum. To what conceivable ends does one put such awesome weapons as these?

To quote from the late, never less than colorful Robert Ruark (an Africa-residing friend of mine, and a collector of Africana, claims to have in his personal possession an unretouched photograph of the magnificently gin-soaked novelist tumbling, in full safari kit, from the seat of a Land Rover, a smile of inalterable southern charm and hospitality on his face as he is about to thud into the red dirt of the Tanganyikan plains) on the raison d'être for the existence of such things as heavy rifles: "For my personal purposes," he wrote, "on anything that can kick me, bite me, claw me, or trample me, I use a Westley-Richards .470 double-barreled express rifle. I notice that most pros use too much gun, and what's good enough for pros is good enough for amateurs." The heavies are, then, not meant for long-range shooting or feats of delicate marksmanship like shooting a cigarette out of the lips of a sideshow performer—on a charging animal, the double rifles are probably not even consciously *aimed,* but pointed like the fowling pieces they were modeled on. The heavies are for stopping—and I emphasize, *stopping,* as in, ideally, "in its tracks"— the largest and the most dangerous of Africa's game.

John Taylor, author of the exhaustive *African Rifles and Cartridges,* devised a secret mathematical formula for describing the "Knockout Value" of heavy calibers. *His* point was that the *entire* point of heavies was not simply to put a bullet into a vital spot— almost any of the calibers described in this chapter could penetrate deeply enough into even the most grandiose of mammals to accomplish that, à la Bell—but to "shock" the animal utterly senseless, particularly the elephant, hitting him so soundly that he is literally made to sit down or even be knocked out cold. Taylor's value for the .600, for instance, translates into an elephant rendered unconscious for thirty minutes or more from a blow to the head, even if the often-hard-to-hit brain is missed. This gives the hunter the welcome opportunity to shoot again, perhaps several times if called for, without having to fret

about being stepped upon. I have fired only three of the heavies myself, that .416, the .458, and the .460, all of them bolt-actions, and
none of them while in Africa, and have killed game only with the .458
(I used one once to kill a blacktail buck for reasons far too convo-
luted to unravel here). And hey, call me whacko, but I actually *enjoy*
shooting these honkers! They recoil, no denying that, but not nearly
so intolerably as their grisly reputations would have one believe; ol'
Elmer would probably have considered them mild. With open sights
and off hand, the .460 Weatherby Magnum, with its, again, factory-
listed 8,095 foot-pounds of muzzle energy for the flat-shooting 500-
grain full-metal-jacket solid, is a very accurate shooter, and not ca-
lamitously uncomfortable. One trick for shooting it with reduced anguish
is for the shooter to tuck his right elbow *down* near his body to
bunch up the shoulder muscle behind the butt to increase the
cushioning.

The only complaint I have heard from some professionals about
the .460 is that it may be too fast for its own good—actually shooting
through game at times and thereby reducing the knockout potential—
and I have also heard suggestions that if the rifle's barrel were short-
ened, an effective recoil reducer added, and the cartridges loaded with
600-grain bullets (or, as some gunsmiths are now doing, building it
as a double rifle), it would be the hands-down choice of *all* PHs, bar
none. Most of those who have shot wounded, infuriated, dangerous
game with it, though, are unstinting in their praise for the cheerful
way the bullet can solve that minor workday difficulty.

With the utmost of pragmatism, then, what guns would *I* take
on a several weeks', mixed-bag African safari?

If I could take only one, then it would be, without question, my
.375 H&H Magnum. Two guns? Now the question is changed. Under
those circumstances I believe I would set aside the .375 in favor of
one of the bolt-action .400s that I have shot, probably the .416 Rigby,
to provide me with a 400-grain bullet for the heavy dangerous game,
and add to that a .338 or .340 for all the other game from antelope
up to eland, and lion and leopard as well. Three guns would allow
me to carry a light for the light game; while if my resources were
unlimited, and I could afford both to own, and to pay the overweight-
baggage charges for, a Nitro Express double, I would tote it, being
delighted to do so mainly for the sheer joy it would bring me to be
able to use it, even if only once.

With regard to the heavies, most professionals prefer the doubles because their side-lock and box-lock actions provide them with the most reliable sequence of two shots (*BOOM, BOOM*) they can conceivably hope for. In bolt-action rifles, heavies or otherwise, the Mauser-type action is held in far greater esteem than more "modern" design innovations, primarily because of the bolt's extraction system: a clawlike attachment on the inletted bolt face that takes positive hold of the cartridge from the very moment the bolt is worked forward— whereas on most newer bolt actions all you get is a sort of, in the words of a PH to me, "rinky-dink little spring" extractor that only sees fit to take hold of the cartridge when the round is fully chambered and the bolt closed. With the Mauser-type extractor, a cartridge could be slipped halfway into the chamber, then, merely by working the bolt back, be pulled free and cleared. This could not be done with a cheaper, spring-type extractor, the cartridge having to be completely chambered before the bolt could manage to extract it—and there is with this system the increased likelihood of jamming up the whole works, a not overly pleasant prospect when something meaning to do you serious hurt is coming your way, rapidly.

An added note should be made on the exercise of care in the selection of bullets. For African game I believe that good penetration is to be more highly valued than excessive expansion, and that a hunter most certainly wants a bullet that holds together. When a hunter starts getting up into the mediums, his bullet is already cutting such a wide wound channel that solids will perform nearly as well as soft-nosed bullets. Some of the finest bullets for African game, though, are H-type partition bullets with an expanding front half and a solid back half that drives the projectile forward after it has entered the animal.

No matter what rifle or bullet a hunter chooses, of course, it will make no difference if he cannot hit what he is aiming at. So, again, he must learn to take a rest before firing, whenever possible, or use a shooting stick, and above all practice, practice, practice with his rifle, his hunter's weapon, before ever setting foot in the hunter's home of Africa.

Certain guns seem to fit better with certain game animals of Africa, and it might be good to look at some examples.

Elephant. The ultimate African animal. Finding good ivory— these days fifty pounds per tusk and above—is always a difficult undertaking, involving miles and miles of walking following the spoor of a big bull. The elephant is what the heavies, .460, .470, and above, were made for, but a .416 with solids, and a professional hunter backing up a hunter with one of the larger heavies, are quite adequate for the surgical brainshot, and even a .375 is not absolutely out of the question under those same circumstances.

Lion. Here the size of the animal is gauged by a thick full mane as much as body size. A .300 Magnum, Winchester or Weatherby, would, I think, be approaching the marginal, but a .338 or .340, or the ubiquitous .375, would be "good medicine," while a .458 with soft-nosed bullets, if a hunter does not mind recoil, will generally always settle the question most satisfactorily. Using the gun he shoots best is always the best advice that can be offered any hunter.

Cape buffalo. A good bull—one with a forty- to forty-five-inch, or greater, spread across his horns—is not nearly so hard to kill as his publicity releases would have it, though if he is wounded and still on his feet, all bets are off! The Cape buffalo lives in .375 territory, at a minimum. A 400-grainer out of one of the .400 calibers would be better—some even viewing *that* as the minimum for buffs—and if one can shoot something even heavier, there would be no harm in it. Whatever a hunter shoots, he should always aim for bone on a buffalo, preferably the shoulder, to break the bull down, the hunter ready to shoot again, even after the buffalo has collapsed.

Eland. The elk of Africa. Yet for so huge an antelope—the largest in Africa, larger than the buffs—the eland does not take a lot of killing. Still, a .375 works well for this beautiful, elusive, and delicious— arguably the finest meat animal to be found on the continent—creature.

Kudu, sable, roan, waterbuck, and oryx. These medium to heavy antelope will usually succumb to the attentions of a hard hit from the welterweights or mediums, but stretch the capabilities of the lights.

Impala. Everyone safariing in sub-Saharan Africa should hunt one of these graceful, most African of antelope. A hunter should be prepared for a longish shot in open country. This, and the like-size gazelle, are the reasons for taking a flat-shooting light caliber. A pronghorn gun would be most apt.

Zebra. A disconcertingly hardy beast. A PH once told me that he spends more time on safaris chasing poorly shot zebra than any other animal. Perhaps it is all the stripes. A .375 with good soft-nosed bullets is about right, in my opinion, but as with all game, that *first* shot must be the one that counts.

African elephant tusker. (*Photo: Daniel Hernandez*)

The Cape buffalo is one of Africa's most lethal animals. (*Photo: Daniel Hernandez*)

Leopard. It is that accurate first shot, and not overwhelming knockout power, that is needed to bring down this cat. Anything from the lights upward is fine, as long as a hunter is confident that he can hit a *killing* spot the first time he pulls the trigger. A wounded leopard in the bush is every PH's worst nightmare.

What does it feel like, though, when a hunter steps away from the guns and is *there,* not knowing whether there is a leopard in the bush or not, knowing only that he is finally in Africa and that the track at his feet is no longer that of rabbit, and that he is no longer a boy? To know, I hunkered down and touched my finger to the pugmark in the red volcanic dust. First, I shivered; then I smiled.

We found the carcass of the impala doe hanging on the limb of a tall tree near the Njugini River the next afternoon. I had killed a buck that morning, and now we hung his forequarters from the limb as well. We built the blind twenty yards from the tree, weaving it out of cut brush—a screen with gunports. That night in camp we ate peppery slices of impala roast.

Before dawn, Jbwani came to my tent with the tea tray. Ten minutes later I was eating breakfast with the broken-nosed PH under the propane lamp in the large dining tent. Thirty minutes after that, the night bleeding from the sky, the PH, his gun bearer Mmaku, and I dropped from the Land Cruiser and crawled to the blind as the Toyota drove off. The Masai herded cattle and goats in this Rombo country of southern Kenya, where Kilimanjaro bulked on the horizon; and as we sat motionlessly in the blind, we could do nothing about the ticks affixing themselves to our skin. The PH had his .375, I had my .300, and Mmaku had the PH's .500 Nitro Express double, loaded with 578-grain soft-nosed bullets. No one, ultimately, can define what is "too much gun" for a leopard.

When, in first light only a few minutes later, a leopard walked around the edge of the blind and stood two dozen feet from us, staring off in the direction in which the Land Cruiser had driven, I was the first to see it. I moved only my eyes, but was able to see with total clarity the black rosettes branded into the golden hide, and how the lithe, feminine line of the cat's body was broken by loose white fur hanging along its belly. The gunbearer beside me did not see the leopard until I touched his leg. He whispered quickly across me to the PH "*Chui!*"

"Do not move," the PH ordered without turning his head to

look at the cat, even his whisper raspy. Move? I would go on sitting here, watching this first leopard I had ever seen in the wild—who, because we were motionless, could not see us—until the ticks made a dry husk of me. Then the leopard snapped its head toward us— perhaps having detected the flick of an eyelash—and I was staring into bottomless panther eyes. The cat was frozen there for a full minute or more before crouching and spinning and slipping off through the tall dry grass.

We saw the leopard an hour later, stretched out on the limb bearing the impala.

"Female," the PH said after studying her for a few minutes through his binoculars. "And she has a cub with her." I reset the .300's safety. For the next two hours, until the Land Cruiser came back for us, we watched the she-leopard in the tree, her big cub curled near her in the crotch of the limb.

The next blind was a cavity cut into heavy brush. It was so big inside that four of us could stand up and walk around, like aimless guests at a dull cocktail party. We hung the hindquarters of a kongoni in a small acacia in front of the blind. By the next day the leopard who had left the pugmark was feeding on it. We were in the blind in the late afternoon.

The trouble with leopard blinds is that when they are properly constructed, not only can leopards not see you, none of the *rest* of Africa's dangerous game can either. This has led to everything from lions to elephants to stumble onto hunters who were minding their own business in leopard blinds. The PH, back when black rhinos were numerous enough to be nearly a nuisance, had once had to kill one in full charge at the entrance to a leopard blind, while the gun bearers had forcibly to detain the hunting client who was trying to bolt from cover. This afternoon, I sat in the blind until it was too dark to shoot, careful all the while not to move even my eyes too much, wondering what might stumble onto us.

As we waited in the darkness for the Land Cruiser, I heard the leopard come to feed on the bait. I could hear meat being torn from bone, then bone being cracked by a leopard's teeth. The strangest, and happiest, feeling of my life passed up the column of my spine, as if I had heard this sound somewhere before along the way, maybe four hundred generations ago. Then the Land Cruiser's lights began to play through the grass and trees and the leopard went and in a little while we were riding back into camp.

That night, the PH hunched forward in his camp chair, a drink of rum in his hand, and stared into the fire, "dreaming" it, as the Masai say.

"We could have had a light out there tonight," he said to the flames. "A light doesn't matter to a leopard. He'd have just gone on feeding. Lots of other professionals I know use lights," he added, leaning back in his chair, a decision reached. He looked at me and said, "I hope I never become that kind of hunter."

We covered the last half-mile to the blind on foot the next morning—still night under the bright equatorial moon, the sky's bears replaced by the Southern Cross. Africa at night is true Africa; Africa at night, comforting campfires and safari cars left far behind, is truest. What am I going to step on out here in this timeless dark, I asked myself. More to the point, What is going to step on me? I could feel my soul crouching, ready to spring out of me with each step I took into Africa at night.

Then we entered some brush and I found myself inside the large blind again. In the darkness I felt for the rest for my .300 and set the rifle in place. I knelt on one knee and waited. I could not see, so much as feel the dawn spreading outside. The feeding sound came again.

"The leopard's here," the PH whispered. I took up my rifle slowly, like raising a shotgun on a turkey. The big male leopard, his head short and square, his thick muscles sharply defined, was standing on his hind legs in the tree, his front claws in the kongoni and his jaws tearing at the flesh. He chewed, then took his claws out of the carcass and dropped back down onto the limb. He stood with his head pointed down and tail curled up. I laid the cross hairs on the center of his left shoulder, and gave the trigger a straight-back squeeze to break the sear, a dull yellow flame licking toward him.

When we return to camp later this morning the Turkana tracker will sing a warrior's chant that will lift the hairs off the back of my neck, Jbwani will come running to meet me with a glass of whiskey—neat—in his hand, the skinners will painstakingly scrape all the clean white fat from the cat's hide and body so they can take it home to rub on their children's throats in the rainy season when they come down with the croup, and there will be pale pink leopard meat to cook and eat. Now, though, as we drag the cat's heavy body out of the deep grass at the base of the acacia and the PH and the gun bearers clap me on the back, I just want to look at this leopard, to run my hand over his warm fur, to spread open his sharp claws, to see that

The way of the hunter led to the leopard. (*Photo © by George H. Harrison*)

my single bullet passed completely through him, and to touch my finger to the center of one of the black rosettes on the golden hide of the only leopard I will kill along this way of the hunter.

The PH, with only a few more years to his life than I, but an old hunter—older than I—smiles at me and says, "Good shot, lad!" And it all comes back to me.

CONCLUSION

The way of the hunter does not end there, of course, not in Africa, not anywhere. The way just goes on.

When I set out to write a book about "what I am," about a feral enthusiasm I shared with any number of others, it was in hot dry days when chukar flushed wild from sagebrush. Now, a season and a half later, the days are January's, and I have found a northern field where geese, cupped and set, come skidding out of the overcast sky and drop into the dekes as I rise up out of the frozen pit. I fire the heavy 10-gauge, and the geese disappear under the snow when they fall; and when I run out and reach down to retrieve them there is the aching cold, then the secret warmth.

In the extended turn of this hunting season there have been wild boars for me, and whitetails and mule deer, caribou and mountain sheep, ducks and quail and pheasants and rabbits and bears, *and* elk and wild turkeys who got clean away, coyote runs that ended with the long dogs getting nothing more than a good workout, sharptails who went unseen, cougars I never saw who saw me, and forest grouse I just stood and stared at. This book went along with me through all that season, and the spirit of all that season has found its way into these pages.

Why does someone still measure his life in seasons of predation? In a time when hunters' numbers grow smaller in a world where the wild continues to be pared away and where every day more steps are taken to bring it under some final, "rational" subjugation? Why doesn't someone know any better than to do this?

Although my father would hunt doves, and showed me my first glimpses of hunting, he was at best a haphazard sportsman; and out of the last generations of my people that I know of, I am the first to hunt with any sort of reckless fervor. So it was not family tradition that made me a hunter. What could it be?

Maybe it is that million years sticking up through the last ten thousand, the way an arrowhead of knapped flint will float to the surface of a plowed field. Maybe it is the only way I have to make sense of the world because my intelligence—such as it is—is, like all humans', a hunting intelligence. Maybe it is because my hands and legs and eyes and teeth and nerves and heart are, and could only be, a hunter's hands and legs, and so on, as a leopard's can only be a leopard's, and not a sparrow's. Maybe it is that I, unlike others who do not know what it is they love in this world, know that besides family and friends and words, what I love in this world is wild animals and wild lands and the wild life of hunting. Maybe I simply *refuse* to know any better.

Whatever the case may be, when next season comes, as long as *I* am able, and something wild can be found to give chase to, I will find my way to the hunting grounds once again. I will do that because that is my passion. And maybe that, and not our hunter's shape and mind, is the single greatest gift our ancient hunting fathers bequeathed us: the ability to live life the only fit way for it to be lived, with true passion.

The way of the hunter is, then, the way finally of passion, a passion that *is* every bit as old as those hills it carries us through and into our home in the game fields filled with real life.

September 1986
January 1988
While hunting.

BIBLIOGRAPHY

AUDUBON, JOHN JAMES. *The Bird Biographies of John James Audubon*. New York: The Macmillan Company, 1957.

BACK, JOE. *Horses, Hitches and Rocky Trails*. Denver, Colo.: Sage Books, 1959.

BARSNESS, JOHN. *Hunting the Great Plains*. Missoula, Mont.: Mountain Press, 1979.

BEAUMONT, RICHARD. *Purdey's: The Guns and the Family*. London: David & Charles, 1984.

BODDINGTON, CRAIG. *Campfires and Gametrails*. Piscataway, N.J.: Winchester Press, 1985.

———. *From Mt. Kenya to the Cape*. Long Beach, Calif.: Safari Press, 1987.

BODIO, STEPHEN. *Good Guns*. New York: Nick Lyons Books, 1986.

———. *A Rage for Falcons*. New York: Nick Lyons Books, 1984.

BRANCH, E. DOUGLAS. *The Hunting of the Buffalo*. Lincoln, Neb.: University of Nebraska Press, 1962.

BRYANT, EDWARD R., ed. *Rowland Ward's African Records of Big Game*. 19th ed. San Antonio, Tex.: Rowland Ward Publications, 1984.

BURCHER, RUTH, ed. *The Book of Hunting*. New York & London: Paddington Press Ltd., 1977.

BURKE, EDMUND. *The History of Archery*. New York: William Morrow, 1957.

BURRARD, MAJOR SIR GERALD. *The Modern Shotgun*. New York: A. S. Barnes, 1961.

———. *Notes on Sporting Rifles*. London: Edward Arnold & Co., 1953.

BURROUGHS, RAYMOND DARWIN. *The Natural History of the Lewis & Clark Expedition*. East Lansing: The Michigan State University Press, 1961.

CALEF, GEORGE. *Caribou and the Barren Lands*. Toronto: Firefly Books Limited, 1981.

CAPSTICK, PETER HATHAWAY. *Death in the Long Grass*. New York: St. Martin's Press, 1977.

———. *Safari*. New York: St. Martin's Press, 1984.

CARMICHEL, JIM. *Jim Carmichel's Book of the Rifle*. New York: Outdoor Life Books, 1985.

CHURCHILL, ROBERT. *Churchill's Shotgun Book*. New York: Alfred A. Knopf, 1955.

———. Hastings, Macdonald, ed. *Game Shooting*. Harrisburg, Pa.: Stackpole Books, 1967.

CLARK, JAMES L. *The Great Arc of the Wild Sheep*. Norman, Okla.: University of Oklahoma Press, 1964.

COON, CARLETON S. *The Hunting Peoples*. Boston: Little, Brown, 1971.

COX, HARDING, and LASCELLES, THE HONORABLE GERALD. *Coursing and Falconry*. London: Longmans, Green, and Co., 1899.

CRAMOND, MIKE. *Of Bears and Man*. Norman, Okla.: University of Oklahoma Press, 1986.

CROCKETT, DAVID. *Davy Crockett's Own Story*. New York: Citadel Press, 1955.

DARY, DAVID A. *The Buffalo Book*. New York: Avon Books, 1975.

DORST, JEAN, and DANDELOT, PIERRE. *A Field Guide to the Larger Mammals of Africa*. London: Collins, 1970.

EAST, BEN. *Bears*. New York: Outdoor Life, Crown Publishers, 1977.

FAULKNER, WILLIAM. *Big Woods*. New York: Random House, 1955.

FORBUSH, EDWARD HOWE. *A Natural History of the American Birds of Eastern and Central North America*. New York: Bramhall House, 1959.

GEIST, VALERIUS. *Mountain Sheep: A Study in Behavior and Evolution*. Chicago and London: The University of Chicago Press, 1971.

GREENER, W. W. *The Gun and Its Development*. 9th ed. London: Arms & Armour Press, 1972.

GRESHAM, GRITS. *The Complete Wildfowler*. New York: Winchester Press, 1973.

HACKER, RICK. *The Muzzleloading Hunter*. Tulsa, Okla.: Winchester Press, 1981.

HALLS, LOWELL K., ed., *White-tailed Deer: Ecology & Management*. Harrisburg, Pa.: Stackpole Books, 1984.

HARBOUR, DAVE. *Hunting the American Wild Turkey*. Harrisburg, Pa.: Stackpole Books, 1975.

HAYNES, BESSIE DOAK, and HAYNES, EDGAR. *The Grizzly Bear: Portraits from Life*. Norman, Okla.: University of Oklahoma Press, 1966.

HELD, ROBERT. *The Age of Firearms*. New York: Harper & Brothers, 1957.

HERRERO, STEPHEN. *Bear Attacks: Their Causes and Avoidance.* New York: Nick Lyons Books, 1985.

KEITH, ELMER. *Big Game Rifles and Cartridges.* Onslow County, N.C.: Small-Arms Technical Publishing Company, 1936.

KELSALL, JOHN P. *The Migratory Barren-ground Caribou of Canada.* Ottawa: Queen's Printer, 1968.

KINKEAD, EUGENE. *Squirrel Book.* New York: E. P. Dutton, 1980.

KURTÉN, BJÖRN. *The Age of Mammals.* New York: Columbia University Press, 1971.

———, and Anderson, Elaine. *Pleistocene Mammals of North America.* New York: Columbia University Press, 1980.

LAUBACH, DON, and HENCKEL, MARK. *Elk Talk.* Gardiner, Mont.: Don Laubach, 1987.

LEOPOLD, ALDO. *A Sand Country Almanac.* New York: Ballantine Books, 1984.

MCDANIEL, JOHN M. *The Turkey Hunters Book.* Clinton, N.J.: The Amwell Press, 1980.

MADSON, JOHN. *The Mourning Dove.* East Alton, Ill.: Winchester Press, 1978.

MATTHIESSEN, PETER. *Wildlife in America.* New York: Penguin Books, 1977.

MELLON, JAMES. *African Hunter.* New York: Harcourt Brace Jovanovich, 1975.

MERRILL, SAMUEL. *The Moose Book.* New York: E. P. Dutton & Company, 1920.

MOCHI, UGO, and CARTER, T. DONALD. *Hoofed Mammals of the World.* New York: Charles Scribner's Sons, 1953.

MONSON, GALE, and SUMNER, LOWELL, eds. *The Desert Bighorn.* Tucson: The University of Arizona Press, 1980.

NESBITT, W. H., and WRIGHT, PHILIP L., eds. *Records of North American Big Game, Eighth Edition.* Alexandria, Va.: The Boone and Crockett Club, 1981.

The New Hunter's Encyclopedia. Harrisburg, Pa.: The Stackpole Company, 1966.

O'CONNOR, JACK. *Complete Book of Rifles and Shotguns.* New York: Outdoor Life–Harper & Brothers, 1961.

———. *Game in the Desert Revisited.* Clinton, N.J.: The Amwell Press, 1977.

———. *Hunting in the Rockies.* New York: Alfred A. Knopf, 1947.

ORMOND, CLYDE. *Bear!* Harrisburg, Pa.: The Stackpole Company, 1961.

ORTEGA Y GASSET, JOSÉ. *Meditations on Hunting.* New York: Charles Scribner's Sons, 1985.

———. *The Revolt of the Masses.* New York: W. W. Norton & Company, 1960.

PLUMMER, DAVID BRIAN. *Tales of a Rat-Hunting Man.* Ipswich, Eng.: The Boydell Press, 1978.

ROOSEVELT, THEODORE. *African Game Trails*. New York: Charles Scribner's Sons, 1910.

————. *Outdoor Pastimes of an American Hunter*. New York: Charles Scribner's sons, 1905.

————. *The Wilderness Hunter: An Account of the Big Game of the United States and Its Chase with Horse, Hound, and Rifle*. New York: G. P. Putnam's Sons, 1893.

RUARK, ROBERT. *Horn of the Hunter*. New York: Doubleday & Co., 1953.

————. *Use Enough Gun*. New York: New American Library, 1966.

RUE, LEONARD LEE, III. *The Deer of North America*. New York: Crown Publishers, 1978.

————. *Sportsman's Guide to Game Animals*. New York: Outdoor Life Books, Harper & Row, 1968.

RUFFER, JONATHAN GARNIER. *The Big Shots*. New York: Arco Publishing Co., 1977.

RUSSELL, FRANKLIN. *The Hunting Animal*. New York: Harper & Row, 1983.

SALMON, M. H. *Gazehounds & Coursing*. Saint Cloud, Minn.: North Star Press, 1977.

SCHORGER, A. W. *The Wild Turkey: Its History and Domestication*. Norman, Okla.: University of Oklahoma Press, 1966.

SHEPARD, PAUL. *The Tender Carnivore and the Sacred Game*. New York: Charles Scribner's Sons, 1973.

————, and Sanders, Barry. *The Sacred Paw: The Bear in Nature, Myth, and Literature*. New York: The Viking Press, 1985.

SMITH, RICHARD P. *The Book of the Black Bear*. Piscataway, N.J.: Winchester Press, 1985.

SNYDER, GARY. *Turtle Island*. New York: New Directions Publishing Corporation, 1974. (To be especially noted is the poem " 'One Should Not Talk to a Skilled Hunter About What Is Forbidden by the Buddha'— Hsiang-Yen," for its title, if nothing else.)

STORER, TRACY I., and TEVIS, LLOYD P., JR. *California Grizzly*. Lincoln, Neb.: University of Nebraska Press, 1978.

TAYLOR, JOHN. *African Rifles & Cartridges*. Highland Park, N.J.: The Gun Room Press, 1977.

THOMAS, JACK WARD, and TOWEILL, DALE E., eds. *Elk of North America: Ecology and Management*. Harrisburg, Pa.: Stackpole Books, 1982.

TREFETHEN, JAMES B. *An American Crusade for Wildlife*. New York: Winchester Press, 1975.

WHISKER, JAMES B. *The Right to Hunt*. Croton-on-Hudson, N.Y.: North River Press, 1981.

WHITEHEAD, G. KENNETH. *The Deer of the World*. New York: The Viking Press, 1972.

ZUMBO, JIM. *Hunting America's Mule Deer*. Tulsa, Okla.: Winchester Press, 1981.

INDEX

Page references for illustrations are in underlined italic figures.

Accipiters, 182–83
Adams, James Capen (Grizzly Adams),
   123–25
Adams, Nick, 14
Addax, 63
Aesop, 122
Afghans (dogs), 183
Africa, 5, 150, 179, 186, 187–204
   big game, 57n
   guns for hunting in, 188–200
African Rifles and Cartridges (Taylor),
   195–96
Agriculture, 11, 152, 179
   damage done by, 24, 35–36
Agriocharis ocellata
   see Ocellated turkey (*Agriocharis ocel-*
   lata)
Aiming, 12, _56_, 57, 95

wild boars, 68–70
wild turkeys, 168–69
Alaska, 143, 152
Alces alces
   see Moose (*Alces alces*)
American bighorn sheep, 172
American buffalo (*Bison bison*), 72, 151–
   52, _151_, 193
Animal(s)
   confirming death of, 94–95, 126–27,
      134n, 141–42, 144, 187–88
   innate superiority of, 179
   see also Wounded animals
Antelope
   African, 198
   lesser, 191
   see also Pronghorn antelope (*Antilo-*
   capra americana)

Antelope jackrabbit (*Lepus alleni*), *9,*
10
Antilocapra americana
see Pronghorn antelope (*Antilocapra
americana*)
Antilocapridae, 72
Antlers
caribou, 142–43
coronet (burr), 72, 133
deer, 4, 71–73, 81, 83–87
dichotomous, 85, 87
elk, 132, 133–34
gauging size of, 86–87, 133–34
moose, 139, *140*
mule deer, *86*
pedicels, 72, 73, 92
Aoudad, 63, 65
Arctic, 179
Arctic hare, 9
Argalis, 172
Arrows, 54, 55
Art, 84
Artiodactyla, 65, 146, 147, 151
Asiatic bighorns, 172
Audubon, John James, 163, 165
Aztecs, 163

Bacon, Roger
*Epistola de Secretis Operibus Artis et
Naturae,* 39
Baiting
bears, 117–19, 125
Band-tailed pigeon (*Columba fasciata*),
22, 24–26, *25, 26*
Barasingha deer (*Cervus duvaucelli*), 64
Barnum, Phineas Taylor, 125
Battue, defined, 44
BB shot, 32, 168
Beagles, 13
Bear, The (Faulkner), 116
Bear hunting
methods in, 117–21, 125
Bears, 4, 114–28, *117, 124,* 173, 205
danger from, 127
dogs in hunting, 15
estimating size of, 120–21, 123, 125–
26
habitat, 115–16

intelligence, 117
name, 115
species of, 115, 116
Bell, W. D. M. "Karamojo," 192
Beowulf, 122
Beringia, 151
Bestiary, 138–51, 153
Big game, 62, 63
African, *57n,* 187–204
North American, 5, 59–60, 71
Big-game hunting, 169
dogs in, 15, 119–20, 125
guns for, 4, 54, 56–60, 190, *191,* 192–
96
initiation to, 63–64
Bighorn sheep, 72, 172–74, *173*
Binoculars, 76, 77, *78, 122,* 126, *131*
Bird hunting, 39–40
changes in, 40–42
dogs in, 15, 182
Birds, 12
and elk, 136
fascination with, 22–23
see also Upland birds; Waterfowl
Birds of prey, 181–83, *182*
Bison
see American buffalo (*Bison bison*)
Black bear (*Euarctos americanus*), 4, 115,
116–21
judging size of, *117,* 118
print of front paw, *119*
squaring hide of, *128*
Black buck, 63
Black rhino, 193, 201
Blacktail buck, 196
Blacktail jackrabbit (*Lepus californicus*),
10
Black-tailed deer, 73–76
antlers, 87
habitat, 76
Blinds, 27, 28, 29, 30, 165, 166
leopard, 200, 201, 202
Blockers, 154–56
Blome, Richard, *Gentleman's Recreation,
The,* 41
Bloodshotting, 55–56
Bloodthirstiness, 3, 23
Blue grouse, 157, 158

"Blue hide," 93
Blue quail, 156
Bobwhite, 156
Bodio, Stephen, 21*n*, 182
Boone, Daniel, 14
Borzois, 183
Boss, Thomas, 43
Bovidae, 72
Bow and arrow hunting, 38, 39
  black bear, 119
  cougar, 144
  elk, 134*n*
  jackrabbit, 12
Breechloaders, 39
British Columbia, 24, 143
Brown-grizzly bear (*Ursus arctos* and
  Ursus arctos horribilis), 115, 116, 117,
  121–27, *122*
  silver-tipped, *124*
Browning, John M., 43
Buckshot, 10*n*
Buffalo
  see American buffalo (*Bison bison*);
  Cape buffalo
Bugling (elk), *131*, 134–35, *135*
Bull elk, 135–36, *136*
  trophy, 136–37
Bull moose, *140*
Bullets, 98, 190, 192, 193
  drop of, 60
  heavy, 191, 194–96
  killing by, 54, 55–56, 126
  light-caliber rifles, 191
  medium, 192–94
  selection of, 197
  soft-nosed, 198, 200
  trajectory, 58–59
  velocity of, 11–12, 55–56
Burrard, Gerald, 59, 60, 147
  Notes on Sporting Rifles, 55
Buteos, 182, 183

Caliber, 13, 40*n*, 53–54, 58, 59, 69
  cougar hunting, 144
  defined, 53*n*
  elk hunting, 134*n*
  heavy, 194–97
  hunting in Africa, 190–200

Nitro Express, 190–91, 195–96
  welterweight, 193, 198
California, 65, 66
  grizzly bears, 123–25
California quail, 157, *157*, 185
Calivers, 39
Calling
  birds, 153, 157
  geese, 31–32, *32*
  moose, 141
  wild turkeys, 165, 166, 167, 169
Camouflage, 21, 29, 166
Camouflage netting, 31
Canada, 152
Canada geese, *32*, 33
Canada moose, 139
Canadian River, 63
Cannons, 39
Canvasbacks, 32
Cape buffalo, 188, 193, *199*
  guns for hunting, 198
Caping, 88–93
  tools for, 88, *90*, 92
Caribou (*Rangifer tarandus*), 72, 73, 125,
  142–43, *142*, 146, 205
Carnivora, 115
Carnivores, 75, 104
Cartridges, 8, 9, 192
  center-fire, 43
Cat squirrel
  see Gray squirrel (*Sciurus carolinensis*)
Cave paintings, 84, 88
Central Flyway, 33
Cervidae, 71, 72, 73, 81
Cervus (genus), 133
  C. canadensis, 133
  C. elaphus, 133
Cervus duvaucelli
  see Barasingha deer (*Cervus duvau-
  celli*)
Chamois, 148
Charles II, king of England, 41
Choke(s), choking, 21, 24, 43
  full, 26, 32
  defined, 21*n*
  modified, 24, 26, 32
  open, 45
  and pattern, 40*n*

Chukar partridge, 1, 5, 159–61, 205
  hunting of, *51*
Civilization
  hunting and, 185–86
Clark, William, 163
Clay birds, 49
Cleaning
  cranes, 35
  doves, 22
  jackrabbits, 12
Coast Ranges, 66, 69
"Coldblood" sight hounds, 184
Colt Woodsman, 8
Columba fasciata
  see Band-tailed pigeon (*Columba fasciata*)
Columbidae, 22, 24
Consciousness
  limitations of, in hunting, 14–15
  wild-animal protein as source of, 94
Conservation
  animals near extinction, 164
  elk, 130
"Continental" style (shooting), 49
Coon, Carleton S., 179
Cooper's hawk, 182
Coronado, Francisco, 115
Cortés, Hernán, 162–63
Cottontail rabbit (*Sylvilagus floridanus*),
  12–13, *13*, 185
Coues, Elliott, 75
Coues' deer, 75, 81–82, 87
Cougar (*Felis concolor*), 5, 143–46, *145*,
  205
Coursing hounds, 183–85, *184*
Cover, 77, 143
Coyote, 205
Coyote dogs, 184–85
Crakys, 39
Crane, 33–35
"Criminal suspicion," 84–85, 104
Critics of hunting, 15
  see also Moral issue
Crockett, Davy, 14, 116
Cromwell, Oliver, 41
Crossbow, 38, 39
Cross-eye dominance, 46, *47*
Cullen, Tom, *182*

Dalli (sheep), 172
Dall's sheep, 172, 174, 176
  ram, *171*
"Damascus" barrels, 43
Death, question of, 4, 61, 85, 96, 97–
  104
Decoys (dekes, blocks), 28–31, *29*, 34,
  153
Deer, 4, 59, 63, 71–82, 153
  as archetype for game animal, 83
  bone, skin, meat, 83–96
  North American species, 73–75
  and turkeys, 163
Deer hunting, 60–61, 63
  weapons for, 53–54
Depth perception, 45, 46
Desert bighorns, *173*, 174
Desert sheep, 172–74
Dog in hunting, 4, 10, 14–16, 105, 108,
  182, 205
  beagle, 13
  black bear hunting, 119–20
  cougar, 144
  coursing hounds, 183–85, *184*
  upland birds, 1–2, 154, 156, 160–61
  waterfowl, 28
  wild turkeys, 165
Double rifle, 195, 196–97
Dove hunting, 18–26, *20*, *25*, *26*, 166
Doves, 3, 18–26, *25*, 27, 28, 45, 50, 154,
  206
Dray, defined, 14
Dressing
  deer, 95–96
Drive(s), drivers, 81, 154–56
Dromomerycines (Miocene semi-deer), 73
Duck hunting, 27–30, *29*, 32, *34*, *35*
  weapons for, 53
Ducks, 3, *34*, *35*, 37, 182, 205
  shot size, 32
Ducks Unlimited, 35
Duiker, 188, 194

Eagles, 182–83
Earplugs, 21
Eastern Mono Indians, 123
Eland, 193, 194
  guns for hunting, 193, 198

Elephants, 188, 190, 192, *199*, 201
  guns for hunting, 41, 193, 197–98
Elk, 4, 56, 58, 59, 73, 129–37, 141, 205
  bull, 136–37, *136*
  habitat, 129–32
  royal, imperial, monarch, 133
  subspecies, 130–32
  trophy, 136–37
Elk bugle, *131*
Elk hunting, 125
  camp, *137*
  packhorses in, *107*
Enjoyment in hunting, 99–100, 101, 103
Epistola de Secretis Operibus Artis et Na-
  turae (Bacon), 39
Equitation lessons, 107–109
Euarctos americanus
  see Black bear (*Euarctos americanus*)
Evolution, 64, 103
Exotica, 62–70
Exotic-game emporiums, 64
Extinction(s)
  turkeys, 163–64
Eye dominance, 45–46
Eye protection, 21
Eyes of hunter, 75–76, 77

Fables
  bears in, 122–22
Failure at hunting, 136, 175
Falconry, 181–83
Falcons, 5, 182
Faulkner, William, 79
  Bear, The, 14, 116
Ferrets, 185
Fice dogs, 15–16, 185
Firearms, 38–40, 53*n*
  see also Guns; Rifles; Shotguns;
    Weapons
Fitz, Grancel, 173
Flintlocks, 39, 41
Flobert, Louis Nicolas, 8, 9
Flushing
  pheasants, 154, 155, *155*
  upland birds, 157, 158, 159, 161, 182
  wild turkeys, *164*, 165
Flushing dogs, 15, 183
Forest grouse, 157–59, 205

Forsyth, Andrew, 39
Fowling, 41
Fowling (birding) piece, 40–41, 47, 195
  barrels of, 41–42
Fox squirrel (*Sciurus niger*), 14
Foxes, 183
Frazier, Ian, 125
Freezing (hide), 93
Frost, Robert, 116

Gadwalls, 30
Gambel's quail, 156, 157
Game
  African, 57*n*, 187–204
  confirming death of, 94–95, 126–27,
    134*n*, 141–42, 144, 187–88
  driven, 44–45
  see also Big game; Small game; and
    under specific animal names
Game gun, 39, 43–44, 45
Game laws, 40, 41, 61
Game management, 16
Game ranches, 63–64
Gauge, 26, 50–52, 53–54
  defined, 40*n*
Gazehounds, 183–85
Gazelle, 191, 198
Geese, 28, 31–32, 205
Gemsbok, 63
Gentleman's Recreation, The (Blome), 41
Giant panda, 115
"Glassing," 77, *78*, 143
  for bear, *122*
  for elk, 130, *131*, 137
Goats, 173
Golden eagle, 183
Goshawk, 182
Grand Slam, 173, 176
Gray (Hungarian) partridge, 159
Gray squirrel (*Sciurus carolinensis*), 14,
  15–16
Great blue heron, 33
Great Plains, 130, 151, 158, 163
Grey, Lord de, Marquis of Ripon, 44,
  45
Greyhounds, 165, 183, 184
Grimm Brothers, 122
Grouse, 5, 44, 157–59, *160*

"Grunting" (moose-calling), 141
Guinea hen, 162
Gun barrel(s), 41–42, 43
Gun bore, 40
   defined, 40*n*
   grooved, 54
   see also Gauge
Gun dogs, 154, 156, 183
Gun fit, 46–48
Gunfire
   and horses, 112–13
Gunpowder, 39, 54
Guns, 28, 38, 39, 50, 126, 137, 141
   for African game, 188–200
   in bear hunting, 126
   in duck hunting, 28
   in elk hunting, 134*n*
   first, 7–9
   game, 39, 43–44, 45
   heavy, 194–97
   learning about, 8–9
   lever- and pump-action repeaters,
      43
   in musk-ox hunting, 150
   muzzle velocity, 191, 192
   percussion, 39
   semiautomatic, 8, 43
   smoothbore shoulder, 54
   Spanish Laurona 10-gauge, 34
Gunsmith(s), 46–47, 48
Gyrfalcons, 182

Hand-culverins, 39
Handguns, 12, 58, 144
Hares, 9, 183
Harlequin quail, 156
Harquebuses, 39
Harris' hawk, 182, 183
Hawk eagle, *182*, 183, 185
Hawking, 181–83
Hawks, 182–83
Hearing protection, 21
Heart of the hunter, 3, 179–80
Heath hen, 163
Heavy-caliber rifles, 190, 191, 194–97,
   198
Hell, I Was There! (Keith), 58

Henry Mountains (Utah), 152
Hibernation (bears), 118, 121
Hides, 4
   preserving, 93
   skinning, 90–92
Hogganbeck, Boon, 14
Holland & Holland (H&H) (gun
   makers), 126, 137, 187, 192, 194,
   196
Hornaday, William T., 163
Horns, 71, 72
   Cape buffalo, 198
   estimating size of: pronghorn ante-
      lope, 148
   mountain goat, 148
   musk-ox, 150
   pronghorn antelope, 147–48
   white ram, 170
   wild sheep, 172, 175, 177
Horse in hunting, 4, 105–13, 114, 129
Horseback riding, 107–10
"Hotblood" sight hounds, 184
Hounds, 5, 15
   in black bear hunting, 119–20
   "hotblood" and "coldblood" sight,
      184
Human history
   hunting in, 2, 5–6, 38–40, 185–86
Humanity
   and hunting, 5–6, 103–104
Humans
   similarities to bears, 114–15
   unique ability to recognize game that
      is not in motion, 75–76
Hungarian partridge, 5
Hunter-gatherers, 40, 100
Hunters, 206
   attitude of, 77
   commitment to game animals, 81
   early, 2, 84, 104
   elite, 178–79, 186
   market, 29, 163
   objective of, 102
   and question of death, 97–98
   subsistence, 101
   true, 185
   see also Old hunters

Hunting
  as art, 60
  as basic human activity, 5–6, 15
  and civilization, 185–86
  communalness of, 81
  competition in, 175–76
  extreme modes of, 181
  on horseback, 109–13
  in human history, 2, 5–6, 38–40, 185–86
  humanness of, 5–6, 103
  lessons of, 61, 70
  as nature of hunter, 77
  Ortega y Gasset on, 98–104
  possibility of failure at heart of, 175
  primitive, 5
  as privileged occupation, 100
  as social activity, 18
  as sport, 41, 43–45
  true, 11
  uniqueness of, 103–104
  for wrong reasons, 175–77
Hunting etiquette, 176
Hunting intelligence, 206
Hunting methods
  Indians of Great Basin, 10
  illegal, 177
  moose, 139–41
Hunting party, 18–19, 21–22, 27
Hunting peoples, 179–81
Hunting season, 63, 64, 205–206
  deer, 71, 75
  elk, 135–36
  jackrabbit, 11

Impala, 198, 200
Indian chital, 64
Indians
  and buffalo, 151–52, *151*
  Eastern Mono, 123
  of Great Basin, 10
  hunting caribou, 143
  Inuit, 148, 180
  moose hunting, 139–41
  Ojibwa, 13
  Tupi, 144
  waterfowling, 28–29

Intelligence
  hunting, 206
Inuit (Indians), 148, 180
Iowa, 154
Irish wolfhounds, 183
Iron sights, 54, 59, 146

Jackrabbits, 9–12, *9*, 183
  hunting with coursing dogs, 183, 184
  species of, 10
"Jakes," 165, 169
Japanese sika deer, 64
Jobson, John, 192
Jump shooting, 28, 41

Kansas, 154
Keith, Elmer, 57, 58–59, 62
  Hell, I Was There!, 58
Kentucky rifle, 13, 57, 58
Keratin, 72
Killing, 96, 97–104
  deer, 84–85
  methods of, 55
Killing pattern(s), 40
Kinnell, Galway, 116
Kodiak Island, Alaska, 76, 122–23, *122*, *124*
Kudu, 192, 193, 198

Lagomorphs, 9
Layout (mummy) boats, 31
Lead(s), 12, 24, 45, 49
Lead shot
  buildup of, and poisoning of waterfowl, 36–37
Leonardo da Vinci, 39
Leopard, 5, 193, 200–204, *203*
  guns for hunting, 200
Leopold, Aldo, 16
Lepus alleni
  see Antelope jackrabbit (*Lepus alleni*)
Lepus californicus
  see Blacktail jackrabbit (*Lepus californicus*)
Lepus townsendi
  see Whitetail jackrabbit (*Lepus townsendi*)

Lethality (hunter)
  weapons and, 39, 52, 54, 61, 181
Lewis and Clark Expedition, 116, 132
Light caliber rifles, 190–92, 198
Lion hunting, 187–88
Lions, 201
  "dead," *189*
  guns for hunting, 198
Loading, 57
Loads, 50–51
Long dogs, 10, 183–85, 205
Long-horned western bush duiker,
  194
"Longwings" (true falcons), 182
Lurchers, 185
Luring, 28, 153
Lyman Reloading Handbook, 192

McGuane, Thomas, 175
McKenzie Mountains, 143
McKinley's law, 181
Mallards, 28, 30, 32
Man
  "Municipal Paleolithic," 178–86
  as predator, 61, 75–76
  see also Humans
Manitoba elk, 132
Mansell, Floyd, *184*
Manton, Joseph, 43, 47
Market hunters, 29, 163
Markland, George, ix, 42–43, 45, 49
  "Pteryplegia: Or, the Art of Shoot-
    ing-Flying," ix, 42–43
Masai (people), 200, 202
Massachusetts, 163
Master eye, 45–46
Matchlocks, 39
Meat, wild, 16, 60, 81, 93–94, 180
  acquiring, 8
  caribou, 143
  cost of, 104
  cougar, 146
  deer, 4, 85, 95–96
  eland, 198
  elk, moose, 143
  leopard, 202
  loss of, 55–56
  wild boar, 68, 70

Meditations on Hunting (Ortega y Gas-
    set), 4, 14–15, 98, 99–104
Medium-caliber rifles, 190, 191, 192–94,
    198
Meleagris gallopavo, 162
Merriam's elk, 130
Migratory birds, 153
  doves, 18–26
  waterfowl, 27–37
Miller, Henry, 132
Miquelet locks, 39
Modernity
  and hunting, 36–37, 103–104
Montana, 152
Moon bears, 115
Moose (*Alces alces*), 5, 73, 125, 132, 138–
    42, 146
  bull, *140*
  habitat, 139
  range, 138
Moose-calling, 141
Moral issue
  hunting as, 2, 102
Mountain caribou, 143
Mountain goat (*Oreamnos americanus*),
    5, 72, 148, *149*, 150
Mountain lion
  see Cougar (*Felis concolor*)
Mountain quail, 157, *157*
Mountain sheep, 205
Mouflons, 172
Mourning dove (*Zenaidura macroura
    marginella; carolinensis*), 19–22, 24
Mule deer, 56, 73, 76–78, *80*, 191, 205
  antlers, 85–87, *86*, 133
  habitat, 73–75, *74*, 76–77
"Municipal Paleolithic man," 178–86
Musk deer, 71–72
Muskets, 39
Musk-ox (*Ovibos moschatus*), 64, 72,
    148–50, *150*
  habitat, 148–50
Muzzle energy, 196
Muzzle velocity, 191, 192

Nebraska, 154
Newfoundland, 143
Nilgai, 63, 64

Nitro Express, 187–204
  calibers, 195
North America
  bear species, 116
  big game, 5, 56–57, 59–60
  deer species, 73–75
  wild sheep species, 172–73
Northwest Territories (NWT), 122, 123, 143
Notes on Sporting Rifles (Burrard), 55

Ocellated turkey (*Agriocharis ocellata*), 162
O'Connor, Jack, 57–59, 60, 173, 192
Odocoilean deer, 71
Odocoileus (genus), 73
Ojibwa (Indians), 13
Old hunters, 2, 5, 180–81, 204
  and dressing deer, 95–96
Omineca Mountains (British Columbia), 158
Omingmak (musk-ox), 148
Oreamnos americanus
  see Mountain goat (*Oreamnos americanus*)
Ortega y Gasset, José, 84, 98–99, 106–107, 119, 180, 181
  on death, 97
  Meditations on Hunting, 4, 14–15, 98, 99–104
Orwell, George, 84
Oryx, 198
Ovibos moschatus
  see Musk-ox (*Ovibos moschatus*)
Ovis canadensis
  see Wild sheep
Ovis dalli
  see Wild sheep

Pacific littoral, 24
Pacific Northwest, 132
Packhorses, *107*, 129, 142
Packing out, *91*, 96
  bear meat, 120
  elk, 134
  moose, 142
Panther
  see Cougar (*Felis concolor*)

Parallax, 60
Partridges, 45, 159–61
  see also Chukar partridge
Pass shooting, 29
Passion of hunter, 4–5, 206
Patience, 26, 93
Pattern, 40, 40*n* (defined), 50
Peacock, 162
Peccaries, 146, 151
Percussion guns, 39
Peregrine falcons, 182
Peripheral vision, 45, 46
Persian ibex, 64
Phasianidae, 154–57
Phasianids, 156, *157*
Pheasant, 5, 44, 45, 154–56, *155*, 159, 205
Pigeons, 24, 182
Pilgrims, 163
Pintails, 32
Plotts, 119
Plucking (waterfowl), 35
Poachers, poaching, 40, 180, 193
  dogs, 185
Pointers, 15, 156, 160–61
Pointing, 48
Polar bear (*Thalarctos maritimus*), 58, 115, 116, 117, 127–28
Posters, 81, 154
Practice
  with rifle, 58, 59, 197
  with shotgun, 48–49
Prairie chicken, 158
Prairie falcons, 182
Predator(s), 102, 146, 181, 206
  bloodthirstiness, 3
  man as, 61, 75–76
Predator/prey relationship, 44, 45, 61
Professional hunters (PH), 187, 188, 190, 198, 200–204
  gun choice, 196
Pronghorn antelope (*Antilocapra americana*), 4, 5, 56, 63, 72, 146–48, *147*, 151, 156
Ptarmigan, 158
"Pteryplegia" (Markland), ix, 42–43
Puma
  see Cougar (*Felis concolor*)
Purdey, James, 43, 190

Purdey's (gun makers), 46–47
Pygmy rabbit, 9

Quail, 5, 50, 156–57, *157*, 167, 205
Quebec-Labrador caribou, 143

Rabbit fever, 12
Rabbits, 3, 5, 7–17, *9*, *13*, 23, 185, 205
    hunting with coursing hounds, 183–
        84, *184*
    population cycle, 11
Rain forests, 179
Range, 58
    African big game, 194
    sporting, 147
Rangifer tarandus
    see Caribou (*Rangifer tarandus*)
Raptors, 182–83
Ratters, 185
Recoil, 49, 57, 58, 59, 198
    heavy-caliber gun, 196
Red deer, 133
Red-tailed hawk, 102–103, 146, 182
Revolver
    .357 Magnum, 144
Rifle scabbard, 111–12, *111*
Rifles, 4, 7*n*, 39*n*, 53–61, 62–63, 142
    accuracy, 54, 57, 58, 59
    aiming, 45
    all-around, 59
    in big-game hunting, 56–60
    black powder, 144
    bolt-action, 197
    double, 195, 196–97
    double express, 41
    in elk hunting, 134*n*
    flat-shooting, 143
    heavy-caliber, 190, 191, 194–97, 198
    heavy/light, 56–60
    for hunting in Africa, 190–200, *191*
    in hunting pronghorn antelope, 147
    in hunting wild pigs, 66–67
    for killing cougar, 144
    killing power, 59
    knockout potential, 195, 196
    light-caliber, 190–92, 198
    medium-caliber, 190, 191, 192–94, 198
    in sheep hunting, 174

Right/left-handed shooting, 46, 47
Ring-necked pheasant, 154
Risk in hunting, 12
Ritual, 102
Roan antelope, 193, 198
Rock doves, 24
Rock ptarmigan, 158
Rocky Mountain elk, 132
Rodent hunting, 185
Roe deer skull
    classical European mount, *98*
Roosevelt, Theodore, 63, 132–33, 165, 188
Roosevelt's elk, 132
Rooster cock, 162
*Rowland Ward's African Records of Big
    Game,* 190
Royal antelope, 190, 191
Ruark, Robert, 195
Ruffed grouse, 157, 158
Running bears with dogs, 119–20, 125
Rupicaprids, 148
Russian wolfhounds, 183
Rut
    deer, 77–78, 79
    elk, 134
    moose, 141

Sable antelope, 193, *193*, 198
Saddlebags, 112
Safari(s), 190, 192, 194
Safety, 21
Sage-grouse, 156, 158–59, *160*, 182
Salting (hide), 93
Salukis, 183, 184
Sandhill crane, 33–35, *33*
Schwartz, Delmore, 116
Sciurus carolinensis
    see Gray squirrel (*Sciurus carolinensis*)
Sciurus niger
    see Fox squirrel (*Sciurus niger*)
Scopes, 61
    "light-gathering," 59
    spotting, 77, *78*, 126, 134
    variable-power, 59
Scottish deerhounds, 183
Scouting
    for doves, 22
Scrapes, defined, 79

Semiautomatic pistols and shotguns, 8, 43
Sequoia National Park, 125
Serow, 148
Shakespeare, William, 84
Sharps, Christian, 152
Sharp-tailed grouse, 158, 205
Sheep, 59
  see also Wild sheep
Sheep country, 172, 174–75, 177
  "great arc," 172
Sheep hunters, 172
Sheep hunting, 125
  reasons for, 175–77
Shells, for shotguns, 36–37
Shepard, Paul, 104
Shirao moose, 139
Shock, 195–96
  hydrostatic, 55
Shooting
  long-range, 58–61
  right/left-handed, 46, 47
  skeet, 24
  uphill/downhill, 59
Shooting coach, school, 49
Shooting flying, 41–42, 153
Shooting glasses, 21, 46
  protective, 155
Shooting stick, 197
Shooting stool, 19
Shot, 168
  manufacture of, 40
  pattern, 21*n*, 40*n*
  shotgun, 8, 10, 10*n*
  steel, 36–37, 50
  for upland birds, 155, 156
Shotguns, 4, 12, 38–52
  advancements in, 43
  gauge, 50–52
  for hunting jackrabbits, 10
  for hunting wild turkeys, 168–69
  purchasing, 46–48
  range of, 21*n*
  semiauto 12-gauge, 8
  and steel shot, 36
  for upland birds, 156
  in wing shooting, 45
  16-gauge box-lock side-by-side, *48*

Shot size, 40
  in bird hunting, 24–26, 32, 34
  No. 2, 50, 168
  No. 4, 32, 34, 36, 50, 155
  No. 6, 10, 24–26, 32, 36, 50, 51, 155, 156
  No. 7½, 21, 32, 50, 156
  No. 8, 21, 50, 156
Shot tower, 40
Sight hounds, 183–85
Siskiyou County, California, 27
Skeet shooting, 24
Skinning
  deer, 90–92
  jackrabbits, 12
Sky-busting, 32
Sloth bears, 115
Small game, 3, 16–17, 23
  hunting alone, 16, 18
  see also Rabbits; Squirrels
Smith & Wesson, 146
Snaphances, 39
Snares, 39
Sneakboats, 28
Snipe, 154
Snyder, Gary, 76, 116
South Dakota, 154
Southern California, 24
Spear(s), 38, 55
Spectacled bears, 115
Spin, 54
Spirit of the chase, 3–4
Spotting scope, 77, *78*, 126, 174
Spotting-stalking (method)
  in bear hunting, 121, 125, 126
Spruce grouse, 157, 158
Squirrels, 7–17, 23
  name, 14
Staghounds, 184
Stalking, 60, 143
  learning, through hunting jackrabbits, 10
  moose, 141
  waterfowl, 28
  see also Spotting-stalking (method)
Stalking horses, 41
Stance (shooting), 49
Stand hunting, 76, 79–81

Standers
    pheasant hunting, 154–55
Stands
    in hunting black bear, 118, 119
Steel shot, 50
    nontoxic, 36–37
Still-hunting, 14, 79, 135
Stone's sheep, 172, 174
Strike dogs, 119–20
Suasuarana
    see Cougar (*Felis concolor*)
Success in hunting, 101
Sun bears, 115
Sus scrofa
    see Wild boar (*Sus scrofa*)
Swing, 24, 48, 49
Sylvilagus floridanus
    see Cottontail rabbit (*Sylvilagus flori-
    danus*)

Tactics in hunting
    small game, 14
    see also Hunting methods
Taxidermist(s), 88–89, *89*, 91, 93
Taylor, John
    African Rifles and Cartridges, 195–96
Teal, 28, 32
Technology
    of hunting weapons, 38–43, 51–52,
        60, 61
    modern, 36–37, 38
Telescopic sights, 54
Tennessee, 65, 116
Terriers, 15, 185
Thalarctos maritimus
    see Polar bear (*Thalarctos maritimus*)
Thinhorn sheep, 172, 173
Thin-skinned game (Africa), 191–92
Tissue damage, 55–56
    see also Shock, hydrostatic
Tlingit, 122
Tolstoy, Leo, 84
Toxic-shot syndrome, 36–37
Trail hounds, 183
Trapping, 39
    wild turkeys, 163
Tree disguises, portable, 41
Tree squirrels, 9, 13–14

Triggs, 119
Trophies, 88–93, *98*
    head mounts, 88
    ram's heads, 175–76
"Try-gun," 47
Tulare (town), 19
Tularemia (rabbit fever), 12
Tule elk, 132
Tupi Indians, 144
Turkeys
    man-reared, 164
    see also Wild turkeys

Upland birds, 1, 5, 150, 153–61, 182
Urials, 172
Ursus arctos/Ursus arctos horribilis
    see Brown-grizzly bear (*Ursus arctos/
    Ursus arctos horribilis*)

Varmint shooting, 59
Veinte Años de Caza Mayor (Yebes),
    99
Venison, 94, 143

Walkers, 119, 144
Walsingham, Lord, 44
Wapitis, 132–33
Water deer, 71–72
Waterbuck, 198
Waterfowl, 27–37, 50, 153, 154
    poisoned by lead shot, 36–37
Waterfowlers
    commercial, 43
Waterfowling, 28–31
    art of, 37
Waugh, Evelyn, 105–106
Way of the hunter, 2–8, 96, 186, 205–
    206
    competition and, 176
    learning, 3, 4, 5, 11, 16
    start of, 7
    and wild sheep, 170, 172
Weapons, 4
    for hunting caribou, 142
    for hunting jackrabbit, 10–11, 12
    for hunting moose, 141
    for hunting mountain goats, 13
    for hunting squirrels, 13

technology of, 38–43
  see also Bow and arrow; Guns; Rifles;
    Shotguns
Weather, 11, 24, 76, 174
  mountain, 112
Welch, Lew, 116
Welterweight-caliber rifles, 193, 198
Wemyss, Lord, 44
Wetlands, 35–36
Wheel lock(s), 39, 56
Whippets, 183
White, T. H., 181
White, Walter H., 191
White ram, 170–72
White rhino, 193
Whitetail (deer), 73, 78–81, *80*, 132, 191,
    205
  antlers, 87
  habitat, 75, 78–79, 81
Whitetail jackrabbit (*Lepus townsendi*),
    10
White-tailed ptarmigan, 158
White-winged doves (*Zenaida asiatica*),
    22, 23–24
Whooping crane, 33
Widgeons, 32
Wild animals
  restoration of near-extinct, 164
Wild boar (*Sus scrofa*), 4, 65, *66*, *67*, *69*,
    205
Wild boar hunting, 65–70
Wild cats
  dogs in hunting of, 15
Wild sheep, 5, 130, 150, 170–77, *171*,
    173
Wild turkey hunter, *168*
Wild turkeys, 5, 50, 150, 162–69, *164*,
    172, 205

Wilderness (the wild), 2, 5, 84
  hunter's relationship to, 23
Williams, William Carlos, 116
Wilson, Betty, *80*
Wind, 58–59, 60, 67, 70, 79
Wind doping, 59
Wind drift, 59
Wing shooting, 24, 36, 39, 41, 45–47,
    48, 49–50
  as art, 45
  on driven game, 44–45
  weapons for, 51
Wood, William, 163
Woodcock, 50, 154
Woodland caribou, 143
Working dogs, 184–85
Worshipful Company of Gunmakers of
    the City of London, 46–47
Wounded animals, 32, 57, 68, 134n, 192,
    200
  second shots at, 126–27
  see also Animals, confirming death of
Wounding
  killing by, 55
Wyoming, 152

Yebes, Edward, Count
  Veinte Años de Caza Mayor, 99
Yukon Territory, 143

Zebra, 198
Zenaida asiatica
  see White-winged doves (*Zenaida
    asiatica*)
*Zenaidura macroura marginella; caroli-
    nensis*
  see Mourning dove (*Zenaidura ma-
    croura marginella; carolinensis*